Modern France

Society in transition

Edited by Malcolm Cook and Grace Davie

London and New York

First published 1999
by Routledge
11 New Fetter Lane, London EC4P 4EE

Simultaneously published in the USA and Canada
by Routledge
29 West 35th Street, New York, NY 10001

Typeset in Times by Routledge
Printed and bound in Great Britain by TJ International Ltd,
Padstow, Cornwall

British Library Cataloging in Publication Data
A catalogue record for this book is available from the British
Library.

Library of Congress Cataloging in Publication Data
Cook, Malcolm
Modern France: Society in transition/Malcolm Cook and Grace
Davie
Includes bibliographic references and index.
1. France–Civilization–20th century. 2. Social
change–France–History–20th century. I. Davie, Grace. II. Title.
CD33.7.C5965   1999
944.08–dc21   98-21808

ISBN 0–415–15431–6 (hbk)
ISBN 0–415–15432–4 (pbk)

MBC
7/00

Modern France

Modern France is an up-to-date and accessible introduction to the nature of French society at the end of the twentieth century. It examines the transition of France and French life as the nation moves from an industrial to a post-industrial economy, together with the cultural and social dislocations that such an evolution implies.

Sociological concepts and categories are discussed in the first half of the book – class, race, gender, age and region, and how they combine together to produce inequalities and identities. These concepts are then applied to a range of issues such as work, politics, education, health, religion and leisure.

Modern France reveals the nature of French society at a critical mom-ent in its evolution and illustrates how a member of the European Union reflects distinctiveness and commonality in the development of Europe as a whole.

Malcolm Cook is Professor of French and **Grace Davie** is Senior Lecturer in Sociology, both at the University of Exeter.

Contents

PART II
Areas of enquiry

Tables

Contributors

Malcolm Cook (m.c.cook@exeter.ac.uk) is Professor of French Eighteenth-Century Studies at the University of Exeter and is currently Chair of the School of Modern Languages and Head of the French Department. He has published widely on the eighteenth century and is the editor of *French Culture since 1945* (Longman 1993).

He is leading a team which is working on the first critical edition of the correspondence of Bernardin de Saint-Pierre (1737–1814). He is also the general editor of *Modern Language Review*.

Grace Davie (g.r.c.davie@exeter.ac.uk) is a Senior Lecturer in the Department of Sociology at the University of Exeter. She specializes in the sociology of religion and is the author of *Religion in Britain since 1945* (Blackwell 1994) and the co-editor (with Danièle Hervieu-Léger) of *Identités religieuses en Europe* (La Découverte 1986). She has published numerous articles on the religious situations of Britain, France and other parts of Europe and is currently preparing a single-authored text on religion in Europe for Oxford University Press.

She has been visiting lecturer at both the Ecole des Hautes Etudes en Sciences Sociales and the Ecole Pratique des Hautes Etudes.

Howard Davis (h.h.davis@bangor.ac.uk) is Professor of Social Theory and Institutions at the University of Wales, Bangor. He has written and translated several books and articles on class and comparative social structure including, with R. Scase, *Western Capitalism and State Socialism: An Introduction* (Blackwell 1985) and, with C. Rootes, *A New Europe? Social and Political Transformation* (UCL 1994).

Recent publications include research on media and cultures of broadcasting in western and eastern Europe. Currently he is leading a consortium of European sociology departments helping to develop the sociology curriculum in the universities of the Central Volga region in Russia.

Philip Dine (p.d.dine@lboro.ac.uk) is Senior Lecturer in French in the Department of European Studies at Loughborough University. The main focus of his research activity has been the cultural implications of the economic, political and social restructuring of France since 1945. This work has centred on three poles: decolonization, sport and leisure, and popular culture. He is currently working on a cultural history of French rugby football, funded in part by the Nuffield Foundation.

His publications include *Images of the Algerian War: French Fiction and Film, 1954–1992* (Clarendon Press 1994), as well as numerous chapters and articles on decolonization, sport and leisure and popular culture.

Bruno Dumons (bruno.dumons@mrash.fr) is a research fellow at the CNRS (Centre Pierre Léon: MRASH, 14 avenue Berthelot, 69363 Lyon). His work concentrates mainly on the genesis and structure of the welfare state and on élites and local powers under the Third Republic, with particular reference to urban municipalities and parliamentary mayors. He is the co-author (with Gilles Pollet) of *L'Etat et les retraites. Genèse d'une politique* (Belin 1994) and the co-editor (with Gilles Pollet) of *Elites et pouvoirs locaux. La France du sud-est sous la troisième république* (Presses Universitaires de Lyon, forthcoming).

Linda Hantrais (l.hantrais@lboro.ac.uk) holds a Chair in the Department of European Studies at Loughborough University where she is Director of the European Research Centre and convenor of the Cross-National Research Group. Her main research interests are in cross-national comparative research theory, methodology and practice, with particular reference to social policy in the European Union and the relationship between family and employment. Her recent publications in these areas include: *Social Policy in the European Union* (Macmillan 1995), *Families and Family Policies in Europe* (with Marie-Thérèse

Letablier, Longman 1996) and *Cross-National Research Methods in the Social Sciences* (edited with Steen Mangen, Pinter 1996).

Patrick Harismendy (patrick.harismendy@uhb.fr) is Senior Lecturer in Contemporary History at the Université de Rennes II. There are four strands to his research activity: the social history of the political and financial élite of the twentieth century (with Luc Jacob-Duvernet), *Le Miroir des princes: Essai sur la culture stratégique des élites qui nous gouvernent* (Le Seuil 1994); the history of political ideas and moderate political movements under the Third Republic, *Sadi Carnot, L'Ingénieur de la République* (Perrin 1995); the history of technical change (a study of the Citroën factories in Rennes is in progress); and the history of French Protestantism in the nineteenth and twentieth centuries (he is editorial secretary of the *Bulletin de la Société de l'Histoire du protestantisme français*, a society founded in 1852).

Cécile Laborde (c.laborde@exeter.ac.uk) is a Lecturer in French Political Thought at the University of Exeter. She has research interests in the history of political thought and contemporary political philosophy (especially French). She is the author of a book on African Islam and of several articles on French and early twentieth-century political thought. Her most recent work is *Pluralist Thinking in France and Britain, 1900–1925* (Macmillan, forthcoming).

Patrick Le Galès (legales@msh-paris.fr) is CNRS senior research fellow with CEVIPOF, Fondation Nationale des Sciences Politiques, Paris, and Associate Professor of Sociology and Politics at Sciences Po, Paris. He is the editor of the *International Journal of Urban and Regional Research*. His main publications include: *Politiques urbaines et développement local: Une comparaison franco-britannique* (L'Harmattan 1993); *Les Réseaux de politiques publiques* (edited with Mark Thatcher, L'Harmattan 1995); *The Paradox of the Regions in Europe* (edited with C. Lequesne, Routledge 1998); and *Villes en Europe: Les villes comme sociétés locales et comme acteurs* (edited with Arnaldo Bagnasco, La Découverte 1997).

Cathie Lloyd (cathie.lloyd@qeh.ox.ac.uk) is Director of the Centre for Cross-cultural Research on Women, Queen Elizabeth House, University of Oxford. Her current research interest includes women in movements for social justice and human rights, gender and development. She has written extensively on anti-racism in contemporary Europe, particularly in France. Her publications include: *Discourses of antiracism in France* (Ashgate 1998), 'Rendez-vous manqués: Feminisms and antiracisms in France – a critique' (in *Modern and Contemporary France*, January 1998); 'Struggling for Rights: African women and the "sanspapiers" movement in France' (in *Refuge*, Fall 1997).

Susan Milner (s.e.milner@bath.ac.uk) is a Senior Lecturer in the Department of European Studies and Modern Languages at the University of Bath. Her main area of research is trade unions and employment policies in western Europe, especially in France. She is currently carrying out research into collective bargaining on working time in France and into the 'social plan' as an instrument of labour regulation.

Ted Neather (e.j.neather@exeter.ac.uk) is a Senior Lecturer in the School of Education at the University of Exeter. He works on aspects of French, German and English education and is particularly interested in teacher education. His publications include: 'Streitfall Lehrerbildung', in F. Busch (ed.) *Tradition und Erneuerung in der Erziehungswissenschaft – Aspekte einer Sozialwissenschaft* (Technische Universität); 'Education in the New Germany' in D. Lewis and J. McKenzie (eds) *The New Germany: Social, Political and Cultural Challenges of Unification* (University of Exeter Press 1995) and 'Teacher Education and the role of the University: European Perspectives' (in *Research Papers in Education*, 8 (1), 1993, 33–46).

Gilles Pollet (gpollet@compuserve.com) is the co-author (with Bruno Dumons) of *L'Etat et les retraites: Genèse d'une politique* and the co-editor (again with Dumons) of *Elites et pouvoirs locaux. La France du sud-est sous la troisième république*. He is Professor of Political Science at the Université Jean Moulin Lyon III. He is also a member of the CERAT which is the research centre of the Institut d'Etudes Politiques of Grenoble. He is a specialist of public policy and works on socio-historical studies of welfare states and local government. He is the co-author (with Alain Faure and Philippe Warin) of *La Construction du sens dans les politiques publiques* (L'Harmattan 1995).

Catherine Rodgers (c.rodgers@swansea.ac.uk) is Lecturer in French at the University of Wales, Swansea. She specializes in French feminist theories and has several research publications in this area. At the time of going to press, L'Harmattan (Paris) is about to publish a book of interviews between her and eleven leading French feminists on their reaction to Simone de Beauvoir's *Le Deuxième Sexe.* Her research has also been focused on Marguerite Duras, on whom she has published widely. She is the co-editor of *Marguerite Duras: Lectures plurielles* (Rodopi 1998).

Acknowledgements

The editors are grateful to the Research Fund of the University of Exeter and to our publishers, Routledge, for financial support for a small colloquium which allowed the contributors to this volume to meet and to discuss each chapter in light of common themes. Both the Department of French and the Department of Sociology have also contributed to this enterprise. The result is evidence of considerable cross-faculty co-operation.

Each chapter has been written by a specialist in the field, some of whom are English and some French. The editors would like to express their gratitude to each of the contributors and in particular to Sarah Leahy for her elegant translations of Chapters 4, 5 and 10.

The map of France on p. xvi is reproduced from *France 1996*, published by Le Ministère des Affaires Etrangères and La Documentation Française, whose assistance we gratefully acknowledge.

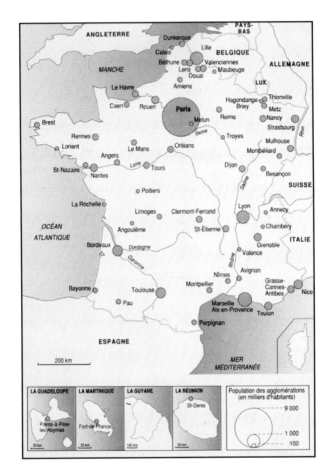

Figure 1 Map of France
Source: Reproduced from *France 1996*, published by Le Ministère des Affaires Etrangères and La Documentation Française.

Introduction

Malcolm Cook and Grace Davie

Our aim in producing this book is to bring together specialists from a variety of disciplines in order to create a dialogue from which a new perception of French society might emerge. The initial task was to provide an up-to-date and accessible introduction to the nature of French society as the second millennium gives way to the third. The following chapters do more than this, however; they catch the transition of French society as it moves from an industrially-based economy to a post-industrial one, with all the economic and social dislocations that such an evolution implies. It became increasingly clear, moreover, that the precise documentation of this transition offered a more helpful *fil conducteur* than a particular decade or time period. It emphasised, in addition, the interdisciplinary nature of the text.

In taking this approach the book adapts itself immediately to the needs of a wide variety of students whose courses require them (a) to understand the structures of neighbouring European societies and (b) to compare such societies with their own. At present, however, most students are unable to do this in any systematic way unless they have a sufficient grasp of French (or indeed any other language) which allows them to use the appropriate sources.

In order for the task to be accomplished in a coherent as well as creative manner the book has been divided into two parts: the first looks at the concepts or categories of analysis that are familiar to teachers and students of the social sciences; the second concentrates on a range of substantive areas to which such concepts or categories can be applied. Both require a little elaboration – so, too, do the connections between them.

First, then, the concepts or categories of social analysis. There are five of these: class, race, gender, age and regional affiliation.

Emergent debates in the social sciences lie behind such choices. Many social scientists have, for example, moved away from assumptions about social class as the essential element of industrial society to considerably more sophisticated analyses based on combinations of class, race, gender, age and region – and indeed other factors as well. Hence the series of chapters in the first section of the book (Davis, Lloyd, Rodgers, Harismendy and Le Galès). Two connected themes cross-cut these categories: first an emphasis on social difference in modern French society and, second, a consideration of changing forms of identity – both French identity itself and the multiple identities of French citizens. Such themes reflect once again the social science literature across a variety of western societies, allowing – where appropriate – wider European or other comparisons.

The complexity of the issues raised by these cross-cutting themes are best explored through a series of questions. By what criteria, for instance, are social differences established in modern French society? How are such criteria measured? To what extent are they changing? How far do social differences depend on the particular history and development of the French nation, or regions within this, or are these inter- or supra-national metamorphoses? Answers can only come through the patient sifting of the evidence; there are no easy or automatic responses to the complexities of social change. Similar questions can be formulated around the theme of identity rather than difference. How, for example, are social identities constructed? What are the resources available to the individual in order to construct an identity? How far are these resources shaped by history? To what extent can they be changed or recreated as French society evolves and mutates? Are such identities simply given or can they be chosen? Can some groups of people make wider choices than others? Why are some forms of identity more important for women than for men, for some minority groups rather than others, or for some regions rather than others? And so on. Combinations of difference and identity provide the essential questions addressed in the first part of the book; each discussion begins from a different starting point, but follows through the argument in relation to alternative possibilities.

With this in mind, each author introduces both theoretical and empirical material in the field, noting the specificities of the French case and the manner in which these have provoked innovative theoretical understanding. A good example can be found in Davis's

discussion (Chapter 1) of social class in the country in which categories of social difference generated at the time of the Revolution
continue to have resonance some two hundred years later; the more
so in view of the fact that France industrialised relatively late,
permitting the endurance of pre-industrial terms well into the modern,
indeed late-modern period. In the more descriptive sections of his
chapter, Davis outlines the occupational structure of modern France;
in so doing he provides a framework in which some of the later
chapters of the book can be placed. The teacher or intellectual, for
example, has a particular status in France, coveted – but rarely
achieved – in the United Kingdom. A second example comes from
Bruno Dumons and Giles Pollet in their chapter on Healthcare
(Chapter 11). French health professionals are clearly preoccupied by
status as well as power, jostling for position and influence within the
medical service in uniquely French ways, never mind the nature of
their relationships with patients. Davis's concluding section picks up
the wider vision of the book, considering new forms of social
inequality in a post-industrial society, a debate which leads
inevitably to theoretical questions concerning the nature of society
itself.

Cathie Lloyd (Chapter 2 'Race and ethnicity') and Catherine
Rodgers (Chapter 3 'Gender'), illustrate questions of identity just as
much as difference. Lloyd, for example, initiates her discussion by
pointing out the inherent conflict between republican (universalist)
ideals of citizenship in France and the particularist nature of racial
or ethnic difference. Given the strongly assimilationist tendencies of
the Republic, the debate about 'race' in France is constructed in
ways very different from its equivalent in Britain (for a start, the
word 'race' is seldom used in the French context). Grasping the
significance of this point requires a degree of imagination on the
part of the non-French reader. Such imagination is necessary,
however, both for this and later chapters. One aim of the French
education system. for instance, is the making of French (republican)
citizens – laudable in many respects but inextricably linked to a
system which has a corresponding difficulty in accommodating
alternative identities, not least religious identities. The chapters on
race and ethnicity (Chapter 2), education (Ted Neather, Chapter 9)
and religion (Grace Davie, Chapter 10), form a close-knit trio in
this respect.

For students of sociology or gender politics in English-speaking
countries, it may come as something of a shock that the French

language does not distinguish linguistically between the terms 'sex' and 'gender'. This does not mean that the French cannot have lively debates about the issues; the nation that produced Simone de Beauvoir is well-placed to consider the nature of female identity. Central to Beauvoir's writing is the notion that 'one is not born, but rather becomes a woman' – an exploration reinvigorated some twenty years later both in theoretical discussion and in policy making. Interestingly, one focus of the theoretical debate has been precisely the complex inter-relationships between sex and gender and the possibility that the latter might precede the former, rather than the other way round. The section on 'Women at work' within the applied sections of Catherine Rodgers's contribution (Chapter 3) provides a natural partner to Linda Hantrais's discussion of paid and unpaid work in Chapter 6, which tackles similar issues from a different starting point.

Considerations of age (the life-cycle) and region as significant markers of social difference or identity are later arrivals in social scientific analysis. The former has been prompted at least in part by the changing demographic structures of modern Europe, and more specifically by the marked increase in life expectancy. The second reflects a widespread debate concerning the shifting relationships between locality, region, nation and supra-nation as globalization impinges on all our lives. The European dimension within this process is self-evident in the post-war discussions of economic and political union across the continent, prompting a certain amount of questioning about the effective units of organization within this. Patrick Harismendy in Chapter 4 captures the particularly French concerns with population size and growth, underlining the role of the French state in promoting the patterns of family life thought to be beneficial to economic well-being and political stability. The concept of 'generation' is also important, illustrated positively, perhaps, in the generation of '68, but much less so in the case of young people alienated on urban housing estates – an indicator, followed up in Part II, of widespread political disenchantment.

The debate about regions in French society is complex. Patrick Le Galès considers this on three levels – the political, the economic and the cultural. What emerges is a constant shifting of fortunes as political identity is achieved for the regions just as the *départements* and cities achieve a dominant status (at the regions' expense). Economic assessments require a careful sifting of the evidence to discover which categories really count, the region as a whole or a significant city within this, itself linked to the capital by the *TGV*. The cultural discussion provides an excellent illustration of the changing nature of social identities – no longer is one obliged to be Alsatian, Provençal, Breton, or indeed anything else, given the mobilities of the modern French society and the increasing access to French, and indeed global culture (through both the education system and the media). But precisely because of these shifts and the anxieties that come with them, new identities are sought – and found – at the regional level. People *choose* to be Alsatian, Provençal or Breton and construct their lives accordingly. Such choices have, however, to be set against the remarkably enduring nature of some regional differences, often reflected in deep-seated and relatively stable social structures.

So much for the categories of analysis which provide a framework for the chapters that follow. The second part of the book looks at a range of topic areas that reflect, or indeed embody the changing nature of all western societies. The contrast between the two sections should not, however, be exaggerated; they are rather different points of entry to the continuing debates about the nature of post-industrial society in general and the French case in particular. The policy implications of social difference provide an obvious link. Who, for example, should or should not have access to health-care, or who does or does not have the right/obligation to work? It is questions such as these that bring the two sections of the book together.

The topic areas presented in Chapters 6–11 are wide-ranging though necessarily selective. In assembling these, we took a variety of factors into account, not least the material that already existed for the English-speaking reader (Flower 1993, Cook 1993). The extensive coverage of a series of cultural themes in the latter was of particular significance – hence the rather more weight given to the economic, the workplace and the life-cycle in this book (topics not covered elsewhere). That is not to say that cultural factors cannot be analysed within the scheme that we have presented here. The evolution of the nature and forms of the mass media, for example, is an essential part of the shift from an industrial to a post-industrial society.

Evolutions in the nature of work and the workplace (Hantrais and Milner, Chapters 6 and 7) provided the natural starting point for our thinking, for it is these shifts that reflect most directly the transitional nature of the French economy. The nature of work, the size and composition of the workforce and the characteristics of the workplace are all indicators of the shift from an industrial to a post-industrial economy; they have different implications for men and for women and for different age categories. The impact of such changes can, moreover, be felt in the home just as much as the economy as men and women come to terms with their changing obligations. Underlying shifts in the economy offer a particular challenge to the trade union movement which becomes, in itself, a barometer of social change. Although small in terms of numbers, trade unions can still bring France to a standstill. As we put the finishing touches to this book French motorways are, once again, blocked by lorries, seriously threatening the economy of France and its pivotal position in Europe.

The divisions of the trade union movement reflect wider political differences, leading naturally to a fuller consideration of politics *per se*. Cécile Laborde's innovative analysis in Chapter 8 introduces some of the new interests and new configurations (or identities) which are beginning to cut across the class-based cleavages of an industrial society. Some of these shifts can be interpreted positively – the Greens, for example, have brought a new agenda to both left and right within French politics. They are, in addition, an excellent example of a single issue politics, a feature of all European societies as the twentieth century comes to an end. More disturbing, in contrast, is the emergence of the Front National as a party of the far right, attracting not only a section of traditionally right-wing voters and the associated occupational categories, but also a size-able section of the young unemployed and the working class – groups of people who fail to prosper in the new economy.

French education is the place where French national identity is not only formed but constantly renewed, a demanding task in a society which is becoming more rather than less diverse and where the changing nature of the economy requires that innovative skills are delivered to the next generation of workers. Old habits die hard, however, and nowhere more so than in a highly centralised education system. In Chapter 9, Ted Neather outlines both the system and the need for change – and the gradual, though at times reluctant, adaptation of one to reflect the other. A recurrent theme of the book, already identified by Laborde, finds a further illustration at this point: the categories of people effectively failed by the education system and excluded from the mainstream of French society. Their location (both social and geographical) can be analysed by means of the categories introduced in the earlier chapters (persistent social exclusion leads to negative forms of identity).

The transmission of society's norms and values to a new generation is an important function of the education system. The French example is particularly interesting in this respect for the republican traditions of *laïcité* and the *école laïque* are clearly coming under strain in a religiously plural society. The links with Chapter 10 on religion are clear enough – paradoxically, in some ways, in that France is the one country in Europe which has systematically excluded religion from the public sphere, the education system included. Religion, however, has not faded as was once predicted. It raises some of the most intractable questions of all in modern societies: how, in particular, to create and sustain a truly tolerant society. The *affaire du foulard* is taken as a touchstone to illustrate this point, and is central to the understanding of modern French identities.

The remaining topics have been chosen because they exemplify the preoccupations of a post-industrial society. Health and health issues (Dumons and Pollet, Chapter 11) are central concerns for all advanced societies; not least the adequate financing of an efficient and equitable health service, able to cater for a population which is living for a longer period of time. In this respect the French healthcare system is (like most others in the west) the victim of its own success as a longer-living population demands more care and better facilities. It has, however, encountered rather more specific difficulties in attempting to resolve these issues, notably a marked tendency to internal fragmentation and an inbuilt resistance to structural alteration, despite successive changes of government.

At the turn of the millennium, all European societies will be engaged in discussions about the meaning of work and leisure. In confronting this debate the final chapter brings the reader full-circle, for it returns to the central issue of the book: the evolving nature of French society as the nature of the economy alters. Philip Dine provides admirable illustrations of these connections. Shopping, for example, has become the major leisure activity of the late twentieth century, just as consumption rather than production dominates the economy. Who shops, when, how, with whom and for what reasons are central questions in the understanding of post-industrial societies. Why, for example, did the Minitel become a dominant instrument of effecting choice in France but not in Britain? What material interests were at stake here? The particular combinations of traditional shops, supermarkets and hypermarkets, in and out of town shopping centres and electronic shopping are different on each side of the Channel. Why this should be so raises important questions of cultural change bearing in mind the parameters set by the past (including patterns of eating and residence).

A number of cross-cutting themes emerge to draw the threads of the book together. One of these relates to the debate about social exclusion and has already been mentioned. Another concerns the similarities to and differences from Britain. Given the commonalities of economic pressures and a shared cultural past, France and Britain have evolved in different ways. An obvious and significant illustration of difference can be seen in the value that the French place on their culture and their language; the latter in fact becomes an increasingly important mission in a world that is dominated by English. For the French, culture and language are products to be nurtured and protected. The process begins in the privileged place given to both teacher and intellectual in French society; it is reinforced by the attention given to linguistic purity and by the resources committed to the projection of French culture overseas. In Britain, for example, an impressive array of cultural and linguistic activities are fostered by the energetic French Institute and the services of the Embassy. This is hard evidence, readily available to the British student, of the value which the French attach to their cultural heritage and to the importance of cultural dissemination.

A second theme can be discerned in the constant contradiction between theory and practice in the evidence that we have presented. France, for example, is a Republic and proud of it. The Constitution lies at the heart of the French state and acts as a governing body over French affairs. Yet the notion of class still exists and there is immense interest in the idea of royalty – other people's royalty that is. The enormous amount of media interest generated by the death of Diana, Princess of Wales, is but one illustration of this preoccupation; it dominated the French press for weeks. It is clear that the French equivalent of the tabloid press has a constant eye to events this side of the Channel, and to the British royal family in particular. How can this paradox be explained? Despite the pressures of both industrial and post-industrial society, it seems that there still exists in France an old-fashioned concept of social difference which is likely to endure. The empirical evidence accumulated in the following chapters reinforces this point – some elements of French society should be noted for their stability rather than their capacity to evolve.

This point in particular needs some elaboration, especially from a British perspective. We tend, in Britain, to think that the French Revolution changed the nature of French society once and for all. This is not the case. Republicans, in fact, might be worried that French society has not changed radically enough since 1789. On the other hand it is evident that the constitutional shifts from the Fourth to the Fifth Republic – while retaining some elements of the First Republic and the revolutionary era – *have* evolved dramatically in the sense that they have produced a regime where the role of the President is paramount and quite different from any of France's European counterparts. This is especially true in relation to foreign policy.

It is also instructive to compare the socialism of Lionel Jospin with the New Labour of British Prime Minister Tony Blair. Both are centre-left politicians of the 1990s, yet the priorities of each reflect the differences of political tradition in either country. It is clear that the tradition of the market economy remains pervasive in Britain despite the dramatic shift in the political fortunes of the Conservative and Labour Parties in the election of May 1997. The French Socialists, in contrast, are a party of the continental left, displaying characteristics very different from their British counterparts (if they can be accurately described as such). A more developed understanding of the role of the state is the most obvious of these. With this in mind both Blair and Jospin are faced with the same dilemmas – is it possible to retain a certain amount of protection and welfare for the worker without depressing the demand for labour too much? Or to put the same point in a different way: what is an acceptable price to pay (in terms of the rate of unemployment) for security at work and the associated welfare benefits? At the end of the millennium, Britain has the edge in terms of competitive labour, France in terms of rather better provision for the worker and his or her family.

How, then, do we envisage the future of French society? We can see that, in common with all western societies, there will be a shift away from male domination; a shift which is already apparent in the workplace, in education and in a growing range of leisure activities. How far that shift gets to the roots of a patriarchal culture remains an open question, in France as elsewhere. There will also be a change in the nature of the population as people live longer; indeed the population of France will change radically when the effects of war disappear and increased longevity is experienced without any modifying factors. France, however, once the most populated country in Europe, enjoys space that neither Britain nor Germany can match, offering a quality of life denied to other populous European countries. Healthcare, already a major concern, will need to adapt to the changing needs of an ever-ageing society. The process of production and supply will be obliged to explore the markets which old people, traditionally, do not occupy. We talk in Britain of life-long learning and there is no doubt that this will be a feature of France too as it has to adapt to a world of rapidly changing technology. Certainly people will move away from industrial centres and reverse the trend of over one hundred years. Jobs will continue to define class and categorize people, though in innovative ways, as the process of wealth creation changes from production to service industries; a feature of all the developed countries of Europe and one to which newly-joined members of the European Union also aspire.

Indeed, a particular concern for the French is the role they play both in Europe and on the world stage. Having led the world in the provision of computer technology with the Minitel telephone computer system, they now trail many of their competitors because they did not adapt quickly enough to rapid growth in the provision of PCs elsewhere. This is a lesson which has been well learnt and it will not be repeated. It is clear, for example, that while Britain drags its feet over monetary union – to the dismay of many Europeans – France is ready to accept the compromises that adoption of the euro will entail. There are visible signs of preparation for this change: it is already possible (in 1998) to see prices in shops marked in both francs and euros, and some French banks are producing statements of accounts in both currencies. Britain, on the other hand, is still justifying her self-exclusion.

In short we have tried to present a picture of France as it is today and as it is changing to meet the demands of the twenty-first century. France and its neighbours have much in common as they rise to this challenge, but it is the particularities which define countries. Those who hold France in particular affection rejoice in the specificities of the French case. A final editorial note emphasizes this point with reference to the text which follows. In a collection such as this, we felt a certain imperative to include a number of French authors. Despite the excellence of the translation, the difference in both content and style of their chapters is evident – the emphasis on history is stronger and there is considerably more detail in the text. They are illustrative of French ways of working and offer to the student an immediate taste of France's intellectual preoccupations.

Bibliography

Cook. M. (ed.) (1993), *French Culture since 1945*, London: Longman.
Flower, J. E. (ed.) (1993), *France Today*, London: Hodder and Stoughton.

Part I

Categories of analysis

Chapter 1

Class and status

Howard Davis

The image of a modern society reflects its historical origins, its stage of economic development, the organization of work and employment, and how it deals with the problems of distributing wealth, income, health, education and other social benefits. At its core are social structures which provide the substantial framework of constraints within which individuals, groups and institutions lead their lives. The distinctive cultural features of a society – its language, customs and characteristic ways of representing the world – are closely linked with the development of its social structures. In this sense, modern France is an industrial society with a well developed economic system, a modern state, and complex social organization which has essential similarities with other west European and industrialized societies. However, to begin to understand the distinctiveness of French society and how it differs from others of the same general type, we need more detailed knowledge of its social structure as well as categories to describe it. In this chapter I describe how the structure of social classes developed as a result of industrialization in France; I then set out the key evidence concerning the recent and present French system of class and status. The chapter concludes with some comments on how the social structure is likely to change and develop, reflecting certain current lively debates among French social scientists concerning new forms of social division, inequality and social change.

The problem of defining social distinctions – especially in terms of social class – has arguably generated more debate than any other issue in the history of sociology. The technicalities of the problem need not detain us here but we do need a working definition of social categories and relations. Traditionally, such a definition has rested on the key concepts of class structure and status distinction in industrial societies – the tradition being represented by the theories of the founders of sociology as well as more than a century of social mapping through censuses and surveys (Crompton 1993). Theories of class were a response to economic and social changes which occurred during the nineteenth century and were intrinsic to the emerging consciousness of industrial capitalism as a hierarchical system prone to crisis and conflict. The vocabulary of class and class structure therefore applies to the system of relations between social categories (for example, the confrontation between the bourgeoisie and the proletariat in Marxist theory), not to individuals as such. Developed versions of the concept of social class are still used to describe the relative position of groups within a system of classes, usually with an emphasis on the potential for conflict or cohesion. In practice, class differences are measured by distribution of wealth, income, occupation and other indicators of social condition such as employment, education and housing. Most of these are continuous variables which means that the measures of social inequality do not precisely match the categories of class. For example, a self-employed plumber, a teacher and a retired business person may all have a similar annual income but according to most theories they would relate to different class positions because of the differences in their wealth, education, life chances and status.

The concept of 'status' refers to the ways in which inequalities and social differences are interpreted in a society. Judgements about status, prestige and relative standing are important for justifying differences and making them legitimate within a moral framework. Thus one society may tolerate a higher level of inequality than another because of a general belief that inequality is the natural outcome of personal abilities or that it is necessary as an incentive to effort. Status differences have to be studied by methods including surveys of occupational prestige, attitudes to wealth and success, or cultural tastes, as well as through interviews. It is not surprising that evidence of the social status in France, as elsewhere, is less systematic than for most other types of social distinction, although the French sociologist Pierre Bourdieu has been a pioneer in this field (Bourdieu 1979).

Foundations of the modern class structure

The foundations of modern French society were established through historical events and processes which lasted several centuries but especially important were those which occurred at the time of the French Revolution. They created the political conditions from which the modern French state could emerge. This history is a combination of developments which were common to all industrialized countries in western Europe and circumstances which were unique to the French case. The first point is that France was not in the first rank of European countries to industrialize, thus important elements of the pre-French Revolution social structures persisted well into the nineteenth century. The naming of social categories was even then according to *métiers*, essentially the artisan and commercial 'trades'. In the censuses of 1866 and 1872, for example, individuals were allocated to categories according to their dependency on a type of activity – whether as a worker, dependent relative or servant. The data therefore reflected an occupational system which was still largely based on family and household production, and concepts of social organization and solidarity inherited from the *ancien régime* (Desrosières and Thévenot 1996: 10). The concept of *métier* still has currency as a way of describing a form of identification with an occupational culture. However, as the impact of the industrial production and modern state organization came to be felt in the latter part of the nineteenth century, social distinctions based on the hierarchy of capitalist entrepreneurs, non-manual employees, skilled manual and unskilled labourers became more apparent. Eventually these social changes were reflected in the categories used for census and survey data as well as collective bargaining over wages and working conditions.

Thus a system of social classification was adopted which was more hierarchical and based on socio-economic criteria (type of income and employment relationship) and less concerned with the collective culture of occupations. It was linked with the trend towards the 'scientific management' of production and the detailed division of labour between tasks. This view was consolidated by national agreements (the Matignon Accords of 1936) between large employers and trade unions designed to standardize categories of work, skill and remuneration. The system of socio-occupational categories (known since 1982 as PCS, the system of *professions et catégories socio-professionelles*) which emerged out of this process is the basis for most data and discussion of the class structure and related questions (such as the shape of public opinion) in modern France. While many of the terms are recognizable to an international audience, there are certain distinctions and nuances which mean that it is useful to take a closer look at the vocabulary. The following account is based on the post-1982 classification which uses a hierarchical scheme of 489 occupations, which can be combined into simpler categories. A summary of the data for the year 1982 (the first year of the current classification) and 1993 is shown in Table 1.1.

The 'economically active' population consists of employees, those in employment, and those seeking employment. The economically inactive population in France includes the retired, children, students and those who are not seeking work.

The first category of farmers (*agriculteurs exploitants*) comprises those working the land on a small as well as large scale but excludes agricultural workers on a wage. The decline in numbers over the decade is part of the long-term shift towards industrialized agriculture, although it is interesting to note that this category of occupation remained larger than either industry or the tertiary sector until the late 1930s, showing that France has been a relatively late developer in this respect – more like Italy than the UK or Germany (see also Chapter 6). The category of artisans, shopkeepers and owners of businesses with ten or more employees consists of occupations which are based on the use of small or large amounts or capital for production and commerce, not salaries or wages from employment. Its size, though in decline, is considerable and it reflects the continuing importance of the small entrepreneur

Table 1.1 Distribution of the economically active population

Occupational category	1982	1993
1. Farmer (owners and tenants)	1,475,000	927,000
2. Artisans, shopkeepers, business owners	1,835,000	1,749,000
3. *Cadres* and higher professions	1,895,000	2,861,000
4. Intermediate professions	3,971,000	4,960,000
5. White-collar workers	6,247,000	7,119,000
6. Manual workers	7,749,000	6,834,000
Unemployed	353,000	299,000
Total active population*	23,525,000	24,748,000

Note:
*Excluding those doing national service.
Sources: *Economie et statistique*, no. 171–172, Nov–Dec 1984; and INSEE, 'Emploi' survey 1994.

in the French economic and social system (see the discussion of the petite bourgeoisie, p. 26). This category, like the first, does not fit easily into the hierarchical system of salaries and wages nor into a system of formal educational qualifications. It is more closely associated with the older system of *métiers* and family production. Thus many small firms and businesses depend on family participation, especially the work of spouses. The category is less stable than those based on higher qualifications and salaried employment. Shopkeepers, self-employed artisans and small business owners move in and out of this category according to their stage in the life-cycle and as economic conditions change. The net effect of these movements, however, has been contraction at the expense of paid employment. The ethos of independence (from 'big' business, the state or the indignities of wage labour) is the most important legacy which this somewhat anomalous category has bestowed on French society and culture (Mayer 1987).

The third category, *cadres* and higher professions, is based on a concept of occupations with a high level of qualification and experience. The skills of this group may be exercised in the public or private sector (or both) but they typically involve *grande école* higher education and a significant amount of managerial responsibility. The term 'cadre' has no direct equivalent in English and many writers on French society leave it untranslated. Indeed, one of the leading French writers on the emergence of the *cadres* declines to give a definition on the ground that it is not a neutral descriptive term but, rather, a social construction which came out of a specific middle-class movement in the 1930s (Boltanski 1987: 37ff.). The category has a social identity and status which brings together elements of executive responsibility, managerial power, public authority and professionalism. The *cadre* concept is an interesting indication of the coherence and importance of the élite of French occupations. The numbers in this category have grown rapidly as the functions of co-ordination and control of the economy and society of advanced capitalism have become more complex. Of course, occupations such as the professions of law, medicine and science have roots which go back well before the emergence of the *cadres* but they are increasingly incorporated into the system of public administration and services. This category is the summit of French society – the technocratic managerial class – and its role has provoked much debate. Some of the themes from this debate will be examined below.

The category of intermediate professions displays similar growth, and for similar reasons. These are the public sector occupations in health, education, social work and public administration which require professional training, as well as technical and supervisory occupations in private commerce and industry. Sometimes known as the *cadres moyens*, these occupations form the core of the middle class. Their incomes, career structure and systems of qualification are superior to those of the next category, the white-collar workers (*employés*). The groups in this sector are engaged in service or clerical occupations in a wide variety of settings: offices, shops, hotels, nurseries, the police, etc. The most distinctive feature of this category is that more than three quarters are women (Desrosières and Thévenot 1996: 84). This points to the significant differences between male and female employment opportunities and is a reminder that occupations and class are not the only source of structural divisions in society. The final category of occupations is the manual workers (*ouvriers*) subdivided by sector and level of skill. The boundaries are relatively well defined: they correspond more or less directly to the manual working class which emerged in the nineteenth century as a social and political movement associated with the conditions of industrial wage labour. Many of the internal divisions are the outcome of the systems of industrial bargaining between employers and workers. Finally, the PCS has a residual category for the unemployed who cannot be assigned to any other category because they have never had employment.

Thus, the occupational system in France is distinct in several ways from its neighbours in Europe: it is the product of relatively late industrialization, it has a strongly centralized system of élite occupations closely linked with the state sector, an active tradition of small-scale entrepreneurs, and a working class with a historically strong attachment to socialism.

Class and social inequalities

The division of the economically active population into occupational categories is an important basis for understanding social structure because work and productive activity are the backbone of the organization of a society in pursuit of its economic goals. However, the occupational classification is not a class structure as such; it is simply a set of categories which are described according to standard attributes. It does not explain how the social relations of class are formed, how the boundaries are constructed, or the movement between them. In reality, the main divisions between social groups are defined by their relative power and their differential access to wealth, income and 'cultural capital', as well as the ways in which they pursue their collective interests (Bertaux 1977). The categories of the French class structure in the twentieth century recognized by the majority of French sociologists are described in the following sections. The most fundamental distinction, between the bourgeoisie and the working class, derives from Marxist class theory which gives priority to the position of social groups in relation to the capitalist system of production. Some of the key French terms in current use are listed alongside the main class categories.

I *Owners of capital, higher level* cadres *and* professions *(class dirigeante, classe dominante, classe supérieure, grande bourgeoisie)*

The differences in terminology reflect the alternative interpretations of the class's role. Together, these categories constitute the uppermost political, economic and cultural stratum. They are not exactly coterminous with the 'ruling' class in the classic Marxist sense that they either own or control the means of reproducing economic wealth. Such a definition would exclude the higher level professions and state employees who exercise power and influence by virtue of their public office. These groups are included in the present definition because the state is the pre-eminent means of economic and social control in modern societies and the highest offices are as important as those in the private sector. However, all of these groups have privileged access to cultural capital including education, and they are most influential in establishing political and social priorities for the society as a whole. The class is very small in numbers compared with others. How much wealth and income do the members of this class receive compared with other groups? National statistics and detailed analyses of wealth and income in France confirm that in the post-war period inequalities have been higher than the average for other western European countries (Marceau 1977: 39–50). In the 1960s the share of income received by the top 20 per cent of the French population was 53.7 per cent compared with 52.9 per cent in West Germany, 44.2 per cent in the United Kingdom and 44 per cent in Sweden (Atkinson 1983: 26). These differences reflect the degree to which wealth and income inequalities are modified by taxation and welfare policies designed to bring about a more even distribution. These results are confirmed in subsequent comparative data based on the index of wealth and income distribution known as the Gini Coefficient.[1] In a ranking produced by Lane and Ersson, France had the highest level of inequality of all the European countries with the exception of Greece (1987:83). The measurement of wealth and income is notoriously difficult because it involves many types of assets. Using wealth (*patrimoine*) to mean ownership of land, property, stocks and shares, material goods and equipment, plus non-material assets such as rights and intellectual property, data from the standard occupational categories produced by INSEE shows the average pattern of distribution (Table 1.2). The table is based on the pre-1982 classification which separates out the category of business owners with significant capital (*industriels* and *gros commerçants*) from the category of artisans and small business owners. The data are therefore more revealing than those from the current classification.

The distribution of wealth is more unequal than the distribution of income. Table 1.2 shows that the households of the wealthiest categories are between three and four-and-a-half times richer than the average despite the fact that the averages in the table mask the

Table 1.2 Average wealth (in millions of francs) by occupational category in 1982

	Average wealth (gross)	Average wealth (net)
Farmers	1,361	1,224
Artisans and small business owners	950	797
Owners of large businesses	2,472	2,297
Liberal professions	1,749	1,545
Higher-level *cadres*	1,011	910
Intermediate *cadres*	439	364
White-collar workers	331	283
Manual workers	268	221
Average	548	494

Source: INSEE, 'Données Sociales' 1987, p. 245. Quoted in Bihr and Pfefferkorn (1995).

differences within categories and therefore understate the degree of inequality. The greater economic resources of the upper class are not only significant for the consumption of goods and services. They give members access to the other forms of power, whether in private industry, public services, culture or the professions. Of course, in each of these sectors there are élite groups which have their own character and interests. However, one of the distinctive features of French society is the cohesion of these upper echelons and the similarity of experience and ideology which is linked with the high degree of centralization of French institutions.

This aspect of the French social structure has attracted the interest of a number of social researchers including Birnbaum (1978) who investigated the origins of the *classe dirigeante* using information from *Who's Who in France*. With the rapid development of industry in the post-war period, the relative importance of the constituent groups changed. Proprietors of businesses and family firms (*patrons*) declined in numbers while the group of directors, managers and salaried professionals expanded. The change was consistent with the current theory that the capitalist ruling class based on private wealth and power was being substituted in modern industrial society by a technocratic élite. This idea was reinforced by the evidence that the most rapidly growing group was the *cadres supérieurs*, boosted by the expansion of industry and large-scale enterprises as well as the expansion of state and public administration. Birnbaum was concerned to find out where the recruits to this class came from and whether the expansion represented an opportunity for upward mobility from other classes.

He cites evidence to show that, while the composition of the upper class changed in line with changes in the industrial structure, more than two thirds of its members were recruited from within its own ranks (Birnbaum 1978: 92). The typical mechanism for recruitment to virtually all élite positions in the civil service and private industry was through the *grandes écoles*, especially the ENA (the École Nationale d'Administration). There is obviously a parallel between the influence of the *grandes écoles* in France and the dominance of the public schools and Oxbridge in the British establishment. Both have been effective mechanisms for the upper class to maintain their dominant position in their respective countries. One essential difference, however, is the relative facility with which the French élite can move between top positions in the civil service, private industry, business and banking. The combination of expertise, close professional networks and prestige allow, for example, nearly one third of all *inspecteurs de finance* to move into private sector positions – mainly in banking – at some stage in their career; hence the term *pantouflage* used to describe horizontal movement of this kind.[2]

To summarize, the upper class has been a distinct and relatively homogeneous component of the French class system. Its élitism is unashamed and widely legitimated by the belief that society as a whole, not just the interests of the class itself, are well served by the corps of mobile, highly trained and politically independent technocrats. Periodically, the élite and its lack of accountability to the rest of society have been attacked both from within and outside the élite. Crozier, for example, in a famous critique, blamed the rigidity of the centralized hierarchy for the 'blockages' in French society which led to the explosion of May 1968 (Crozier 1970). But there is little doubt that the same features were beneficial for centralized economic planning and *dirigiste* policies in the years of economic modernization and rapid growth during the 1950s, 1960s and early 1970s. At a time when all classes were experiencing rising standards of living, inequalities of wealth and income were not as divisive as they would otherwise have been. More recently, as France has moved towards a more 'post-industrial' economic and social structure, some of the criticisms have become increasingly pertinent.

2 Middle classes (classe moyenne, cadres moyens)

The size and composition of the middle classes in France reflects the expansion of occupations involved in the planning, co-ordination and administration of industrial and post-industrial society. This class includes the positions which the PCS from 1982 describes as *cadres*, together with the liberal, intellectual and intermediate professions. They involve a wide range of salaried occupations in research, design and development; professional roles in education, health and the administration of services; accounting; production management; creative roles in media and cultural industries; and a multitude of occupations which fulfil the 'service' functions in a modern economy.[3] There are many fine gradations within the middle-class occupations but most are linked with bureaucratic career structures, and involve delegated authority and autonomy in the workplace. They do not have the inherited property and wealth which sets the upper class apart but they do have the education and cultural capital to invest in the next generation, which maintains their relative advantages. In these respects, the French middle classes are in a similar position to those in other European countries and have comparable education, careers, culture and lifestyles.

The growth of the middle classes means that they not only recruit from within their own ranks but contain a significant proportion of upwardly-mobile members from the petite bourgeoisie as well as the non-manual and manual working class. For example, nearly two-thirds of the other *cadres moyens* born between 1918 and 1935 came from other backgrounds (defined by the father's occupation): 9 per cent farmers, 36 per cent manual workers, 11 per cent white-collar employees, and 8 per cent from the *cadres supérieurs* (Bertaux 1977: 23). Subsequent generations have not experienced such a high level of intergenerational mobility and rely instead more heavily on formal qualifications for their occupational advancement. The culture, traditions and political allegiances of the middle classes are not as sharply defined as in other classes.

If the middle classes are so complex and heterogeneous, how should they be characterized? Boltanski makes the valuable point that a social group's identity is more likely to be articulated through paradigmatic examples of the 'type' than through precise definitions of boundaries. In his research on French *cadres* he finds that the 'exemplary' *cadre* is a male in his forties, a business school graduate, working in sales, marketing or advertising (rather than production), and employed by a successful, well-known organization such as IBM, and likely to be living in Paris (1987: 281–2). This image is revealing because it suggests that the post-'68 generation of *cadres* is more closely identified with post-Fordist consumer capitalism than with public service in the centralized, dirigiste state which was once the main avenue for *cadre* mobility.

There are a number of important social and political issues connected with the evolution of the middle classes. Above all they are the product of their intermediate position in the social structure which – as the nomenclature of the 1982 PCS implies – involves acting as social intermediaries in education, health, welfare, culture and consumption. These occupations have attempted to follow the higher or liberal professions by creating professional bodies and systems of qualification but neither their market position nor their conditions of work allow them to achieve fully independent status. In fact, there is a constant threat of proletarianization among these service occupations as they become relatively less well paid, less skilled and less autonomous. Contemporary debates about social class and political behaviour naturally focus on these developments in the middle class because they often hold the balance of power without being an organized political force. An important dimension is the degree to which occupations among the middle class are becoming feminized; in 1995 women accounted for 45 per cent of employment in the intermediate professions (Desrosières and Thévenot 1996: 105). Because women tend to be under-represented in promoted positions and are more likely to have interrupted careers than men, it is usually assumed that their opportunities for organized action are restricted. However, their concentration in state service occupations may be an encouragement to collective action.

3 Petite bourgeoisie

The petite bourgeoisie, or lower middle class, is a category which hardly figures in most contemporary accounts of class structure in European societies. It does appear in the theory of E.O. Wright as a 'contradictory' class position defined by ownership and control of limited means of production and use of one's own or family labour-power' (1985: 48–9). It is seen as a residual class of small-scale business owners and the self-employed which has been almost completely eliminated by the growth of large-scale capitalism. There is obviously some truth in this: the hypermarket is today at least as important for French shoppers as the traditional small *épicerie* or *boulangerie* despite a certain nostalgia for the latter. The number of small independent retailers declined by 11 per cent between 1968 and 1975 and by 5 per cent between 1975 and 1982. But the decline is not terminal: the *artisans* and *commerçants* categories in the PCS still constitute about 6 per cent of the active population. The number of artisans actually grew by 7 per cent in the 1975–82 period, possibly in response to a harsher economic climate for employment (Mayer 1987: 57).

Although the petite bourgeoisie has its roots in the tradition of household production and *métiers*, where assets are handed down through the family line and expertise is acquired on the job, there is a constant process of renewal. It comes from the widespread desire to work on one's own account and to escape from the restrictions of wage labour and salaried employment. According to surveys reported in Mayer (1987: 42) half the French population in 1984 claimed that 'to be your own boss' was an ideal of success, and, in 1977, 35 per cent (excluding the self-employed) said that they had been 'tempted' or had 'the desire to' set-up their own business, a significantly higher proportion than the European average. For the manual working class and those in routine white-collar employment, artisanal businesses (for the former especially) and shopkeeping are an important channel for mobility and independence. For some, it is only temporary and for most the price of 'freedom' in terms of modest income and long hours is high. However it keeps alive a set of social and political aspirations to be independent from both the state and big business which have regularly found a voice in politics. The rhetoric is most closely linked with the movement led by Pierre Poujade in 1953 and other populist movements up to the present, including Le Pen's Front National, although it is not exclusively right wing.

4 Working class (classe ouvrière, ouvriers, employés)

The French working class came into being with the development of wage labour in the nineteenth century and the new conditions of industrial work and employment. Theories of class formation and class conflict, especially those of Marx and Marxists, see the growing consciousness and organization of the working class as the prime mover of change in industrial society and the vehicle for radical and revolutionary politics. The historical reality is more complex: the working class has its own internal divisions, its identity as a class has never been pure, and it has adopted a variety of strategies to defend its position.

Notwithstanding the decline in the size of the working class from its peak in 1973 (Therborn 1995: 69) following changes in the structure of employment, it is still the largest class grouping. Divisions within the manual working class are reflected in the occupational classification – mainly in terms of skill. Of the 6,834,000 manual workers (*ouvriers*) in the 1993 employment survey (see Table 1.1, p. 18), 61 per cent were skilled (*ouvriers qualifiés*), 35 per cent were unskilled (*ouvriers spécialisés*) and 4 per cent were employed in agriculture. These divisions of skill and occupation are mirrored in the employment conditions, work experience and social milieu of each stratum. The most highly skilled workers have the most secure positions, the highest wages and the strongest organizations to protect their position. They also have better access to education and qualifications. It is no surprise to find that they are more committed to the formal recognition of qualifications and respond more positively to technological innovation. New categories of employment and new forms of union organization persuaded some observers that a 'new working class' was in the making (Mallet 1963). However, these were not conditions likely to generate a revolutionary consciousness or movement. In contrast, the unskilled working class has often endured forms of work which are much closer to the description of alienated wage labour found in Marxist theory: insecurity, low wages, detailed division of labour, and dangerous or unhealthy conditions.

Interpretations of the working class in the 1960s and 1970s were driven by a fascination with the extent of their class consciousness and radical potential. The response of the trade unions and working class as a whole to the events of May 1968, which included a general strike by 9 million workers, provided plenty of fuel for discussion of working-class behaviour. Evidence from a number of sources during this period (for example, Gallie 1983, Hamilton 1967, Touraine 1966) confirms that France had the most radical and politicized working class of all the western European countries. While the working class in Britain and Germany, for example, were equally aware of income inequalities and social disadvantage, they expressed less resentment and were less inclined to criticize the wider structure of society. Their trade union ambitions were limited in practice to bargaining over wages, hours and working conditions. In contrast, the largest trade union in France, the Confédération Générale du Travail (CGT), espoused a class critique of capitalist society and worked to mobilize support for the political left, especially the French Communist Party.

Such a preoccupation with proletarian mass consciousness now seems dated. French society has altered in step with the more global, flexible and consumption-orientated capitalism. Old boundaries, social milieux and identities have been eroded, and theories of class conflict and action have lost their ideological charge with the demise of communism. The occupational categories remain but they have more meaning as personal attributes than symbols of collective organised labour. One of the most important changes in the occupational structure is that the boundary between manual work and routine clerical and white-collar work has dwindled as the manufacturing and service sectors have converged. The lower level clerical and service occupations (*employés*, *employées*) are incorporated into the wider working class. They share increasingly similar occupational attributes because they use information technology, jobs involve personal as well as technical skills, and more training takes place 'off the job'.

The routine white-collar occupations have a higher proportion of women than any other category (76 per cent in 1995). This phenomenon, which is part of the more general increase in women's paid employment, has helped to shift the alignment of the working class from its male and 'Fordist' hierarchy of manual skills towards a more complex mix including service, personal and social communication skills. The emerging structure of working-class occupations is less differentiated, more uncertain and more dependent on social and cultural capital than the traditional industrial proletariat. How far this 'post-industrial' class structure provides opportunities for upward mobility is as yet unclear, although it is likely that the answer to the question will depend on the state institutions which provide income protection, training, equal opportunities on employment, and career pathways (Esping-Andersen 1993: 17–22).

The relatively small group of agricultural workers is classified separately. They have very low wages and the longest working hours. There is a high proportion of workers of foreign origin in this category, which highlights race and ethnicity as a further source of social differentiation, alongside class.

5 *Farmers* (agriculteurs exploitants)

This is one of the oldest occupational categories and the one which has seen the most profound changes in the post-war period. The classification is based on the criterion of land ownership and is subdivided into large-, medium- and small-scale farmers according to the area of cultivation. Small and medium farmers are still numerous in France compared with the UK, Germany and the Low Countries (629,000 in 1990 with land up to 40 hectares). However, the process of concentration and industrialization of agriculture has led to massive mobility out of this sector, mostly into the working class. What remains is not simply a dying *paysan* or country way of life but a more modern and economically integrated class which has an identity linked with the EU subsidy system, improved production and marketing methods, and access to urban lifestyles.

Contemporary critiques of class and inequality

Overwhelmingly, the evidence pertaining to class structure in France confirms that its essential features derive from the types of industrial organization and division of labour which prevail in all modern societies. The similarities between France and other western European societies are far more striking than any of the differences which have been noted in this chapter. Moreover, the class structure and the inequalities which persist in employment, education, housing, consumption, health and mobility chances have endured throughout the twentieth century. According to cross-national research on intergenerational mobility, the relative chances of being mobile between classes were much the same in the 1980s as they had been fifty years earlier in all industrial societies – the only exception being Sweden, whose welfare policies have had a measurable impact on inequalities (Marshall 1997: 3–6). In France, as elsewhere, what has changed dramatically is the shape of the class structure and the relative size of the main class groupings as manufacturing employment has declined and service employment has grown. This has allowed more opportunities for mobility into the upper levels although the relative chances for movement between different class locations have hardly changed.

At the same time it is hard to deny that social class is a less salient topic than it was. Class has lost its importance in political rhetoric: no longer is it the natural core of individual identity and status, and the criteria which social scientists use to classify social groups are harder to apply. Sociologists and social commentators have therefore looked for alternative ways to describe social inequality and its impacts. In France, recent discussion has centred around the idea that society has become more difficult to 'figure out', more diffuse, fragmented and prone to disintegration. The emphasis is less on structure and more on the elusive qualities of a 'society' which seems to be without clear principles of organization. Society is described as 'opaque' (Fitoussi and Rosanvallon 1996) and 'fragmented' (Wieviorka 1996) and keywords include uncertainty, insecurity, exclusion and 'disaffiliation' (Castel 1995).

The issues, and the debate, are complex. The sense of turbulence and change is linked with a number of developments in the economic as well as the cultural spheres. While the French economy has continued to grow and become more closely integrated into the larger European economy, it shares the endemic problems of unemployment and exclusion. The trend towards deregulation since the 1980s has accelerated the processes of restructuring and labour market reform. A 1993 survey found that close to half of the French male population of economically active age (18–65) had experienced at least one period of unemployment in the previous ten years (quoted in Fitoussi and Rosanvallon 1996: 28). Therefore, while class positions may not have changed, work and employment are now experienced as more arbitrary and uncertain. This alone is sufficient to engender doubts about the ability of occupations and careers to deliver a secure position within the wider society. But this is not the only source of uncertainty. As work, employment and careers are compelled to conform to the new system of global competition, so the social institutions which once provided some protection from the arbitrariness of this sphere – the family, neighbourhood, trade unions and local associations – have themselves become more 'privatized'. Individual identity, which is closely linked with social recognition and status, is less firmly rooted in shared social conditions and experiences and has suffered a kind of 'decompression'. From the individual point of view, unemployment, debt, surviving on a pension, or becoming a social security claimant are experiences of inequality which are increasingly likely to be lived in isolation from the traditional sources of personal and social support. Only a biographical approach can show how far this has occurred and how it affects a person's social identity. But the evidence points to a growing problem of social cohesion which is exacerbated by a lack of direction in the political system. Loss of confidence in socialist policies since the fall of communism has combined with uncertainty about the future of the nation state in the European context to cause ambivalence where previously there was a confident approach to the problem of inequality – either to justify it or to struggle against it in the name of progress.

Other chapters in this volume will elaborate on aspects of the 'new inequalities' in France. This chapter has shown that, while the system of class relations is the basic framework within which access to or exclusion from occupations, income, wealth, education, opportunities and even health are worked out, the everyday experience of class and status is becoming less determined by shared ways of life. Alain Touraine speaks for many interpreters when he says that these experiences are the outworking of a long term process of divergence in modern societies between technological or market rationality and the affirmation of freedom by the individual subject. He warns that if this separation is allowed to become a complete divorce 'there will be a break between the inside and the outside, between a society identified with a market and social actors reduced to drives or traditions' (1995: 232). The twentieth-century class system in France, for all its inequalities and conflicts has been a vehicle for individuals and groups to express themselves and act according to an image of society as a whole. Where there is no such image, society 'oscillates between resignation and nostalgia, silent despair and transient protest' (Fitoussi and Rosanvallon 1996: 231). Questions of class unavoidably turn into questions about society as a moral order and the kind of citizenship which can unite a population against both new and old inequalities which lead to exclusion.

Notes

1   The Gini Coefficient is a summary measure of the overall distribution of income and wealth in a society which derives a value between 0 (which represents complete equality) and 1 (which represents total concentration).
2   The existence of the term *pantouflage* (from *pantoufle* meaning slipper) signals the importance and relative ease of movement between the state and private sectors for members of the French élite.
3   In some discussions of the 'service class' (for example, Erikson and Goldthorpe 1992: 40–1) the category includes the higher professions and large-scale employers. Elsewhere, it is subdivided into higher and lower levels which correspond quite closely to the categories of higher and intermediate level *cadres* used by French sociologists. There is a basic similarity of class position at all levels but variations in the extent of expertise, delegated authority and autonomy at work.

Bibliography

Atkinson, A.B. (1983) *The Economics of Inequality*, Oxford: Oxford University Press.

Bertaux, D. (1977) *Destins personnels et structure de classe*, Paris: Presses Universitaires de France.

Bihr, A. and Pfefferkorn, R. (1995) *Déchiffrer les inégalités*, Paris: Syros.

Birnbaum, N. (1978) *La Classe dirigeante française*, Paris: Presses Universitaires de France.

Boltanski, L. (1987) *The Making of a Class:* Cadres *in French Society*, Cambridge: Cambridge University Press.

Bourdieu, P. (1979) *La Distinction: Critique sociale du jugement*, Paris: Editions de Minuit.

Castel, R. (1995) *Les Métamorphoses du social*, Paris: Fayard.

Crompton, R. (1993) *Class and Stratification: An Introduction to Current Debates*, Cambridge: Polity.

Crozier, M. (1970) *La Société bloquée*, Paris: Le Seuil.

Desrosières, A. and Thévenot, L. (1996) *Les Catégories socioprofessionnelles*, Paris: Editions La Découverte.

Erikson, R. and Goldthorpe, J.H. (1992) *The Constant Flux: A Study of Class Mobility in Industrial Societies*, Oxford: Clarendon Press.

Esping-Andersen, G. (1993) *Changing Classes: Stratification and Social Mobility in Post-industrial Societies*, London: Sage.

Fitoussi, J-P. and Rosanvallon, P. (1996) *Le Nouvel Age des inégalités*, Paris: Editions du Seuil.

Gallie, D. (1983) *Social Inequality and Class Radicalism in France and Britain*, Cambridge: Cambridge University Press.

Hamilton, R.F. (1967) *Affuence and the French Worker in the Fourth Republic*, Princeton: Princeton University Press.

Lane J.E. and Ersson S.O. (1987) *Politics and Society in Western Europe*, London: Sage.

Lemel, Y. (1991) *Stratification et mobilité sociale*, Paris: Armand Colin.

Mallet, S. (1963) *La Nouvelle Classe ouvrière*, Paris: Editions du Seuil.

Marceau, J. (1977) *Class and Status in France: Economic Change and Social Immobility 1945–1975*, Oxford: Clarendon Press.

Marshall, G. (1997) *Repositioning Class: Social Inequality in Industrial Societies*, London: Sage.

Mayer, N. (1987) 'Small business and social mobility in France', in R. Goffee and R. Scase (eds) *Entrepreneurship in Europe: The Social Process*, London: Croom Helm.

Therborn, G. (1995) *European Modernity and Beyond: The Trajectory of European Societies 1945–2000*, London: Sage.

Touraine, A. (1966) *La Conscience ouvrière*, Paris: Le Seuil.

—— (1995) *Critique of Modernity*, Oxford: Blackwell.

Wieviorka, M. (ed.) (1996) *Une société fragmentée? Le multiculturalisme en débat*, Paris: Editions La Decouverte.

Wright, E.O. (1985) *Classes*, London: Verso.

Chapter 2

Race and ethnicity

Cathie Lloyd

> The unity of France is hard to keep in sight. Having assumed it
> would be obvious from the start, we find it escaping us: we are
> faced with a hundred, a thousand different Frances of long ago,
> yesterday or today.
>
> (Braudel 1988: 35)

The ideas of race and ethnicity are highly controversial in France,
and are dealt with in complex and sometimes contradictory ways. The
French republican ideal of equality is opposed to the idea of race
which differentiates, classifies and places people in hierarchies. There
is a conflict between the universalist idea of equality and the particularist idea of racial or ethnic difference.

In this chapter I examine the problems of definition of race and
ethnicity which have recently assumed such importance in France,
framing discussions of immigration and multiculturalism in the
broader context of attitudes towards indigenous ethnic identity.
Contemporary debates about race and ethnicity focus on immigration, so I provide some basic information about its main characteristics and examine the principal changes in policy since the 1970s and
discuss how they have contributed to the racialization of certain
groups.[1] In so doing I emphasize the importance of the electoral
success of the Front National in the light of wider political discourses on
race ethnicity and immigration. The chapter ends with a brief assess-
ment of the extent to which France is becoming a pluri-ethnic society.

Definitions

The idea of race was founded on nineteenth-century scientific beliefs
that individuals could be classified on the basis of physical appear-

ance and inheritance. It was thought that physical variations such as skin colour gave rise to distinct behaviour, and that the different races were incompatible with one another. Mixing was undesirable because it was thought to lead to the degeneration of so-called 'pure' races. This idea has been discredited due to numerous reasons, including the unacceptable political practices with which it was associated, such as colonial racist divisions epitomized by the apartheid system of separate development in South Africa or the extermination of specific groups of people, notably Jews, gypsies, homosexuals and disabled people by the Nazis during the Second World War. The United Nations Economic, Scientific and Cultural Organization (Unesco) adopted a moral stand against the doctrine of racism while at the same time demonstrating that it was irrational and unscientific (Kuper 1975). Post-war genetic research, fostered by Unesco, found that human beings have more in common with one another than divides them genetically. This was the theme of an exhibition, 'Tous parents, tous différents', at the National Museum of Natural History at the Musée de l'Homme in Paris in 1992.

In the United Kingdom and other European countries official bodies often substitute the concept of ethnic group for that of race. The idea of ethnicity refers to the criteria by which individuals belong to a particular group through a shared culture, history, language, religion, often emphasising their subjective belief in their common origin (Weber 1969: 395). In France neither the concept of race nor ethnicity are used in common parlance: it is more common to refer to the problem of racism. Academics, government bodies and political movements broadly agree that the ideas of race and ethnicity are difficult to reconcile with the republican ideas of equality. In contrast to countries such as the Netherlands and the United Kingdom, there is no official keeping of ethnic records in France.[2]

The French rarely use the term 'ethnic minority', instead the most frequently used descriptions are 'immigrants', 'foreigners' or 'French'. These descriptions are not very clear or satisfactory because they are based on a legal status, which may change. Strictly speaking, an immigrant is a person living in France but who was not born there. However, during their residence in France, their status may change if they adopt French nationality (Tribalat et al. 1991).

The historical aspects of race, ethnicity and assimilation

The concept of race and ethnicity can be traced back in history to ideas about classification debated during the Enlightenment which inspired the Revolution of 1789. The idea of classification clashed with another key idea of the time which was that all men (sic) were equal. After the Revolution the nation was seen as a voluntary association or contract between free individuals. The Declaration of the Rights of Man of 1789 emphasized this fundamental political equality, an idea which has been enshrined in the founding principles of subsequent republican constitutions. For instance, the constitution of the Fifth Republic states that: 'France is an indivisible, secular, democratic and social Republic. She guarantees the equality before the law of all citizens without distinction of origin, race or of religion' (Constitution of the Fifth Republic: title 1, art. 2).

Writers such as Colette Guillaumin who have analysed the concept of race since the eighteenth century, point to the changing and unstable meaning of the term (Guillaumin 1992). Before the 1789 Revolution, it was claimed that the nobility were the descendants of the Francs who had conquered and protected the commoners or Gauls. The Comte de Gobineau, writing in the 1850s, claimed that the different races of the world could be arranged in a hierarchy of purity and ability. The *hygenists* of the early twentieth century followed this thinking by focusing on the dangers of mixing (*métissage*) of the different races. During the Second World War the logical consequences of the idea of race were shown in France when the Jewish population was singled out first for exclusion from a wide range of employment under the Vichy laws of 1942, and then for extermination when some 76,000 people were sent to death camps by the Nazi occupiers abetted by the Vichy regime. Guillaumin and others point out that because race is such an unacceptable term today, euphemisms are often used. The idea of *culture* has been substituted for race since the 1970s in the writings of the New Right. This intellectual tendency operated through debating clubs, notably the GRECE and the Club de l'Horloge. They argued that France was rooted in Indo-European, pagan culture, criticizing egalitarianism, Judaeo-Christianity and American culture as alien to European values. Racism was reorganized as an idea around praise for cultural difference, the celebration of roots and group identities which supported arguments for separateness while trying to remain distant from the discredited biological idea of race (Taguieff 1994).

In France membership of the nation involves inclusion in a political entity which implies cultural assimilation for regional and cultural minorities and immigrants (Brubaker 1996).The Revolution promoted centralizing and homogenizing ideas which were hostile to expressions of regional and cultural difference such as language, which could threaten the unity of the *République une et indivisible*. This concept of the nation as a political entity differs from the German idea of the nation as based on an ethnic group or *volk*. France and Germany were contrasted in a famous lecture by Ernest Renan in 1882 in which he described the French model of the nation as 'a daily plebiscite' (Renan 1990). The French view of the nation discounts the idea that citizens might be different from one another in any significant way. French nationhood is thus based on a political bond and expressed through its cultural unity.

In practice however, there was enormous variation within France, including that of language. Under the monarchy the regions of France[3] were attached to the Crown under varying arrangements. The Revolution of 1789 changed this, so that the departments of France were ruled directly from Paris (Beer 1977: 144). In order to produce a French nation, certain indigenous ethnic identities were suppressed, in ways which are now acknowledged to have involved an unacceptable denial of human rights (Giordan 1982). Even before the Revolution the state had attempted to control identity. For instance, since 1539 parents had a legal obligation to register their children's names with the state in accordance with an approved list (Bernstein 1991). Successive governments repressed the use of regional languages: Berger (1977) refers to notices in schools during the Third Republic which stipulated 'no spitting and no speaking of Breton'. Negative stereotypes, notably that of Bécassine the dim Breton servant girl, became commonplace:

> The Bretons were the servants, the prostitutes, the cannon fodder of France, and escape from Brittany into French civilization was held out by schools to Breton children as the only route to dignity and self-respect.
>
> (Berger 1977: 166)

The impact of the Jacobin view of the State as a political rather than a natural entity, was that supporters of the Republic felt threatened by ethnic identity. The idea that expressions of ethnicity tended to be reactionary seemed to be borne out in the nineteenth and twentieth centuries. Ethnic regionalists were anti-republican and some even collaborated with the Nazis during the occupation.

Since the 1960s ethnic regionalism has been transformed, forming an important component of the social movements which emerged after the events of May '68. Regional ethnic groups used a Third World rhetoric to draw attention to their demands for economic development, suggesting that regions like Brittany were underdeveloped and peripheral to the Parisian core. The upsurge in regional ethnic identities has been analysed as a response to the conditions of modernization, or linked to the growing concern with environmental issues. In the 1980s, new regional policies were introduced following the publication of the Giordan report (1982) reinforcing demands for the recognition of the right to be different. It was thought that ethnic minorities should be allowed to use their own language in school as part of cultural democracy (see also Chapter 5).

Even today, however, the expression of ethnic difference sits uneasily alongside republican ideas of equality through individual assimilation. The Jacobin view of equality runs the risk that real inequalities between citizens might be ignored: if all citizens are equal what space is there to understand social stratification based on gender, ethnic group or income? Neither does the idea of an equal citizenry provide any guidance regarding the position of foreigners living in France who are the main subjects of contemporary debates on race and ethnicity.

It was thought that republican ideas embodied the universally desirable goals of Liberty, Equality and Fraternity. The French claimed to encourage these ideas in their foreign policy, but it was a short step from believing that their values should be fostered throughout the world to thinking that French culture was superior. As France built up its empire, especially in the 1880s, it was inspired by the idea of a worldwide mission to foster French culture. Spread of French ideas was often used as a façade behind which lurked the economic and military aims of colonialism, which had nothing to do with the enlightenment of colonized peoples. During the first part of the twentieth century, the ideals of the French Revolution, particularly the idea of liberty and the right to self-determination, were taken up by anti-colonial movements and turned against the French colonizers.

Unlike the British, the French tended not to settle their colonies, with some exceptions, notably Algeria. Low birth rates, compounded by the heavy loss of life during the First World War meant that France needed to attract immigrant labour to work in its growing industries. Throughout the nineteenth and early twentieth centuries workers were recruited from other European countries: Italy, Poland, Germany and Belgium. Refugees came, fleeing anti-Semitic persecution in Eastern Europe, and fascism in Italy, Spain and Germany. Many immigrants worked on a seasonal, temporary basis, but others stayed and became French through naturalization. This long history of immigration distinguishes France from most of its European neighbours. It is often said that about a third of French citizens are the children, grandchildren or great-grandchildren of immigrants.

Becoming French involved people *assimilating* into French society. Assimilation was defined at the time of the emancipation of the Jews in 1791 who on becoming French, were expected to set aside public manifestations of their religious, cultural and other particularities. Clermont-Tonnerre summed up these ideas in a famous statement:

> We must reject the idea of the Jews as a nation, but we must give them everything as individuals...they must neither form a political corps nor an order in the State; they must be citizens individually.
>
> (*Archives Parlementaires* 23 December 1789: 756)

In practice, assimilation only provided an illusion of equality. Although individual Jews were supposed to be equal citizens, they were still affected by anti-Semitism notably at the end of the nineteenth century, culminating in the Dreyfus Affair (Winock 1982). In colonial policy the idea of assimilation applied only to the educated élite and when workers from the North African colonies came to work in France they were treated with disdain and sometimes violence (Macmaster 1995).

After the Second World War the French government, advised by the demographer Alfred Sauvy, sought migrant workers from nearby European countries such as Italy, Yugoslavia and Portugal who were thought to be close enough in cultural terms to the French to settle and assimilate into French society.[4] However, from the late 1950s recruitment for unskilled construction and factory work turned increasingly to North Africa. Immigrants from the

French colony of Algeria had been entering France freely since the early twentieth century, but those who came experienced considerable hardship and bad living conditions, and lived segregated from the rest of French society (Etcherelli 1994). The tension and violence arising from these arrangements was intensified during the war for national independence in Algeria (Lloyd and Waters 1991: 54–5, Stora 1991). Police and auxiliaries raided the homes of North Africans living in France, and it became a common sight to see North African immigrant workers being stopped by the police in the streets of Paris. By the end of the Algerian war in 1962 'all the feelings of battered national pride, bitterness and disillusionment that remained...became centred on the Algerians in France' (Macmaster 1997: 211). They were stigmatized, seen as undesirable and potentially criminal, and they were frequently the target of violent right-wing racist groups.

The main characteristics of immigration in France in the 1990s

The numbers of immigrants has grown from 1.74 million in 1946 to 4.16 million in 1990 (Haut Conseil à l'Intégration 1992) but immigrants still represent roughly the same proportion of the population (between 6 and 8 per cent) as they did in 1931. About 14 million people – a quarter of the population of France – are the children or the grandchildren of immigrants. While in 1946 there were only 22,000 Algerians in France, in 1992 they now form the second largest immigrant group in France after the Portuguese. Although they are not immigrants but French citizens born on French territory overseas, we should also note that 340,000 people born in the Overseas Dominions and Territories (DOM-TOM) are now living in metro-politan France.[5]

Immigrants came to work in construction, automobile, mining and other heavy industries. Concentration in these sectors and in certain geographical regions, about one-third in the Paris region, made them vulnerable to economic fluctuations, which has meant that they experience high levels of unemployment, this is compounded by a lack of qualifications. Foreigners are excluded from many jobs in the public sector, although this has now been partly modified for European Union nationals. Earlier forms of cyclical, seasonal migration have given way to a more settled form of migration, especially with family reunification since the mid 1970s.

There are three main legal categories of people referred to as immigrants in France: those who are French by birth, those who are French by naturalization and those who retain their foreign nationality. The status of some migrants has changed over time. For instance, Algerians were considered as French until their country became independent in 1962. Today they are foreigners to whom special bilateral arrangements apply to their right of entry and their rights to French nationality. Unique among the people from Algeria are the *harkis*, who stayed loyal to France during the war of independence and migrated to France after 1962, when they were given French nationality.

In recent years there has been considerable debate about illegal immigration partly because there is uncertainty about their numbers. Recruitment in the 1950s and 1960s tacitly depended on migrants entering France on an undocumented basis and becoming legal after finding a regular job. There would be periodic, official amnesties during which they could apply for legal documents. This form of *post hoc* regularization has now officially ended, but many people continue to find precarious, badly paid work with employers willing to exploit 'illegal' workers (Haut Conseil à l'Intégration 1992). There are several categories of 'illegal' workers in France, most of whom entered the country legally. The biggest category are French nationals: many cannot be deported because they are the parents of French children, or are rejected asylum-seekers, over-stayers and people whose status has changed because of changes in the law.

Although the question of indigenous regional ethnic minorities remains, when discussing race and ethnicity in France the main issue is usually immigration. However not all immigrants are regarded in quite the same way. As we have already seen, some groups are singled out, particularly North Africans. I will now turn to consider how such racialized groups have also been produced by immigration policies.

Political approaches to immigration, integration and racism

While public opinion seems to understand the economic need for immigration, there has been more resistance to the wider acceptance of immigrants in French society (Schain 1994: 263). As immigrants from North Africa became increasingly integrated in social housing, there were debates about the acceptable number of immigrants who could be accommodated in a locality. What constituted the threshold of tolerance?

Within the past twenty years there have been major changes in the policies adopted towards immigration in France. In the period following 1945, often known as the *Trente Glorieuses*, immigrants were regarded as an economic necessity for the industrial reconstruction of the country. Since the 1970s, with major industrial restructuring and growing unemployment the need for immigrant labour has been questioned. Driven by the xenophobic pronouncements of the extreme right political party, the Front National, immigration has become synonymous with virtually every social evil.

Immigration has thus become a central political issue in France. Even minor amendments to the law are subject to fierce debate, and this has led to the impression that there is fundamental disagreement between the main political parties, whereas a careful examination of legislative and administrative change reveals more of a consensus (Weil 1997: 6). Governments of both the right and left have tended to placate the supporters of the far right by acceding to demands for restrictions on immigration. No student of France's changing immigration policy will fail to be struck by the massive increase in regulations since the early 1970s: the law of 1945 has been amended twenty times and there has been a much larger number of decrees, orders and circulars.

During the 1950s and 1960s as we have seen, immigration was largely uncontrolled, regulated by administrative circular or *infradroit* (Wihtol de Wenden 1988). Most people entered France as tourists and sought regular papers once they had found work. It only seemed necessary to control immigration from the early 1970s when the economic downturn precipitated by the oil crisis, meant that there was a fall in the demand for labour. This coincided with a series of violent attacks on Algerian workers. From the 1970s the main emphasis has been on restricting immigration while making provision for the proper integration of people already in the country and the arrival of their families. The *Calvez* report in 1969 expressed concern as to the future impact of the bad living conditions of foreign workers. It recommended that non-Europeans should only be given temporary work permits. Circulars issued by two Ministers, Marcellin and Fontanet, made residence in France conditional on having employment and decent housing. Shortly after these restrictions were introduced, the Government agreed to a long-standing demand for a law against racism which had been drafted by anti-racist associations.

In the late 1970s all the main ingredients of later debates about immigration came into play. Like many other European countries the policy was a mixture of control and integration with an emphasis on the former. The Government proposed to reduce the number of immigrants in France by 200,000 a year by increasing deportations and introducing financial incentives to encourage repatriation. Immigrants who were settled in France found their lives destabilized by the replacement of the five- or ten-year residence card by an annual permit. Residence cards could be refused for a number of reasons including late return from paid holidays, the suspicion that a person was a threat to public order or loss of employment. From a status centred on employment which had been generally tolerated, the immigrant was being transformed into a person surrounded by a climate of suspicion and illegality. This was confirmed when the Government announced measures against clandestine immigration in 1980. Many of the measures introduced at this time were either found to be illegal by the Conseil d'Etat or proved ineffective (Wihtol de Wenden 1988: 255) but this only created the impression that the Government was powerless to reduce immigration.

By the time of the Presidential election of 1981 immigration had become an important issue. The idea of a 'threshold of tolerance', above which numbers of unassimilated immigrants could not be accepted into particular areas without undue social tensions, was widely accepted by local authorities. Left-wing, particularly Communist municipalities had the largest populations of immigrant workers and they found it difficult to balance the different interests of French and immigrant workers. These conflicts came to a head during the election campaign when one Communist mayor evicted West African immigrants from a hostel and exploited popular fears by associating North Africans with drug-dealing (Lloyd 1981, Marcus 1995: 77–8).

In their manifesto the Socialists had promised to give immigrant workers the vote in local elections. In government they failed to take a principled stand when these proposals proved controversial, although they did lift restrictions on the right of foreigners to lead associations thereby encouraging immigrants' participation in civic life. Many undocumented immigrants were regularised during an amnesty in the first months of the new government. The Government introduced a more liberal ten-year residence and employment card for immigrants in 1983 which made their lives in France more secure.

These gains for immigrants rights were short-lived. In the first few years of the Socialist Government there were a number of disturbances on outer-city housing estates arising from reactions to racist attacks and confrontations between young people from immigrant families and the police. The recession began to give rise to higher levels of unemployment and insecurity about future job prospects. In the spring and autumn of 1983 came the first signs of the growing electoral influence of the extreme right Front National which had won votes by campaigning on an anti-immigration platform. All the mainstream political parties responded defensively. The Socialists stressed that a successful integration policy for immigrants already living in France depended on strict control of entries and they speeded up the deportation of 'illegals'. Immigration thus moved to the centre of the political agenda.

When a new right-wing Assembly was elected in 1986–8 a period of cohabitation began between a neo-Gaullist Prime Minister (Jacques Chirac) and a Socialist President (François Mitterrand). The Minister of the Interior, Charles Pasqua, introduced legislation to make it more difficult to obtain the ten-year residence permits and increased the number of deportations and refusals of entry. In October 1986 the police rounded up illegal immigrants and deported 101 Maliens by charter flight. Many people were shocked, and some politicians became increasingly aware of the dangers of stirring up racism in their attempts to answer the Front National's anti-immigrant strategy.

The right-wing Government, however, continued to respond to Front National demands by proposing to reform the French Nationality law to end the automatic right to nationality for people born in France: the *droit du sol*. They responded to mounting opposition by establishing a Committee of Experts whose hearings were widely followed on television and radio. The Long Commission report (Long 1988) acknowledged the need to simplify the existing nationality law and proposed that children born in France to foreign parents should make a voluntary application for citizenship with a declaration of loyalty to France. This gave rise to a major debate about what it meant to be French and enabled many young people from immigrant families to make their views known. In the face of a wide mobilization against these changes, the law was not implemented until 1993 (*Loi Méhaignerie*).

With the Socialists back in government between 1988 and 1993, the emphasis passed to policies favourable to the integration of immigrant populations. The desecration of the Jewish cemetery at Carpentras in 1990 revealed to the nation's horror the continuing influence of anti-Semitism. This led to a number of initiatives including the reform of law against racism and the establishment of organizations which focused on the struggle against racism and integration of immigrants (see p. 47). However, the outbreak of the Gulf War in early 1991 and the fear of terrorist attack connected to Muslim fundamentalists in 1994 led to a tightening of regulations on the issue of visas and the introduction of Draconian identity controls.

In 1993 legislative elections returned a right-wing National Assembly and a second period of cohabitation began with the Socialist President Mitterrand. In 1995 the right-ward shift was confirmed by the election of the neo-Gaullist Jacques Chirac as President. Since the 1980s the right had been seriously divided over the attitude to take towards the extreme right Front National. In 1993 the Minister of the Interior, Charles Pasqua, announced that his goal was zero immigration and then enacted a series of restrictive measures on immigration which were complemented by rigorous identity controls and a reform of the nationality code which meant that young people born in France of foreign parents were no longer automatically French citizens (GISTI 1995, *Libération*, 30 April 1993). These measures enormously increased the amount of law, circulars and decrees which regulated the lives of foreigners in France. They instituted a regime of suspicion, enabling mayors to make an investigation before permitting marriage between a French citizen and a foreigner (*Libération*, 8 June 1993). The laws created new categories of people who were not entitled to full residence permits, and all the attached social rights, but who could not be deported because they were the parents of French children. Ambiguity and arbitrary administrative measures gave rise to many cases where people who had been living and working legally in France for many years, found themselves denied a legal status and at risk of deportation. Their position was aggravated by a virulent media debate against *clandestins* who were spoken of in the same breath as crime, drug-dealing and terrorism.

The Socialist Government elected in June 1997 commissioned Patrick Weil to review immigration law. The report, published within a month, emphasized the need to be more conscious of the human rights dimensions of immigration law, proposing a reduction of the redundant aspects of administration such as repeated checks for foreigners on entering the country or claiming welfare benefits (Weil 1997). Repeated checks are part of the mechanism of racialization as they help to identify a particular group subject to suspicion, and while the Weil report can be criticized for not going far enough, these dimensions may contribute to a change in the administrative culture operating towards immigrants.

Since the early 1970s, popular perception of immigration has changed. Unemployment and the economic crisis has superseded earlier views that migrants were needed to help in rebuilding France's prosperity. Government policy has focused on introducing new controls while migrants from North and West Africa were slowly gaining access to social housing, a combination that was bound to meet with hostility. Debates about the need for zero immigration and unsubstantiated scare stories about clandestine immigrants have kept racism alive. At the heart of this syndrome was the North African Muslim, who seemed to epitomize unassimilability (see also Chapter 11).

Is France a pluri-ethnic society today?

Despite restrictions on immigration and a reluctance to speak about ethnicity, there is some evidence that France might be becoming pluri-ethnic. On the one hand there has been a right-wing form of celebration of difference which aims to isolate a particular group from mainstream France, while on the other we can see evidence that a vibrant, mixed culture may be emerging. Such change would involve a reformulation of the idea of integration in the sense that French society is becoming more global.

Resources for the teaching of mother-tongue and cultures of origin were provided in the 1970s by the Gaullist governments but they were not intended to create a multi-ethnic France. Instead they aimed to support (rather unsuccessful) repatriation policies by facilitating a smoother transition on return to migrants' countries of origin. At the same time the new right placed questions of culture on the political agenda by emphasizing the importance of difference which underlined the incompatibility and unassimilability of certain cultures. In the last two years the Front National has implemented these ideas in the municipalities it controls by removing books by Developing World authors from libraries and refusing to invite ethnic minority artists and performers to cultural festivals.

In 1981 the Socialist Government emphasized integration as well as cultural difference. It was thought that France no longer possessed its earlier capacity to absorb immigrants. In the past integration had taken place earlier through institutions such as trade unions, political parties, the education system and even working-class neighbourhoods. Economic restructuring and disillusionment with mainstream politics had undermined the authority of these institutions (Leca 1985). The Government sought alternatives, notably in the sphere of civil society, where groups could develop their own resources. Civic life was strengthened when restrictions were lifted on the right of foreigners to form associations. By 1991 the *Fonds d'Action Sociale* (FAS) was funding more than 4,000 such associations which accounted for about a third of its total budget.

Although France has had an anti-racist movement for many years, during the 1980s it became a fashionable activity which attracted much media interest (Lloyd 1998). The rock concerts organised by *SOS Racisme* drew huge numbers of young people and youth culture emphasized mixing. At the same time *SOS Racisme* and *France Plus* were strongly integrationist, they both adopted critical attitudes towards the young women wearing the Muslim headscarf (the *affaire du foulard*). Recent research on associations suggests that they have become increasingly involved in local community work, oriented towards support for education, literacy and the prevention of juvenile delinquency (Wihtol de Wenden 1997).

In 1990 the *Commission Consultative des Droits de l'Homme* began work on a series of reports on racism, commissioning surveys which gave an overview of public opinion. The Commission includes representatives of human rights and anti-racist organizations and can make recommendations to government. The *Haut Conseil à l'Intégration* (HCI) was set up at the same time to clarify the debate about immigration by producing accurate statistical information about foreigners in France (HCI 1991). They identified areas for potential reforms and planned co-ordination at different levels of government. Integration operated 'according to a logic of equality, not a logic of minorities' thus rejecting the idea of specific policies aimed at particular ethnic groups (HCI 1991: 10). The HCI has produced indices of the level of integration according to the number of mixed marriages, the level of unemployment, the numbers of people in particular groups who are employed in supervisory, professional employment, the proportion of women in employment and the percentage of the population in prison. In their most recent reports the HCI continues to be concerned about the hardening of ethnic groupings within what they see as an increasingly segmented population, suffering from insecurity (HCI 1997). Their proposals focus on schools, giving powers to school councils to deal with problems of discipline or relations between pupils. In 1981 the government introduced a programme of Educational Priority Zones (ZEP) which made available special resources for mainstream education in areas where large numbers of children from immigrant backgrounds lived. An official week of anti-racist education has provided an opportunity for anti-racists to discuss directly with pupils.

The attitude of the French to minority religions does however illustrate the limitations of its toleration of other cultures. France was deeply divided across and within traditional left/right political fractures about the Muslim headscarf affair (see Chapter 10, this volume). Behind the rhetoric about the need to maintain French secular traditions (which contradictorily, also include national holidays for all the main Christian holidays and until recently the approved list of children's names which were mainly those of Catholic saints) lay a deep suspicion of Islam, shored up by fears of fundamentalism. Successive governments have recognized that Islam cannot be reduced to fundamental- ism and they have attempted to establish a Muslim representative body with which they could establish a dialogue and periodic consultations. The *Conseil Répresentatif des Musulmans de France* was established under the guidance of Charles Pasqua who, at the opening of the new mosque in Lyon, said that the time had come to establish an independent French Islam (*Le Monde*, 1 October 1994; *Le Monde*, 21 January 1995).

French debate about integration is deeply ambiguous, and remains bound up with the older discourse of assimilation. Sometimes the meaning shifts from one to the other, although integration is usually taken to be more respectful of ethnic differences than assimilation. However, integration policies do not tackle the issue of the racial discrimination faced by certain groups in France. Instead, policymakers who are concerned to promote equality talk of the struggle against social exclusion. Yet there is considerable evidence that certain groups suffer specific discriminations in the labour and housing markets. Foreigners are twice as likely as French to be unemployed, for example. Recent changes in immigration law have introduced identity checks for foreigners claiming welfare and health benefits, which stigmatizes particular people.

Despite these serious reservations there is evidence that a multicultural France is emerging. The North African dish of *cous-cous* has become part of the French diet in a similar way to curry or chow mien in the UK. Throughout France, especially over the summer months, local arts and music festivals include artists from North and West Africa or invite performers from the *banlieue* who are developing their own syncretic art-forms. *Rai* and *rap* music have become part of the contemporary scene. A growing number of film-makers and other media workers have come from immigrant families and there is a respected body of literature produced from the experience of immigration.

Conclusion

We have seen that questions of race and ethnicity are debated in a very particular way in France. While policy-makers refuse to recognize the existence of particular ethnic groups in theory, they are forced to do so in practice in order to respond to specific problems such as racism. While the idea of the ethnic minority community may be rejected, the State helps to fund civic associations based on ethnic criteria such as religion, language or other cultural activities. At the time of the Gulf War the Government referred to the Muslim community in France and has subsequently attempted to establish a suitable consultative body.

Recent immigration policy, based on the idea of zero immigration has failed to neutralise racist currents in society. Instead, repeated controls and a regime of suspicion seems to have confirmed the views of the Front National. The considerable inroads into the French electorate made by this organization suggests that immigration and racism are likely to remain hotly debated subjects and that France is likely to continue to be divided on the subject.

The question of culture is of enormous importance in France and tends to mask the more structural problems of racial discrimination in housing or employment about which relatively little is known. The law against racism is relatively powerless to deal with covert or institutionalized forms of discrimination. While there is a lobby for more effective provisions against racism, enunciated through the different anti-racist associations and the *Commission Nationale des Droits de l'Homme* (CNCDH), it finds it difficult to be heard and the argument for *individual* integration into French society remains powerful.

However, there are signs of a shift. Some of the original reasons for racism have disappeared, although their echoes remain. France is no longer an imperial power and recent governments have been seeking a role more centred on Europe and the Mediterranean. Gradually we may see that immigration is adding yet another layer to the many different identities of France identified by Braudel (1988) in his famous study of the diversity of French identity in the *longue durée*.

Notes

1 The term 'racialization' refers to the process by which social relations between certain groups of people have been structured according to certain (real or imagined) biological characteristics which signify different places in a hierarchy (Miles 1989: 75).
2 The collection of ethnic data is very strictly regulated by the National Commission for Information and Freedom established in 1978. However, the Renseignements Généraux do collect data about the personal appearance of suspects, which appears to include skin colour (*Le Monde*, 8 Juillet 1997).
3 The main regions of mainland France with their own language and ethnic regional movement are: Alsace-Lorraine, Flanders, Brittany, the French Basque country, French Catalonia, Occitania (Beer 1977).
4 In 1911, 3 per cent of the French population was foreign and by 1931 this had grown to over 6 per cent (mainly Italians and Poles). The Spanish population increased from 302,000 in 1946 to 607,000 in 1968 to 216,000 in 1990, while the Portuguese became the largest group growing from 50,000 in 1962 to 296,000 in 1968 and 758,000 in 1975.
5 The DOM-TOM comprise Guadeloupe, Martinique, Guyana in the Caribbean; La Réunion in the Indian Ocean and St Pierre and Miquelon, New Caledonia and French Polynesia.

Bibliography

Beer, W.R. (1977) 'The social class of ethnic activists in contemporary France', in M.J. Esman (ed.), *Ethnic Conflict in the Western World*, Ithaca: Cornell University Press.

Berger, S. (1977) 'Bretons and Jacobins: Reflections on French Regional Ethnicity', in M.J. Esman (ed.), *Ethnic Conflict in the Western World*, Ithaca: Cornell University Press.

Bernstein, R. (1991) *Fragile Glory*, London: Bodley Head.

Bonnafous, S. (1992) 'Le terme "intégration" dans le journal *Le Monde*: Sens et non sens', *Hommes et Migrations*, May: 24–30.

Braudel, F. (1988) *The Identity of France: History and Environment*, Paris: Arthaud-Flammarion.

Brubaker, R. (1996) 'Civic and Ethnic Nations in France and Germany', in J. Hutchinson and A. Smith (eds), *Ethnicity*, Oxford: Oxford University Press.

CNCDH (1996) *1995: La Lutte contre le racisme et la xenophobie*, Paris: La Documentation Française.

Etcherelli, C. (1994) *Elise ou la vraie vie*, London: Routledge.

Giordan, H. (1982) *Democratie culturelle et droit à la différence*, Rapport présenté à M. Jack Lang, Ministre de la Culture, Février, Paris: Commission des Cultures Régionales et Minoritaires.

GISTI (1995) *Entrée et séjour des étrangers. La Nouvelle foi pasqua*, Paris: GISTI.

Guillaumin, C. (1992) 'Usages théoriques et usages banals du terme *race*', *Mots*, no. spéciale: 59–65.

—— (1995) *Racism, Sexism, Power and Ideology*, London: Routledge.

Hargreaves, A. (1995) *Immigration, Race and Ethnicity in Contemporary France*, London: Routledge.

HCI (Haut Conseil à l'Intégration) (1991) 'Premier rapport', February, Paris: HCI.

—— (1992) 'Rapport statistique', 9 December, Paris: HCI.

—— (1993) *L'Emploi illégal des étrangers*, Paris: Documentation Française.

INSEE (1986) *Les Étrangers en France*, Paris: Documentation Française.

—— (1992) *Rencensement de la population de 1990: Nationalités*, Paris: Documentation Française.

Jones, P. (1991) 'Race, discourse and power in institutional housing: The case of immigrant workers' hostels in Lyon', in M. Silverman (ed.), *Race, Discourse and Power in France*, Aldershot: Avebury.

Kuper, L. (1975) *Science and Society*, London: Unesco/Allen & Unwin.

Leca, J. (1985) 'Une Capacité d'intégration défaillante?', *Esprit*, Juin, 102.

Lequin, Y. (1988) *La Mosäique France: Histoire des étrangers et de l'immigration*, Paris: Larousse.

Lloyd, C. (1981) 'What is the French CP up to?', *Race and Class*, XXII (4), Spring: 403–7.

—— (1998) *Discourses of Antiracism in France*, Aldershot: Ashgate.

Lloyd, C. and Waters, H. (1991) 'France: One culture, one people?', *Race and Class*, 32 (3) January–March: 49–65.

Long, M. (1988) *Etre Français aujourd'hui et demain*, Paris: 10./180.

Macmaster, N. (1994) 'The rue Fondary murders of 1923 and the origins of anti-Arab racism', in J. Windebank and R. Gunther (eds), *Violence and Conflict in Modern French Culture*, Sheffield: Sheffield Academic Press, pp. 149–60.

—— (1997) *Colonial Migrants and Racism: Algerians in France 1900–62*, London: Macmillan.

Marcus, J. (1995) *The National Front and French Politics*, London: Macmillan.

Miles, R. (1989) *Racism*, London: Routledge.

Quiminal, C. (1991) *Gens d'ici, gens d'ailleurs*, Paris: Christian Bourgeois.

Renan, E. (1990) 'What is a nation?', in H.K. Bhabha (ed.), *Nation and Narration*, London: Routledge.

Schain, M. (1994) 'Immigration and politics', in P.A. Hall, J. Hayward and H. Machin, *Developments in French Politics*, London: Macmillan.

Silverman, M. (1992) *Deconstructing the Nation: Immigration, Racism and Citizenship in Modern France*, London: Routledge.

Stora, B. (1991) *La Gangrène et l'oubli*, Paris: La Découverte.

Taguieff, P.-A. (1994) *Sur la Nouvelle Droite*, Paris: Descartes et Cie.

Tribalat, M., Garson, J.-P., Moulier-Boutang, Y. and Silberman, R. (1991) *Cent ans d'immigration: Etrangers d'hier, Français d'aujourd'hui*, Paris: PUF/INED.

Weber, M. (1969) *Economy and Society*, vol. 1, New York: Bedminster Press.

Weil, P. (1997) *Pour une politique de l'immigration juste et efficace*, Rapport au Premier Ministre, Juilliet: Paris.

Wihtol de Wenden, C. (1988) *Les Immigrés et la politique*, Paris: Presses de la Fondation Nationale des Sciences Politiques.

—— (1997) 'Que sont devenues les associations civiques issues de l'immigration?', *Hommes et Migrations*, 1206, Mars–Avril: 53–66.

Winock, M. (1982) *Drumont et Cie. Antisémitisme et fascisme en France*, Paris: Seuil.

Chapter 3

Gender

Catherine Rodgers

Sociologists, anthropologists and psychologists would agree that sexual difference is fundamental in defining one's identity, in structuring thought and organizing society. As Françoise Héritier notes: 'a society without difference between the sexes is inconceivable' (quoted in Perrot 1995: 47). For Lévi-Strauss, gender was inherent in thought itself, a notion which Perrot expands on when she writes: 'it is a cognitive structure which controls symbol systems and the categories of language' (ibid.). Héritier, again, says in her book *Masculin /Féminin*: 'observation of the difference between the sexes underlies all thought, traditional as well as scientific' (quoted in Lapierre 1996: 6). She shows that this difference seems always to have been interpreted in men's favour, and that such a hierarchical approach is deeply rooted in human thinking.

It is crucial to understand what is meant by 'sexual difference', given the importance of this concept in the definition of identity, culture, thought and society. An appreciation of how this concept has evolved over the past fifty years or so will help us to a better understanding of a country like France, and the changes it has undergone. The evolution of this concept can be apprehended at different levels: an abstract one consisting of the mainly feminist reflection on sex and gender, and a more concrete level, corresponding to the way in which sexual difference manifests itself in society, in the law, in institutions (education, work, family), in the media, and in discourses and ideologies.

One point must, however, be made from the start, which is that the term 'gender' (*genre*) is still little used in French. In English, it tends to denote the social and cultural component of sexual difference, while the term 'sex' refers to the natural, physiological and anatomical element. In French, because the term gender (except for grammatical *genre*) is not widely used, it is difficult linguistically to distinguish between the social and cultural construction of sexual identity and the biological, anatomical one. *Femelle* and *mâle* are not used in French, except to refer to animals, or in a derogatory, suggestive or ironic tone. The term *femme* refers therefore both to woman and female, *homme* to human being, man and male. This can give rise to ambiguity. For example, when Simone de Beauvoir wrote: 'On ne naît pas femme, on le devient' ('One is not born, but rather becomes, a woman') (Beauvoir 1988: 295), she was using *femme* in the sense of woman; whereas some of her detractors ridiculed her by interpreting *femme* as meaning 'female'. This lack of linguistic clarity – perhaps in itself revelatory – does not mean however that the question of sexual difference has not been analysed in France.

In writing *The Second Sex* in 1949, Simone de Beauvoir was perhaps the first to devote an in-depth and extensive study to the definition of femininity. With her suggestion that, 'One is not born, but rather becomes, a woman', she argued for an overwhelmingly cultural and social dimension to the construction of woman. In fact, most of *The Second Sex* is spent analysing the idea of 'becoming' a woman. Although Beauvoir does not negate the anatomical dimension of sexual difference, detailing at length female handicaps such as menstruation, pregnancy and the menopause, she refuses to allow anatomy a deciding role in determining a woman's fate. Nature may hand a worse deal to women (and this is certainly Beauvoir's view) but women can transcend it. She also points out that anatomy becomes meaningful only when interpreted by society. If young girls and women have such bad experiences with their periods, it is mainly because of the way society views menstruation, and because periods signify femaleness in a society where being a woman means being a second-class citizen (ibid.). Beauvoir's constructionist conception of sexual identity is coupled with a claim for equality between the sexes.

Her vision of equality has, however, become increasingly problematic. Although she writes in *The Second Sex* that woman must be accepted as a sexed being (ibid.: 692), the bulk of her thesis works towards a remaking of women in the image of men. It leads her to reject maternity as the key factor in women's oppression, since during pregnancy women become subject to bodily processes, which may serve the species but which are detrimental to them as individuals, while as mothers they have to sacrifice their independence to the family. Beauvoir's ideal is that of the independent, well-educated, working woman, who, if she has children, has them looked after by society. It goes without saying that Beauvoir supported contraception and abortion. If she was so vehement in her rejection of any feminine nature or essence, it was perhaps because patriarchy, for centuries, had been sending women back to a supposed female nature, something which was used to justify the worst inequalities in women's social status.

The Second Sex did not have any immediate follow-up in France, although it was widely read privately. It was not until the beginning of the 1970s that a feminist movement developed: the Mouvement de Libération des Femmes (MLF). Some of the demands of the MLF (easy access to contraception and the right to abortion, for example) certainly seemed to adopt Beauvoir's ideas of twenty years earlier. Some egalitarian, constructionist feminists, such as those of the collective *Questions féministes* (in particular Christine Delphy and Monique Wittig) or Gisèle Halimi, or later Elisabeth Badinter, also appear to be the descendants of Simone de Beauvoir in their analysis of patriarchy and their claims for equality between the sexes. However, the MLF was far from unified, and there was also a wave of differentialist feminists, such as Chantal Chawaf, Hélène Cixous, Antoinette Fouque, Xavière Gauthier, Luce Irigaray and Annie Leclerc, who insisted on the specificity of a feminine nature – essentialism was back, in a more or less overt form. This group often reclaimed a female nature in the name of the superiority of women over men. They insisted in their writings on the female body, its *jouissance*, its possibility of giving life. Their key word was *différence*.

At the same time, many changes such as those of sexual liberation, greater equality in marriage, in education and at work were taking place in France, changes which I shall consider in more detail later on in this chapter, and which were making women and men more equal, at least in principle.

As sexual equality has developed, and reflection on identity and sexual difference has matured, the idea has been expressed that gender might in fact precede sex, a claim made, among others, by Michelle Perrot: 'there are many of us, of both sexes, who think that gender, as a category of thought and culture, precedes sex and shapes it … that the body is not the fundamental starting-point' (Perrot 1995: 39). The same idea has been developed by the sociologist Christine Delphy in her article, 'Rethinking Sex and Gender' (1993). Delphy puts forward the idea that not only gender is a social construction, but sex is too, and she reverses the widespread idea that sex determines gender:

> gender precedes sex ... sex itself simply marks a social division; ... it serves to allow social recognition and identification of those who are dominants and those who are dominated. That is, that sex is a sign ... [which] has historically acquired a symbolic value.
>
> (ibid.: 5)

As a historian, Michelle Perrot reminds us (Perrot 1995: 42) that it is only in the eighteenth century, with the development of biology and medicine, that a sexualization of gender has taken place, and that up until this point, masculine and feminine identities were thought of in terms of ontological and cultural identity rather than of physical differences.

Theories about the concept of sexual difference have therefore moved between three main standpoints: a confusion between sex and gender, one encouraged by patriarchal ideology which could thus pass off social traits as natural ones; a distinction between the two, but one where sex still preceded and determined gender; to a realization that it might be gender which is the chief determinant.

The interest expressed abroad in French feminism is misleading with respect to the importance feminist studies have in France. As the first appendix to *La Place des femmes* shows, women's studies and research – 'études féministes et études sur les femmes en France' – receive little recognition from the university system or the government (Ephesia 1995: 701), and as a consequence much research on women and gender is carried out in a near clandestine manner. Of the several feminist journals that existed from the mid-1970s until the mid-1980s, *Nouvelles Questions féministes* is the only one still to be published today. Les Éditions des femmes is the sole remaining feminist publisher in France, and most of the feminist collections in other publishers have ceased to exist. French feminist academics look at the British and American situation with envy.

Compared with Anglo-American feminism, French feminist activism can appear rather mild and not overtly political, apart from *Choisir*. Another particularity of the French scene is the ambivalent role the State has played in women's progress. On the one hand, in providing good education for women, good childcare facilities, and through its welfare policy – of which women benefit much more than men – the State has improved women's condition. On the other hand, the State seems reluctant to envisage the specificity of women's needs. For example, French women work the least part-time in the European Union (Ozouf 1995: 380). Ozouf puts forward the thesis that if French feminists are less vehement than American feminists, it is because French women 'see themselves first of all as equal and free individuals ... spurred on by this conviction they can experience sexual difference without resentment, cultivate it happily and with irony and refuse to essentialise it' (ibid.: 383).

The attraction of the universalist republican model for the French may also explain another French particularity. In Anglo-American countries, whereas recent years have seen the emergence of lesbian and gay movements, and many publications on homosexual identity, in France, by comparison, lesbian and gay movements remain fairly discreet, although they do hold regular demonstrations. In 1995, the Lesbian and Gay Pride March in Paris attracted 50,000 people for the first time; in 1996 gay rights demonstrations took place not only in Paris but in other towns in France. Although they are divided over the question of difference – some claiming the right to difference, others the right to indifference – all want the 'contrat d'union sociale' which is the legalization of couples of the same sex. A bill was presented to the Assemblée Nationale in January 1997.

French society has changed considerably since the Second World War: more people are being educated, and more people work outside the home as employees. The past twenty years have seen rising unemployment, as well as deep transformations in family structure. Women have played an important role in these developments. They have been at the origin of socio-demographic changes, controlling their own sexuality through contraception and abortion, something which has led to lower marriage and fecundity rates and new types of family life (single-parent families). Women have entered the education system in significant numbers, right up to university level, and have come to form an increasingly important part of the work-force. In spite of persisting inequalities, these modifications have, to a certain extent, redefined the relationship between the sexes, although the *real* extent of the changes is a debatable point.

Changes in the law are a good indication of changes in society. The text of the French Constitution states that: 'the Law guarantees women, in all domains, equal rights with men' (preamble to the Constitution of 27 October 1946, incorporated in the 1958

Constitution). This sentence marks a huge advance from the Napoleonic Code (1804) which treated women as minors. The Napoleonic Code was a regressive step for women, especially married women. It resulted, for nearly a century and a half, in the private subordination of women and their low legal status. Married women were declared irresponsible – like the insane or children: they could not create a company, sign a work contract, decide on their own incomes, open a bank account, or be responsible for their children. In fact, in the nineteenth century women were entirely confined by law to their domestic roles of wife or mother. The public sphere was reserved for men. Although the principle of equality is inscribed in the 1946 Constitution, it took years for specific laws to be passed ensuring the equality of men and women in different domains.

Women gain control of their sexuality

Sexuality is the domain which has seen the most dramatic changes over the last forty years. In 1920, anti-conception propaganda was forbidden, and abortion was declared a crime. In 1942, under the Vichy régime, which idealized the roles of housewife and mother, abortion was a crime against national security and punishable by death. One woman was executed on these grounds in 1943, and criminal proceedings against women practising or undergoing an abortion survived until the 1970s.

One of the rallying slogans of the MLF in the 1970s was: 'The children we want, when we want them'. They were on their way to obtaining a series of laws which would bring about the following changes:

- In 1967, the Neuwirth Act legalized the use of contraception. Contraceptive methods, although legal, continued to be poorly advertised at first, and it was only in 1991, under the threat of AIDS, that advertisements for contraceptive methods were made legal. In the 1990s, modern contraceptive means are widely known and available, with only 4 per cent of women who do not want to become pregnant not using any method at all (Aubin and Gisserot 1994: 35). The situation is helped by the fact that French Social Security reimburses the cost of the contraceptive coil and most types of contraceptive pills.
- In 1975, the Veil Act, at first provisional then made definitive in 1979, de-criminalized abortion. In 1983 the cost of abortion

was made reimbursable through Social Security. In 1993 failure to respect the right to abortion became a crime. The law was passed in response to the increasingly violent opposition of pro-life movements in France like 'Laissez-les Vivre'. The number of abortions in France has reached a ceiling of 200,000 a year (ibid.).

Contraception and abortion mean that, on the whole, French women are choosing to have fewer children, and to have them later in life. In contrast to Britain's average of 1.8 children, by 1996 fecundity in France had declined to 1.7, but still remains higher than in other European countries (INSEE, Institut National de la Statistique et des Etudes Economiques). Women become pregnant later in life: in 1960, the average age of a mother at the birth of her first child was twenty-five, as against 28.4 in 1991 (INSEE). Women are not refusing to have children, rather they are choosing the moment to have only one or two, and attempting to combine maternal and professional lives.

If women refuse multiple maternity, they also expect to be able to conceive when they wish to. New procreative methods, such as *in vitro* fertilization and artificial insemination, give women greater control over their fecundity. Whereas repeated, imposed pregnancies and dangerous, painful childbirths were once the lot of women, contraception, abortion, better medical care and epidural anaesthesia (now completely paid for by Social Security) have revolutionized the feminine condition.

These medical advances and legal changes have tipped the balance in favour of women when it comes to procreation. Whereas in the past, the woman was at the mercy of the man, in a sexual relationship, it is now she who directs the procreative process. This redistribution of power, combined with other factors such as the greater economic independence of women – to which I shall return in a moment – has had considerable consequences for the organization of family life.

Redefinition of the family

France, like other European countries, has over the last few years seen the emergence of a greater diversification of family models: fewer marriages and more unmarried couples, more divorces (60 per cent initiated by women) (Aubin and Gisserot 1994: 42), more births outside the nuclear family (one in three in 1993) (ibid.: 41), and more one-parent families, which tend to consist of the mother and her children, since in 89 per cent of divorces women keep the children (ibid.: 42). This has been made possible by the greater economic self-sufficiency of women, better education, and a desire for independence.

However, women are more at risk of poverty than men. Women divorcees generally experience a lowering of their standard of living, which on average they only manage to make up ten years after their divorce (ibid.: 43). They are, generally speaking, less well equipped than men to find good jobs, often having prioritized non-professional activities over career and further training.

The care of children can be a heavy burden for women, especially since 35 per cent of men do not make their required maintenance payments regularly (ibid.: 43), but they also value this responsibility. It should perhaps be stressed that French childcare facilities, although not perfect as far as crèches are concerned, are greatly superior to British ones: *l'école maternelle* cares without charge for all children aged between 2 and 6, and after 6 years of age children go to a primary school (*école primaire*), where they can be looked after until six o'clock in the evening.

Women acquire more legal protection from violence

Although specific laws aimed at protecting women against violence have been passed – especially those against rape and sexual harassment, French women are still victims of men's violence. The precise extent of this violence is not known. The number of official complaints made to the police has certainly risen since 1985, but the figure is difficult to interpret. Women are better informed about their rights thanks to the work done by various feminist organizations, and are less intimidated than in the past, so are more likely to bring charges of sexual harassment. In 1985 there were 2,823 charges of rape, as against 5,068 in 1991; 6,594 charges of indecent assault in 1985, and 9,164 in 1991 (Aubin and Gisserot 1994: 77). However, it is estimated that these figures should be quadrupled if they are to approximate to the real level of violence perpetrated against women by men. Domestic violence is still very much a taboo subject in France, and it is extremely difficult to quantify.

Women acquire more rights within marriage, and greater equality between spouses

As mentioned before, French married women were severely restricted by the Napoleonic Code. Achieving greater equality with their spouses has been a slow process.

- In 1965, married women acquired the right to work, and to open a bank account without authorization.
- In 1970, the notion of paternal authority (*puissance paternelle*) was replaced by the concept of parental authority.
- In 1975, divorce by consent was introduced.
- In 1985, 'each spouse can freely exercise a profession, receive his or her salary, and make use of it as he or she wishes, after having taken care of marital responsibility' and each 'alone has control over and can dispose of his or her personal property' (article 225 of *Code Civil*). The child acquired the right to have the surnames of both mother and father.
- In 1987, an act was passed facilitating the joint exercise of parental authority.
- In 1993, the principle of joint parental authority was established for all children, whatever the parents' situation.

From this abbreviated list of legal changes, it can be seen that married women now have more rights, and that the law has been altered to ensure greater equality with regard to the authority each parent can exercise over a child.

Women and work

In principle, equality at work between women and men has now been achieved. A law of 1972 guarantees equal pay in theory; since 1993 professional equality has also been promulgated. In practice, too, there are signs of progress. Over the past thirty years, women have achieved significant entry into the workplace. The percentage of working women has steadily increased, and has not declined even with the recent economic crisis and generally high level of unemployment. Women constitute 44 per cent of the working population, and in 1994, 77 per cent of women aged between 25 and 49 were in work (Aubin and Gisserot 1994: 26). Women no longer choose between work and family: they no longer give up work when they have children (80 per cent of women aged between 30 and 34, with a child under 2 years of age, are in work) (ibid.: 28). It is only when women have three children or more that this figure declines. Women's work profiles have come closer to those of men: most women work outside the home, and their work activity is increasingly stable and continuous. However, if we take into account the distribution of full-time and part-time work, we find that women begin by working full-time, change to part-time work between the ages of 25 and 35, then return to full-time employment when their children have grown up.

If we compare the percentage of both sexes in employment, we can see that whereas the percentage of women has steadily increased since 1960 (rising from 28 per cent to 47 per cent in 1993), that of men has decreased (from 58 per cent to 48 per cent) (Majnoni 1996: 216). This trend looks set to continue, and has had a profound change, not only on the status of women in France, but on the whole structure of French society.

The percentage of women in higher status occupations has increased during the 1990s. For example, whereas in 1982, 13 per cent of company executives were women, this figure has now risen to 22 per cent (Aubin and Gisserot 1994: 51). The percentage of women who have started a company has gone up from 18 per cent to 30 per cent over the last fifteen years (Majnoni 1996: 235). Overall in France, 20 per cent of companies are headed by a woman (ibid.). However, it is still too often the case that when women are promoted to posts carrying considerable responsibility, real power still eludes them. Indeed, these figures mask many inequalities. Highly qualified women may tend to enjoy work conditions similar to those of men, but poorly qualified women are often relegated to lowly paid and precarious jobs, and are at a greater risk of unemployment.

Moreover, men and women do not occupy the same type of job. Women are in the majority when it comes to part-time jobs (85 per cent), fixed term contracts (52 per cent), subsidized jobs (*emplois assistés*) and *stages* (60 per cent) (Aubin and Gisserot 1994: 51). Part-time jobs are still not deemed respectable. As a consequence, part-time employees find promotion more difficult, and are often under a greater threat of redundancy. Women are therefore the first to suffer. Working women are also concentrated in certain activities: the public sector, administrative work, domestic work, primary-school teaching, the health sector (especially nursing), and social work. In general, they occupy jobs which are less time-consuming and are of lower status.

In spite of the law, inequality of pay persists. Women on average earn 24 per cent less than men (ibid.: 53). In particular, women executives earn 27 per cent less than their male counterparts (INSEE 1992). On the positive side, the gap between the salaries earned by men and women has been closing. But women are more likely to be unemployed than men: since 1974, the difference in unemployment rates between men and women has remained more or less stable, 8.6 per cent for men, 12.9 per cent for women in 1992 (INSEE).

The recession, the high level of unemployment, and the decline in the birth rate have all contributed to a revival of the debate about the legitimacy of women's work. The question of a possible maternal salary has also been formulated. This indicates that even if the younger generation is convinced of the necessity of work for women, it is not considered by the population as a whole to be on an equal footing with men's work. The model for employment is still a masculine one: an uninterrupted, full-time career. Society has not yet adapted to the new forms of work, nor to women working. Part-time and temporary work is denigrated, and devalued; jobs with responsibility tend not to be part-time. Promotion is often linked to a change of workplace, something that few women can achieve, their careers generally being considered as secondary to those of their male partners. On the other hand, the work market is evolving: all jobs have become more precarious, variable and fragmented. Women have shown that they can adapt to these new patterns; they may have a head start, and the general trend might benefit them in the long term. Although the majority of women are now in employment, society still seems to hold women responsible for the care of children. Women tend to be the recipients of parental leave, leave for sick children, and flexi-time; and it is women who stop working or go part-time to look after the children.

The distribution of domestic tasks has hardly changed over the last ten years: men spend only 10 minutes more per week than they used to on domestic chores, whereas women spend 5 minutes less (Aubin and Gisserot 1994: 66). On average, mothers have an hour less leisure time than their companions (ibid.: 67), spending two-thirds of their time caring for children. Mothers carry out the most repetitive tasks whereas fathers take charge of the more occasional jobs, such as the shopping. This inequality seems to be absorbed and accepted by girls at a very young age, and girls in secondary education choose careers which will allow them greater flexibility and more free time, hence their choice of less prestigious careers.

Women and education

The most striking area in which women have made significant achievements is that of education. It was only in 1882 that primary education was declared compulsory for girls as well as boys; in 1924 that the boys' and girls' secondary school curricula were harmonized and that the female and male *baccalauréats* were made equivalent; and in 1975 that co-education became the norm in primary and secondary schools. And it is only comparatively recently (1978, for example, for the École de l'air) that some *grandes écoles* have opened their doors to female students.

In spite of these serious handicaps, girls in France have managed to catch up with, and even to overtake, boys on several counts.

- In 1940 there were half as many girls in French secondary schools as boys: this gap had been closed by 1971.
- The numbers of both girls and boys in education increased greatly between 1982 and 1990, but since 1990 the figure for girls has been even greater than that for boys, especially in higher education (48.3 per cent as against 45.2 per cent for the 16 to 25 age group).
- Girls perform better at school than boys. There are more *bachelières* (57 per cent) than *bacheliers* (43 per cent). They choose to prolong their studies more than boys, in 1993 representing 54.3 per cent of the higher education student population. They enter all disciplines: not only the Humanities, Pharmacy and Law, where they have for some time been in the majority, but also Economics and Medicine where the proportions are now equal. They are attending the prep schools and the *grandes écoles*.

Nevertheless it is important to interpret these figures with a certain degree of caution:

- Girls choose a more limited number of curricula, and still do not often take scientific courses, choosing the Arts and the Humanities, or the Biological Sciences, whereas boys tend towards 'hard' science, such as Mathematics, Physics, Chemistry and Engineering. There may be more *bachelières* than *bacheliers*, but the former tend to confine themselves to literary (that is, less valued) *bacs*. They may constitute 80 per cent of total candidates, but only one-third of candidates for the more prestigious Mathematics Bac C.

- There are marked differences in training courses: 85 per cent of girls choose courses in the tertiary sector, and of the 15 per cent who opt for courses in the secondary sector, most choose those in the textile industry.
- Female students tend not to enter the most prestigious *grandes écoles*: the figure is only 10 per cent in *l'école polytechnique* and in *l'école normale supérieure*, and only 25 per cent – and falling – in *l'école nationale d'administration*.
- At university level, girls constitute the majority of students in the first two years, but thereafter their numbers drop – a paradoxical situation, given the fact that female students certainly enter university with better grades than their male counterparts. Furthermore, at the end of their university studies, women emerge less qualified than men.

The marked segregation between feminine and masculine educational choices does not seem to correspond to innate intellectual differences, which are in any case unproven, but rather to the expectations of parents and society, and to role internalization. Feminine qualities are still associated with literary studies, and masculine qualities with science and mathematics. In an education system where mathematics is used as a means of selection, girls are at a disadvantage. Not that the slight differential in mathematical ability between the sexes – boys are marginally better at spatial orientation – justifies their shunning of scientific studies. The reluctance of girls to pursue scientific studies is much more likely to be the result of other factors: for example, scientific studies are more competitive and boys are better equipped with the necessary aggressivity and self-confidence to succeed; they are also boosted by greater parental expectations. This concentration of female students in courses which do not lead to the best and most secure jobs is a real problem, a problem which several school information programmes are trying to remedy.

Of major concern too is the fact that with equal qualifications, girls find it more difficult than boys to find a job: they remain unemployed for longer, and the jobs they obtain are often inferior to those of their male counterparts. Further, female employees tend to benefit less than male employees from training, and even when this is not the case, their chances of gaining promotion are lower.

Women and politics

Politics, and nowhere more so in the developed world than in France, has proven to be an extremely misogynist domain. French women acquired the right to vote relatively late (1944). They now constitute 43 per cent of the electorate and take part as much as men in the electoral process. Their vote is increasingly autonomous, whereas in the past it was heavily influenced by their spouses. But they are very poorly represented in elected bodies. The following figures indicate the percentage of women in elected assemblies for 1993.

- Assemblée nationale (National Assembly): 6.1 per cent.
- Sénat (Senate): 4.8 per cent.
- Conseillers municipaux (Local councils): 17.1 per cent.
- Maires (Town Halls): 5.4 per cent.
- Conseillers régionaux (Regional councils): 12.3 per cent.
- Conseillers généraux (Departmental councils): 5.6 per cent.
- Parlement européen (European parliaments): 29.9 per cent.

Women tend to be under-represented in politics throughout Europe, but the problem is more acute in France than in its partner states. This under-representation is also visible in the higher echelons of the public service: the percentage of women in the *Grands Corps de l'État* (Conseil d'État, Cours des Comptes et Inspection Générale des Finances) is less than 10 per cent. Political power still eludes women, whether it's in elected assemblies, the public service, political parties or in trade unions.

Several reasons can be put forward for this discrepancy. For example, French women are relative latecomers to legal and political rights, and political power in France is especially conservative: it is a masculine area *par excellence*, and women entering it cannot rely on the necessary network of contacts. Gisèle Halimi (1995), in *Une embellie perdue*, has documented the misogyny of the political world, and her struggle as a woman and as a feminist to have her ideas recognized and taken seriously. Political power – especially given the French system of plurality of mandates – is extremely time-consuming: it requires availability and mobility, both of which are difficult to combine with family life. Mona Ozouf (1995), in *Les Mots des femmes*, in her essay titled, 'La singularité française', advances the idea that it is paradoxically in the name of 'universalism', so dear to the French mind, that women have been kept out of power. The perception of women as deviants from the norm, as too specifically feminine, meant that they could not be considered as universal citizens, and were, therefore, kept outside the egalitarian system which applied only to citizens. In Britain, on the other hand, women were allowed the vote much earlier because they could do so in their capacity as women, not as individuals.

It seems also that women may hold a different relationship with power, that their priorities are not the same as those of men: they are certainly less militant than men, more suspicious of political discourses and ideologies, and more interested in concrete humanitarian and social actions. This different approach to power is one of the reasons why so many feminists, such as Antoinette Fouque (1995) in 'Demain la parité', argue for qualitative parity, that is to say a parity not defined merely in terms of numbers of women being present in elected assemblies, but rather in terms of these women being allowed to implement different ideas and to choose a different style of power.

For all the reasons given above, there also exists some self-censorship on the part of women. They do not in general wish to enter the world of politics which remains alien to them, which is so little suited to their aspirations, and which conflicts with the demands already made on their time. The injustice of the political scene has, however, prompted several groups (*Choisir, Club parité 2000*) to ask for quotas to be implemented and for different forms of parity. In December 1996 the Socialist Party decided on a system of quotas for the legislative elections, reserving 30 per cent of the seats for women candidates. This resulted in more women being elected to the Assemblée Nationale in June 1997, bringing the proportion of women members to 10.91 per cent.

Survival of sexual stereotypes

Legal changes accompany and reinforce social changes, as well as changes in mentality. As we have seen, progress, both on paper and in reality, has been made. But a sense of sexual hierarchy is deeply embedded in the French psyche and survives in modern myths, in the fashion world, publicity, the press, films and literature. An analysis of advertisements shows that contradictory images coexist: the representation of women in domestic roles cohabits with images of independent career women. Women are still often portrayed as sexual objects to be possessed. The female body is still exposed in order to enhance product desirability. If anything, with sexual liberalization, the female body (if young and slim) has become even more exposed, made more available than it once was. Male sexuality is still represented as an irrepressible force, to be willingly complied with by women.

In women's magazines, the same ambiguities persist: inequality at work may be denounced, but many articles are devoted to the crucial role that mothers play in the upbringing of small children, and stress the need for their presence at home. Worried voices are heard about the uncertainty felt by men, and the crisis in masculine identity as a result of women's new assurance and independence. The women's press continues to encourage women to remain young, slim and attractive in order to seduce Prince Charming. Women are still encouraged to think of themselves first and foremost as bodies. The attraction of supermodels symbolizes the cult of the perfect body, and it is significant that top models should have replaced film stars as the main object of fascination. If women no longer constrict their bodies with bodices, they are now lured into plastic surgery, silicone implants, and liposuction in order to attain the perceived perfection of Pamela Anderson's physique, born as it is of masculine fantasy. One hesitates to see as progress the fact that men are also now increasingly considered as sex objects.

Romantic novels, television soap-operas and women's magazines continue to promote stereotyped images of the sexes and of their relations. Men and women are surrounded by images which cannot fail to have an influence on their sense of identity, and on their perceptions of the opposite sex.

The question that arises is why these stereotypes should be so vivid and potent. The persistence of the relationship of domination of masculine over feminine is explicable, as Bourdieu demonstrates in 'La Violence symbolique' (1995), in terms of the internalization by the dominated of the dominant viewpoint. In society, tasks are still heavily divided according to sex. Some trades and professions, like that of building, are considered masculine. Given a patriarchal ideology, this social order seems self-evident and natural, and therefore reproduces itself. Women have incorporated the structures of this symbolic domination, and perpetuate them unconsciously.

Part of this symbolic domination places women in a constant state of corporeal insecurity: they are judged on their appearance, on whether or not they conform to men's desires. Their appearance – dress, make-up, hair, body, attitude – must show their compliance and sexual availability. By contrast, women who refuse to comply are deemed unfeminine. Another effect of the adoption by the dominated of the dominant framework is feminine masochism: social and sexual domination become eroticized. In a patriarchal society, power is seductive. Only a radical change in social organization will bring about a change in the power relation between men and women.

Nevertheless, Elisabeth Badinter, in *L'Un est l'autre*, written in 1987, analyses change in French contemporary society from a more optimistic perspective. In her book, as in the later *XY, de l'identité masculine* (1992), she puts forward the thesis that differences between men and women are diminishing, each gender incorporating elements of the other, and that the new emergent human being is made up of masculine and feminine elements which he/she can draw on according to the situation. This sexual levelling, which Badinter sees as a positive force, leads to a better understanding between individuals; passion which feeds on the opposition between the sexes gives way to tenderness. Yet if there are signs in contemporary French society that men and women are becoming more like each other, this move towards unisexism does not seem to be the model most French people desire. If both sexes claim equality, they also want to retain differences; women fear a uniformity that would amount to alignment on the masculine model, and men seem to be experiencing an identity crisis as they respond to changes in social roles and sexual identities.

Conclusion

French society has evolved rapidly since the Second World War. Relationships between men and women have changed, and these changes have been recognized institutionally and in the new laws in an attempt to redress the misogyny of the *Code Napoléon*. Theoretically, the conditions for equality between the sexes have, more or less, all been met. In practice, woman's place in society has improved, and French society in general seems to have become more egalitarian as far as gender is concerned. Masculine domination is certainly not as obvious as it once was. Women have become more independent and have acquired more control over their lives.

But many inequalities continue and in all domains. The social and cultural domination of men is still ubiquitous, even if, individually, many men have found it difficult to adapt to the new powers of their female partners. The most tenacious aspect of the hierarchy between the sexes is also the most deeply internalized: that is, the way the sexes are represented, all around us, in the media and in advertisements. How to combine difference and equality is the question that has dominated French thinking in the first half of the 1990s.

It is possible that France at the end of the 1990s is at a turning point, that the French model which has always been one of uniformity, and integration of difference by difference being subsumed under the norm, may be giving way to a more differentialist model, where differences are allowed to exist. The late 1980s and 1990s have seen a greater awareness of the need for reflection about the shaping of sexual identity. Positions appear less entrenched. Most feminists – like Gisèle Halimi or Simone Veil (Halimi 1994) – now recognize that difference must be part of the equation or there will be no equality. In the preface to *La Place des femmes*, Annie Labourie-Racapé affirms in a rhetorical question:

> Does not the granting to women of the same capacity to act as men presuppose the need for equitable measures? And does not positive discrimination, fair inequality, unequal rights for an unequal class of people, impose itself as necessary?
>
> (Ephesia 1995: 33)

This recognition may also have been prompted by the fact that many groups in France are campaigning for their difference to be respected, whether they are religious (Islamic groups), cultural (North African, *Beur*), or sexual (gay, lesbian) minorities. The advantage of the universalist model is that it upholds a more workable notion of equality. On the other hand, within the differentialist model the notion of equality has to be modified so that there can be equality and difference, a balance which as yet has not been achieved, at least as far as gender is concerned. As Michelle Perrot notes: 'Looking back to the dawn of history, there is nothing but masculine domination, for as far as the eye can see' (Ephesia 1995: 40).

Bibliography

Albistur, M. and Armogathe, D. (1977) *Histoire du féminisme français du moyen âge à nos jours*, Paris: Des femmes.

Aubin, C. and Gisserot, H. (eds) (1994) *Les Femmes en France: 1985–1995*, Rapport établi par la France en vue de la quatrième conférence mondiale sur les femmes, Paris: La Documentation Française.

Badinter, E. (1980) *L'Amour en plus: Histoire de l'amour maternel du XXVIIe au XXe siècle*, Paris: Flammarion.

—— (1986) *L'Un est l'autre, des relations entre hommes et femmes*, Paris: Odile Jacob.

—— (1992) *XY, de l'identité masculine*, Paris: Odile Jacob.

Beauvoir, S. de (1988) *The Second Sex*, trans. and ed. by H.M. Parshley, London: Pan Books Ltd, (first published as *Le Deuxième Sexe* (1949), Paris: Gallimard).

Blöss, T. and Frickey, A. (1994) *La Femme dans la société française*, Paris: PUF.

Bourdieu, P. (1995) 'La violence symbolique', in M. de Manassein, *De l'égalité des sexes*, Centre national de documentation pédagogique, 83–7.

Delphy, C. (1993) 'Rethinking Sex and Gender', *Women's Studies International Forum*, 16 (1): 1–9.

Duby, G. and Perrot, M. (eds) (1992) *Histoire des femmes en Occident*, vol. 5, le XXe siècle, Paris: Plon.

Duchen, C. (1986) *Feminism in France: From May 68 to Mitterrand*, London: Routledge & Kegan Paul.

—— (1994) *Women's Rights and Women's Lives in France, 1944–1968*, London: Routledge.

Ephesia (1995) *La Place des femmes; les enjeux de l'identité et de l'égalité au regard des sciences sociales*, Paris: Editions de la découverte.

Fouque, A. (1995) 'Demain la parité', in M. de Manassein (ed) *De l'égalité des sexes*, Paris: Centre national de documentation pédagogique.

Fraisse, G. (1996) *La Diffférence des sexes*, Paris: PUF, coll. Philosophies.

Guillaumin, C. (1992) *Sexe, Race et Pratique du pouvoir, l'idée de nature*, Paris: Côté-femmes.

Halimi, G. (1992) *La Cause des femmes*, Paris: Gallimard (first edition, Grasset, 1974).

—— (1994) *Femmes: moitié de la terre, moitié du pouvoir*, proceedings of the international colloquium organized by Choisir at Unesco, 3–4 June, Paris: Gallimard.

—— (1995) *Une embellie perdue*, Paris: Gallimard.

Héritier, F. (1996) *Masculin/Féminin, la pensée de la différence*, Paris: Odile Jacob.

Lapierre, N. (1996) 'La Différence des sexes à l'origine de toute pensée', *Le Monde*, 2 February.

Laubier, C. (ed.) (1990) *The Condition of Women in France; 1945 to the Present; A Documentary Anthology*, London: Routledge.

Léger, D. (1982) *Le Féminisme en France*, Paris: Le Sycomore.

Majnoni d'Intignano, B. (1996) *Femmes, si vous saviez...*, Paris: Éditions de Fallois.

Manassein, M. de (1995) *De l'égalité des sexes*, Paris: Centre national de documentation pédagogique.

Marks E. and Courtivron, I. de (eds.) (1981) *New French Feminisms: An Anthology*, Hemel Hempstead: The Harvester Press.

Mathieu, N.-C. (1991) *L'Anatomie politique: Catégorisations et idéologies du sexe*, Paris: Côté-femmes.

Montreynaud, F. (1992) *Le 20e siècle des femmes*, Paris: Nathan.

Nahoum-Grappe, V. (1996) *Le Féminin*, Paris: Hachette, coll. Questions de société.

Negrón, M. (ed.) (1994) *Lectures de la différence sexuelle*, Paris: Des femmes.

Ozouf, M. (1995) *Les Mots des femmes, essai sur la singularité française*, Paris: Fayard, coll. L'esprit de la cité.

Perrot, M. (1995) 'Identité, égalité, différence, le regard de l'histoire', in Ephesia, Paris: Editions de la découverte.

Picq, F. (1993) *Libération des femmes, Les années-mouvement*, Paris: Seuil.

Rabaut, J. (1978) *Histoires des féminismes français*, Paris: Stock.

Remy, M. (1990) *De l'utopie à l'intégration, Histoire des mouvements de femmes*, Paris: L'Harmattan.

Tristan, A., and A. de Pisan, (eds) (1977) *Histoires du M.L.F.*, préface de Simone de Beauvoir, Paris: Calman-Lévy.

Veil, S. (1994) 'Elles gouvernent...elles aussi', [round table] in Halimi, G. (1994) *Femmes: moitié de la terre, moitié du pouvoir*, proceedings of the international colloquium organized by Choisir at Unesco, 3–4 June, Paris: Gallimard, 217–67.

Chapter 4

Age

The life course

Patrick Harismendy

Like most other European societies, France has for twenty years now been undergoing a 'second demographic transition' (Lestaeghe 1995), marked by low birth, death and infant mortality rates. The break, however, is both relatively recent (after the long baby boom of the 1940s to the 1960s) and distinctive – accompanied as it is by profound sociological changes. In particular, the traditional family, up to now the only stable environment for procreation, has given way to various forms of the couple, in which the child no longer has the same status. In addition, the prolongation of life has had an influence both on the economy and on the relationships between generations, while the duration of professional life has been shortened. This chapter will study the nature of these changes, identifying certain developments specific to France, among them a long tradition of State intervention which has increasingly been called into question – by French citizens in terms of its application, and by French governments in terms of its principles.

A longer – and safer – life?

At 58.2 million inhabitants, France's population is close to that of the United Kingdom and represents 15.5 per cent of the European total, but, in terms of density, it is still sparse (105 inhabitants per square kilometre, compared with 239 in the UK or 228 in Germany). However, after the demographic depression of the nineteenth century, exacerbated by the Malthusianism of the 1920s, France underwent an early baby boom (from 1942 onward) which maintained its intensity until 1967; an average of 850,000 births per year providing the '12 million beautiful babies' called for by General de Gaulle at the time of the Liberation. There was, in addition, a high level of labour immigration into France, quite apart from the return of the French from North Africa in the late 1950s and 1960s (see Chapter 2). Thus, between 1936 and 1968 the French population rose from 42.1 to 49.7 million inhabitants, that is an annual growth rate of 1 per cent (or a birth rate of 1.2), 72 per cent of the increase being due solely to natural growth. This resulted from a variety of favourable factors: a large number of early, stable marriages guaranteeing maximum fecundity (between three and four children per fertile woman) combined with the positive image of the house-wife, and finally a lack of enthusiasm for emigration.

Such dynamism was accompanied by sustained urbanization and changes in the living environment. Many young couples formed at the Liberation took part in the overwhelming migration from country-side or medium-sized towns to the cities. Moreover, housing construc-ted during the 1950s corresponded to standards of comfort to which most French people were unaccustomed, in a country still largely living with cold water and oil lamps. Far from considering them-selves dependent on their husbands, young mothers – many of whom were of rural or working-class origin – experienced during the period 1946–1965 a feeling of liberation, of being less downtrodden than their mothers. The standardization of French society at this time found its origins in the emergence of a middle-class lifestyle; so much so that the sociologist Henri Mendras spoke of a 'second French revolution'. The image of the housewife, although outdated today, remained however of paramount importance for advertisers, who neglected working woman apart from commercials for deodorants or medicine.

Since 1975, the birth rate has been slowing down: the population has increased by only 250,000 from 1993–97 compared with 300,000 in the period from 1988–92. The role of immigration has become almost negligible, given the framework of restrictive legislation introduced in August 1993 (the *lois Pasqua*), following the earlier phases of regularization or family reunifications (1973–82). In 1995, only 45,000 legal entries were recorded set against 93,000 in 1993. These, moreover, were almost all people coming to join the rest of their family from the French-speaking countries of black Africa. What is more, North African and black African women – who, along with the Portuguese constitute the majority of the female immigrant population – are adopting the French demographic model of two children (Desplanques and Isnard 1993). Their repro-ductive rate, between 4.26 and 5.25 in 1980, dropped to 3.23–4.78 in

1990; that is, halfway between the French rate and that of their country of origin. Marriage rates have also been disturbed: immigrant women are marrying later in life.

The drop in birth and reproduction rates after 1967 can be explained, therefore, mainly by new social values – one of the highest rates of female employment in Europe (37 per cent in 1968, 47.2 per cent in 1996) which complicates maternity, and a relaxation of attitudes towards contraception and abortion. It was, in fact, only in 1967 that the Neuwirth law revoked the anti-Malthusian legislation of the 1920s and the Vichy regime, and authorized the sale of contraceptives, albeit with great difficulty until 1972. Resistance from the Catholic Church also held up the passing of the Veil abortion bill (January 1975). This bill was passed due, at least in part, to the extremely lively media campaign run by the Mouvement de libération des femmes (MLF) and certain intellectuals and actresses from the New Wave movement in the art and cinema world of the 1960s; such people as Catherine Deneuve, Delphine Seyrig (a special favourite of Marguerite Duras) or Françoise Sagan, all of whom had clandestine abortions in Great Britain or the Netherlands. If the number of reported abortions seems low – only 13.9 per cent of births or 166,000 terminations per year (compared with 23.1 per cent and 184,000 terminations in the UK) – the actual figure is estimated at 31.5 per cent, that is, an average number of 0.53 abortions per woman (0.67 in 1976). Despite the drop in the birth rate, such figures demonstrate that methods of contraception have still not been fully mastered, especially in the south of France.

The problem of an ageing population is an entirely different matter, for if the rate of female replacement (that is, the number of female babies born compared with the number of female deaths) was still 120 per cent in 1970, it is now no more than 87.3 per cent. The renewal of generations is at stake (Calot 1992). For French demographers, there are two alternative explanations: are we (a) experiencing the emergence of greater infertility – as is happening everywhere else – or (b) will the generation of French women born around 1960 and brought up in a climate of sexual liberation and independence (with the pill and abortion) make up for a late start towards the end of their fertile lives (Prioux 1996). The small increase in birth and marriage rates in 1996 (279,000 in 1996, 257,000 in 1995) begins to point to the second of these explanations, especially as the average age for a woman to give birth to her first child has now reached 28.9 years. What is more, even if 35 per cent of women of all ages are single, 90 per cent of them share a desire for maternity, compared with 80 per cent some forty years ago. In addition, the studies carried out on *in vitro* fertilization, in particular those of Professor Frydman, have revealed the desire felt by many mothers who have difficulty in producing a child, a desire intensified by the strictness of French legislation on adoption (only 2,778 foreign children were adopted in 1993). Thus 15,000 children have been born from artificial insemination, and 2,000 by *in vitro* fertilization. Militant feminists demanded: 'the children we want, when we want them' (a slogan that became famous). For all that, France remains at heart a country dominated by men, and is having difficulty in acclimatizing to controlled fertility and programmed maternity.

French population growth remains, however, more rapid than that of Germany or the UK (see Tables 4.1 and 4.2), countries both with similar demographic patterns to France (Guibert-Lantoine and Monnier1996). With equal fertility rates (1.7 children per woman), analogous birth rates (12.5 per cent), similar levels of infant mortality (4.9 per cent in France and 5.3 per cent in the UK), France and the UK have very different death rates. In the United Kingdom life expectancy for men is slightly higher (74.2 versus 73.7 years of age). French women, however, hold the European record for longevity (81.8 years, compared with 79.4 in the UK and 79.6 in Germany). The radical drop in mortality, and in particular infant mortality during the 1950s and 1960s, allowed the effects of the baby boom to be felt for longer in France than in other countries.

One year of life expectancy has been gained every five years since 1960, but men have benefited less than women. There is a higher rate of masculine mortality at all ages, and this is not due only to physiological causes. In 1993, 6,346 men died in car accidents and 3,736 of AIDS, compared with 2,437 and 813 women, respectively.

Table 4.1 General reproduction rates per woman in France, Germany and the UK

	France	*Germany*	*UK*
1970	2.47	2.03	2.43
1990	1.78	1.45	1.84
1995	1.70	1.24	1.70

Sources: INED (1996); INSEE (1997).

Table 4.2 Birth, death and infant mortality rates in France, Germany and the UK per thousand inhabitants (1994–96)

	France	Germany	UK
Birth rate	12.5	9.4	12.5
Death rate	9.1	10.8	11.0
Infant mortality rate	4.9	5.3	5.2

Sources: INED (1995); INSEE (1996).

In the UK, men are 3.5 times more likely than women to commit suicide (Lassalle 1996), but in France, too, the gap is pronounced: that is, 8,861 versus 3,390 (a factor of 2.6). It should also be pointed out that France has the highest rate of violent death (Bourgoin and Nizard 1994) – similar to Europe's ex-communist countries – a fact which reveals certain deficiencies in the area of crime prevention. A reluctance to take the AIDS pandemic seriously was – regrettably – manifested at the highest levels of government, a fact demonstrated by the contaminated blood affair; the legal wrangles of which are still continuing. This affair was surrounded by a kind of hysteria, rather similar to the infinitely less deadly 'mad cow disease'. The same is true of legislation in a country where the car manufacturing lobby prevents the passing of any effective laws to reduce the number of deaths on the road. Road deaths, along with suicide and AIDS, have given rise to a high male mortality rate between the ages of 20 and 35, weakening this age category. The French consumption of psychiatric medication is three times higher than that in the UK or Germany; a fact that cannot be accounted for solely by the alleged laxity of doctors with regard to the prescription of medicine. Behind the welcome figures showing a drop in the death rate, there are, therefore, worrying levels of morbidity.

For the most part, however, causes of death have changed greatly. Before the Second World War, tuberculosis, multiple parasitic and professional diseases accounted for 66 per cent of adult mortality. In the 1990s, 25 per cent of non-accidental deaths are due to cancer, and, even more significantly, 50 per cent to 'the degeneration of vital functions' following the International Classification of Diseases; in other words, half of all deaths in France are now due to old age. This is due not only to medical progress, but also to the prevention of disease, notably through the education of the general public (see Chapter 10).

Global trends towards increased medicalization are demonstrated by the growing importance of the hospital – the normal place of birth and death. Giving birth at home was still commonplace thirty years ago in a predominantly rural France. In the same way, religious beliefs required that visits were made to the deceased on their death bed; for people of note houses were singled out by ostentatious canopies covering the façade. Horse-drawn hearses – ridiculed by Georges Brassens in some of his songs – have disappeared as well. An apparent new equality in the face of death, has, however, been displaced from the social to the physiological. Differences in mortality rates can no longer be discussed in terms of one's ability to commemorate a death, or in terms of revenue ensuring better health, but in terms of culture and hardness of work. For example, even with comparable incomes, a primary school teacher will, on average, live eight years longer than an unskilled worker who is subjected to stress, bad weather and the deviant sociability of the café – which encourages alcoholism and smoking without the compensation of outdoor recreational activities.

The structure of the French population draws these observations together. The 20–59-year-old age group remained at approximately 53 per cent in 1996 (as it was in 1987); the 0–19 age group had, however, gone down from 28.6 to 26 per cent; conversely, the over-60s had gone up from 18.4 to 20.1 per cent, bearing in mind that the generations of the 1920s and 1930s were heavily depleted, thus minimizing these distortions. These proportions will be shattered when the baby boom generation reaches retirement age, when France will experience an explosion in the numbers of the elderly population. Already, in 1990, France counted 4 million people in the categories of 'fourth and fifth ages', two thirds of whom were women. In certain areas, elderly people outnumber the young; in this respect there are notable disparities between the north and the south.

The crisis of the family: Real and imaginary

Beyond these purely numerical observations, developments of a sociological or behavioural order can be discerned which explain, at least in part, the lower levels of reproduction and an ageing population (without losing sight of the demographic particularities of this geographical area). First, the questioning of the institution of marriage must be addressed. The number of weddings per year has dropped from 350,000 during the period 1946–1970 to 210,000 in the 1980s. With 4.4 marriages for every thousand inhabitants, 16.1 per cent of which are remarriages, France has one of the lowest marriage rates in Europe (7.45 per cent in 1975 and 5.1 per cent in 1990). The crisis can be seen in various ways: fewer people are getting married, and later; marriages are less stable; finally, the 35 per cent drop within ten years in the marriage rate of immigrants demonstrates the degree to which this phenomenon has penetrated (Launay 1996).

The 1960s, and above all the 1970s (with the reduction in the age of consent to eighteen) ushered in cohabitation among the young. To this must be added a relaxation of moral codes, especially with regard to sexuality (Spira *et al.* 1993). In twenty years, the average age at which young French women have their first sexual experience has dropped from 21.3 to 18.1 (19 for 75 per cent of them), and although still higher than in the UK, this has broken several taboos, among them, cohabitation. Only 15 per cent of couples getting married in 1963 had cohabited, this rose to 50 per cent in 1978, and now applies to 84 per cent of couples. It is worth noting that this form of union is well adapted to the needs of a country where twice as many young people aged between 19 and 24 are at school or college than in the UK, and are, therefore, financially dependent on their parents. This is why 45 per cent of young French cohabiting mothers have reached *baccalauréat* level, compared with only 9 per cent in the UK (Kiernan and Lelièvre 1995). The postponing of the future by young French people – the result of a prolonged education and difficulties in establishing a professional career – has the effect of raising the average age of marriage by one year every three years; it has now reached 28.3 for first marriages. Patterns of cohabitation, however, are changing. During the 1970s, only 7 per cent of couples split up after two years and only 4 per cent did not marry after ten years of living together. Now, a third break up within ten years, and 16 per cent reject marriage (Toulemon 1996). Formerly a prelude to marriage, cohabitation has now become an alternative, since only 10 per cent of couples living together get married after the birth of a child.

Twenty-five years ago, marrying late might prevent child-bearing, but today the average age of unmarried mothers at the birth of their first child is 27.5 (58 per cent are students). More than 37 per cent of births take place outside wedlock, compared with 6.8 per cent in 1970, far fewer than in Iceland (59.6 per cent) but more than in the

UK (32 per cent) and in a more traditional Germany (15.4 per cent). The acceptance of children who would formerly have been called illegitimate, is also related to divorce rates, since 25 per cent of female managers have a child outside marriage. We have come a long way, then, since the scandal caused by Louis Calaferte's novel, *Septentrion*, which advocated sexual freedom outside marriage. Today the real difference is no longer between legitimate and illegitimate children, but between legitimate or legitimized children and unrecognized children (Couet 1996). Fourteen per cent of children born outside marriage find themselves in the latter category after five years, and their infant mortality rate is more than double the national average (11.6 per thousand).

Divorce has also become commonplace. Infidelity does not explain everything. In practical terms, with the lengthening of life expectancy, the theoretical duration of marriage has tripled in a century, and doubled in forty years; statistically speaking, a couple married at 25 could expect fifty-five years together. Golden wedding anniversaries, still rare twenty years ago when they constituted a story for the local press, are no longer mentioned. The psychological factor must now be taken into account and divorce has become a means of regulation in the economy of couples, just like any other, bearing in mind the moral considerations. Although it has remained more or less stable for the last 15 years (81,000 divorces granted in 1980, 104,210 in 1984 and 115,650 in 1994), the French divorce rate is among the highest in western Europe with 33 per cent of marriages breaking up, generally after ten years. The corresponding decrease in the proportion of religious weddings also demonstrates the intensity of the process of secularization and shows just how necessary the divorce law – adopted in 1975 on the initiative of the commission presided over by Jean Carbonnier, Dean of the Law Faculty of Paris – was. Before this (and since 1884), divorce was granted only for adultery or violence, both extremely difficult to prove. Mutual consent, the reason for 85 per cent of current annulments, is very loosely defined, and allows a quick settlement as long as there is no disagreement over the custody of children. On the other hand, the system of justice is relatively powerless to enforce alimony payments and many divorced women experience conditions of great poverty, especially when unemployment plays a part. This is often the case, in that unemployment is – indirectly – the cause of a quarter of divorces granted.

In the 1990 census, out of 21.5 million households (defined in fiscal terms) 5.8 million were made up of one person only, to which must be added 2.5 million re-constituted families and of course the one million single parent families which represent 4.6 per cent of the total number of households. Recognized for the first time by INSEE in 1981 – that is, later and less pervasive than in Germany and the UK – this phenomenon (which is still growing) affects 13.2 per cent of families with children and, in 85.5 per cent of cases, these are families headed by women. Until the end of the 1960s, most were widows, but now the largest section is among the 30–50 age range. Producing fewer children than a stable home, single-parent families are socially discriminating. Fifty-eight per cent are formed of female workers and employees; usually married before the age of 24 and having only one child, they rarely remarry and suffer a marginalization similar to the rest of the '*Rmiste*' population (that is those who receive Income Support – *Revenu minimum d'insertion* (RMI). Chapter 6 discusses this point in more detail.

Families created by a second marriage are, conversely, more common in higher social and intellectual sections of society, and therefore in towns. Out of 14.1 million young people under the age of 19, 1.7 million come from single-parent families and 12.4 from couples, 750,000 of which are second marriages. The phenomenon is complex, but there are a number of common characteristics (Desplanques 1994). Most of these families have known single-parent phases; remarriage usually happens when the children are over 14 years of age; and, paradoxically, it is more common among families with two children than with one. This demonstrates both higher social class – hence greater financial resources, but even more perhaps, the capitulation to the social norm of bringing up children within a stable environment.

The ability of France to contain the growing number of elderly people in view of the demographic legacy of the inter-war years has already been mentioned, but France has been very backward in recognizing the place of senior citizens in society (Bourdelais 1993). One could even go so far as to speak of a taboo, in, for example, the absence of retired people in television advertisements – beyond those concerning cars…or sweets! If the elderly constitute a suitable target for successive finance ministers, who panic about alarming numbers of dormant bank or savings accounts, and periodically have to reduce interest payments in order to deflate this unproductive hoarding, it needs to be said that consumerism is not really part of the elderly person's way of life. Many lived through the deprivation of war and were affected by it. Their free time, in consequence, is spent in pursuits which will lead to self-sufficiency, like gardening (practised by 30 per cent of retired men), but especially television. The greatest consumers of images, and above all of television news – more so even than children – the elderly read very little except the newspaper (usually a regional one) (Delbès and Gaymu 1995). Apart from some specifically targeted services or products, the elderly do not constitute a significant economic sector, contrary to what some people declare or would like to believe.

Because there are still relatively few elderly people in France, coupled with the fact that they are, on retirement, entitled to social benefits established in the 1940s and 1980s, this age group has, sometimes, a standard of living bordering on indecency. In 1984, 34 per cent of couples over 60 were considered poor, compared with 24 per cent today. It is important to remember, however, that the same statistic for couples aged under 30 has increased from 14 per cent to 22 per cent. In short, the standard of living of a retired couple (and not the degree of wealth remembering that two thirds own their own house) is clearly higher than that of a couple with one child and one working adult, or even than that of a couple with two children where both partners work (Legris and Lolliviers 1996). Taking account of the expenses they incur, young people entering the employment market late have enormous difficulties in creating a home, and they know that they will never have a standard of living comparable to that of their parents. With this in mind, the increase of life expectancy also has economic implications. On the one hand, medicalization during the last year of life is extremely expensive, as every Social Security report confirms. On the other, deficiencies in French legislation make it almost impossible for grandchildren to inherit directly from their grandparents; such legacies are taxed at 55 per cent. Those who inherit are, therefore, usually retired or about to be. Consequently, inheritance no longer has the same function as it used to, as the main source of wealth, but has now become an extra bonus, to be enjoyed after many years of work.

Today, the balance of French society rests on two generations. First, young people under 40, in employment, whose domestic economies are squeezed dry by taxes, who are educating their children and maintaining a home. Second, there is the generation of 55–65 year olds, who are wealthy, but do not wish to part with their assets, despite the tax benefits of a settlement made during the donor's lifetime (dividing assets between the children), in view of the precarious nature of current pension schemes. This group has to compete for aid with young parents, to whom 3–4 per cent of the total revenue is distributed (from Barny *et al.* 1996), thus reducing the disparities between generations. This older generation also has to assume responsibility for very elderly dependants who, contrary to general assumptions, are being looked after more and more by the family or a daily help (Joël and Bungener 1990). The cinema has taken up this theme which is becoming increasingly a fact of our society. From a comic angle, in *Tati Danielle* (1990) the director, Etienne Chatiliez, depicts a terrible octogenarian who makes life impossible for her nephews when she moves in with them. From the opposite viewpoint, the director Cédric Klapisch, a specialist in youth and housing estates, in his film *Chacun cherche son chat* (1995), examines the emerging relationships between young and old in an old quarter of Paris. Although somewhat New York-influenced in terms of its approach to the Parisian 'village' and a little too idealistic, this film proposes a pleasant alternative to the estates, with the city resuming its former function of bringing individuals together. Whatever the case, it is possible to observe the appearance of poly-nuclear families – not part of the French tradition – throughout the whole of France and not just in the south (Kaelble 1988). Today, 20 per cent of over 65 year olds are dependent, 40 per cent are semi-dependent but only 16 per cent are housed in purpose-built accommodation.

Is French society very different now from what it was forty years ago? Yes and no. In fact, different social milieux have evolved, rather than the structures themselves. In the past, the traditional opposition lay between the north and west of France, Catholic and demographically productive, and the south, de-Christianized or Protestant, and Malthusian. The split now runs between rural France and areas surrounding small towns (where the birth rate is 2.65), and large cities like Paris (where the birth rate is 1.5). In addition, the birth rate remains higher at the two extremes of the social scale. In families of modest income with one salary, the rarity of divorce and of abortion and a resistance to contraception lead to traditional patterns of behaviour, while for the upper middle-classes, more faithfully religious and with larger incomes and a pleasant environment, material obstacles do not get in the way of having children. These same disparities are found in the choice of partner, and especially in meeting places (Bozon 1996). If, for the majority of French society, 33 per cent of couples met through the intermediary of the family in 1959 and as many at dances or by chance, now schools and universities are becoming the most common venues. The higher one moves up the social scale, the more private the meeting places become. The street, the cinema, and the night-club of the working classes are replaced by holidays abroad or the sports clubs and associations of middle management. As for the upper-middle classes and the aristocracy, discretely arranged marriages remain very much part of the scene. For behind the democratic and egalitarian front, France has retained her hierarchies, rituals and titles, even if they have no legal value. *Rallyes*, a form of ball organized by the parents of upper-class youth, are still the best way of avoiding a misalliance (Mension-Rigau 1990). It goes without saying that within these milieux, the crisis of the family is non-existent. On a more general level, only 6 per cent of male managers are single, the figure for agricultural workers, however, is 32 per cent. Job prestige is a sure winner in terms of finding a partner for men. For women the situation is more or less reversed: 7 per cent of manual workers are single, compared with 16 per cent of female managers.

Family politics: A very French obsession

A sizeable proportion of what has been said here would only be of minor interest were it not situated in a political or even ideological context. Nineteenth-century demographic depression, caused by the revolutionary and Napoleonic wars – themselves possible at a time when France was the most populous state in Europe – has prompted a recurring theme of decadence in France, associated occasionally with the idea of a secret plot; this in turn has motivated an otherwise very rational people to think in emotional terms. For the government of France, the regulation of family is part of the job. Governments are, therefore, able to legislate, regulate, forbid or permit on this subject, but they are also partisan (Debré and Sauvy 1946, Dupâquier and Biraben 1981). What might be called the populationist tendency in France is even stronger, given the opinion of both economists and historians regarding the four positive factors of the *Trente Glorieuses*[1] (Jean Fourastié 1979). These form a 'virtuous circle' of development: that is, protectionism, dynamism of the internal market, the regularity of productive investments and of training and, finally, the demographic impulse. In a country still tempted by apparently simple solutions, in the form of universal panacea, the idea of encouraging the birth rate appears to some as the key to activating the economy. In fact, powerful groups exist in the numerous family associations – from the most conservative to the most liberal – which form a variety of lobbies hoping to defend this or that family value or benefit, and to whom the State lends a willing ear. As late as 1993, the State was still pouring thousands of millions of francs into family benefits, making up 15 per cent of the total amount of state benefits, or 4.3 per cent of the GNP.

In 1996, an extra-parliamentary debate on the family was organized as a result of a study by the Advisory Commission on Population (*Haut Conseil de la Population*). Without going into detail about its conclusions, the existence of such a commission illustrates the State's attachment to this subject. Public action has shown itself to be more effective in other areas, however. For example, the *Institut national des études démographiques*, INED (the National Institute for Demographic Studies), is the only state organization of its type in Europe. For many years INED was led by the distinguished demographer, Alfred Sauvy; it publishes, among other things, the scholarly journal, *Population*. It is the sole supplier of demographic statistics, and anyone questioning its birth rates or fecundity too loudly is liable to discipline or dismissal from the Institution (Le Bras 1991). 'Much ado about nothing', some will say. Maybe; but this is the way it is in a country convinced of its 'exceptional' nature, and which needs to think of itself from now on in terms of 'exemplary' status, but no more than that (Duhamel 1994).

A populationist approach, then, inherited from the inter-war years and Vichy – which created a Ministry of the Family headed by the disconcerting Jean Ybarnégaray – became part of the universal planning project instituted at the time of the Liberation. Based on incentives, these policies introduced benefits for large families: family allowances with a special social security fund, including the notion of tax shares from which income tax allowances based on the number of people in a family could be calculated. Conversely, the fortunes of single people or childless couples were adversely affected. In the 1970s a new wave of measures responded to social change in the form of 'back to school' allowances and the recognition of single parents' tax status. An evolution in attitudes had, however, taken place. Until this point, the State was targeting the third or even the fourth child. From 1979–81, incentives for a third child were lost. Maternity leave was extended to twenty-six weeks from the second child onward, and the scale of family benefits was restructured around the second and third child, no longer applying to any others (Singly and Commaille 1996). Equivalent patterns can be found with regard to aid for the elderly.

Are such measures still effective in metropolitan France when social values have clearly evolved (indeed were they ever)? In other words, to what extent are such incentives taken into account by parents and future parents in terms of the family economy? A comparison with the United Kingdom which has a similar demographic development has been attempted (Hantrais 1992), but this no longer has any real meaning. In fact, the State never really possessed the means to achieve its ambition. Even at the Liberation no social security contributions were introduced and no Social Security Ministry created, much less a Ministry for the Family. Despite this, the objectives set by the technocrats and politicians remained in force (Levy 1992). The proof of the unworkability of these objectives lies in the fact that only 40 per cent of child-care needs are provided for throughout the whole country; and in Paris, the waiting lists are so long and the methods of selection so rigorous that some kind of political clout is necessary. Today, demographic questions are no longer put to families, with surprisingly few consequences. 1996 is a particularly instructive example. A whole series of factors – the progressive suppression of benefits for the first child, non-deductible maternity leave, the creation of a ceiling on the deduction of the cost of placing children with a nanny, and the new basic tax rate which is less favourable to couples with children, especially unmarried parents – failed to prevent a rise in the birth rate. The latter is not due to State incitement, but to each couple's personal wishes, a fact equally well demonstrated by the increase in the birth rate in 1942, at the height of German power and with one million French prisoners of war!

Finally, is French society becoming more individualist than it was? Does the creation of a Ministry for Solidarity between Generations in 1995, or alarming talk about divorce or suicide among the young, really reflect what is going on? The Government has, in fact, convinced itself that the family no longer exists, and that it has a duty to help individuals (Lesemann and Martin 1993). But – as the sociologist Agnès Pitrou pointed out some time ago (Pitrou 1978) – family solidarity *does* exist, as we have seen with regard to old people and to young parents. This does not mean that there is no risk of isolation. In Paris, 27 per cent of retired people are single with no children, and only 50 per cent have a child who can help them in practical ways. And if 8 out of every 100,000 young people aged between 15 and 19 commit suicide, 114 per 100,000 elderly people (aged 80–84) choose to end their lives (Surault 1995). On the other hand, since the mid-1980s when the economic crisis worsened, suicide – which had become increasingly commonplace in most levels of society – became less frequent. And instead of the trilogy 'religion, patriotism and work', surveys have shown that essential values are now connected with the family, which has become (rather than remains) the principal place of social regulation. Life crises, such as the exceptional prolongation of education, tighten the links, albeit at the price of a growing moral burden and feelings of dependence. If the cry 'I hate my family' can still be heard, it is no longer for the same reasons.

It is, perhaps, easier to understand the very particular relationship between the French political classes and the press with reference to young people. Electoralism is an obvious element, but things go deeper than that. For France owes part of its nineteenth- and twentieth-century history to crises, some serious, some less so, which shook the country or saved it. It is for this reason that the 1968 episode provides a reference point of the utmost significance. The May crisis gave birth to a 'generation' (Hamon and Rotman 1988) – that is a cohort of young people sharing common aspirations, starting with objections about the model of the family and paternal authority, embodied metaphorically by General de Gaulle. Those in power had no choice but to take an interest in the subject. But with the exception of Jacques Chaban-Delmas – a prime minister of Georges Pompidou, who, in a keynote speech inspired by the analyses of the sociologist Michel Crozier (author of *La Société bloquée* in 1970), tried to integrate young people as an active element in his 'new society' project – no one really did anything. Every student demonstration, however, reactivates the hope or fear that another 'generation' might emerge. The newspaper *Libération* ran the headline 'Birth of a Generation' in December 1986, at the sight of a million university and high-school students demonstrating against a modest proposal of selection for university entry, which did at least have the consequence of blocking Jacques Chirac's candidature for the 1988 presidential election. We must admit, however, that young people today, aged between 28 and 36 have never been unified, nor have they been catalysts for a new social model.

On the other hand, as in many other countries, the experience of the housing estates – with rap music as their means of expression – is far more structured, albeit negatively. First, this is due to a feeling of exclusion, or, alternatively, to a desire to 'get out', either by leaving the area, or by being able to display one's success. Second, it is revealed on a daily level by delinquency which starts younger and younger, where murder takes place in schools – something never before seen in a country where education is regarded as a universal value (Dubet 1995). But leaving violence to one side, the standardization of words, gestures and attitudes from Lille to Marseille, the *hauts lieux* of rap, is far more meaningful than sporadic demonstrations about specific projects. The Government's response, whether in the guise of the police or the education system, has to come to terms with the disillusionment of young people who have never known anything but recession, unemployment and boredom, and who can spot the difference between well-meant speeches and patent ineffectiveness. It is hardly surprising that these young people put their faith in clubs, even religious ones, in sport or in individual initiatives rather than in the old administrative system, in order to answer to the question that the whole of French society is asking – how to secure an income? This means that the problem of relations between generations can no longer be summed up by the juxtaposition of solidarity versus individualism, which lay at the heart of the welfare state plans which emerged from the Resistance and the Liberation, but must now be looked at in terms of the dilemma posed by social cohesion versus selfishness. In other words, it is up to the Government to reassert itself in order to avoid a communitarian landslide which could also create gulfs between generations. For communitarianism is totally alien to principles of integration or of a French identity founded, since the time of the Revolution, on the idea of nationality derived from the ownership of French property.

Note

1 A period of rapid social and economic growth and modernization between 1946 and 1975.

Bibliography

Barny, C. de, Eneau, D. and Houriez, J.-M. (1996) 'Les aides financières entre les ménages', *Insee première*, 441, Paris: INSEE.

Bourdelais, P. (1993) *L'Âge de la vieillesse*, Paris: Odile Jacob.

Bourgoin, N. and Nizard, A. (1994) 'Mortalité violente: la France mal placée', *Population et sociétés*: 289.

Bozon, M. (1996) 'Le choix du conjoint', in F. de Singly (ed.), *La Famille, l'état des savoirs*, Paris: La Découverte, pp. 22–32.

Calot, G. (1992) 'La relève des générations', *Population et sociétés*: 265.

Couet, C. (1996) 'Les naissances hors mariage', *Données sociales 1996. La société française*, Paris: INSEE, pp. 22–9.

Debré, R. and Sauvy, A. (1946), *Des Français pour la France*, Paris: Gallimard.

Delbès, C. and Gaymu, J. (1995) 'Le repli des anciens sur les loisirs domestiques. Effet d'âge ou de génération?', *Population*, 3: 689–720.

Desplanques, G. (1994), 'Les familles recomposées en 1990', *Population et sociétés*: 286.

Desplanques, G. and Isnard, M. (1993) 'La fécondité des étrangères en France diminue'. *Données sociales 1993. La société française*, Paris: INSEE, pp. 46–53.

Dittgen, A. (1994) 'Les formes du mariage en Europe. Cérémonie civile, cérémonie religieuse. Panorama et évolution', *Population*, 2: 339–68.

Dubet, F. (1995) *La Galère, jeunes en survie*, Paris: Le Seuil.

Duhamel, A. (1994) *Les Peurs françaises*, Paris: Folio.

Dupâquier, J. (1995) *Histoire de la population française*, vol. 4, Paris: PUF.

Dupâquier, J. and Biraben, J.-N. (1981) *Les Berceaux vides de Marianne*, Paris: Le Seuil.

Fine, Mark A. and Fine, David A. (1994) 'An examination and evolution of recent changes in divorce laws in five Western countries. The critical role of values', *Journal of Marriage and the Family* 56 (2) : 249–63.

Fourastié, J. (1979) *Les trentes glorieuses ou la révolution invisible*, Paris: Fayard.

Garibal, M. (1991) *La France malade du vieillissement*, Paris: Economica.

Guibert-Lantoine, C. de, and Monnier, A. (1996) 'La conjoncture démographique. L'Europe et les pays développés d'Outre-Mer', *Population*, 4–5:1005–30.

Hamon, H. and Rotman, P. (1988) *Génération*, vol. 2, Paris: Le Seuil.

Hantrais, L. (1992) 'La Fécondité en France et au Royaume-Uni: Les effets possibles d'une politique familiale', *Population*, 4: 987–1016.

Haut-Conseil de la Population et de la Famille (1992) *Avenir de la population*, Paris: La Documentation française.

Insee (1994), *Les Familles monoparentales*, Paris: INSEE, coll. contours et caractères.

Joël, M-E. and Bungerer, M. (1990) *La Prise en charge de la dépendance*, Paris: Legos-Cermès.

Kaelble, H. (1988) *Vers une société européenne? 1880–1980*, Paris: Belin.

Kiernan, K. and Lelièvre, E. (1995), 'Devenir parent hors-mariage en France et en Grande-Bretagne: Les différentes facettes d'un statut particulier', *Population*, 3: 821–8.

Lasalle, D. (1996) 'Les suicides en Grande-Bretagne de 1971 à 1992', *Population*, 3: 766–75.

Launay, C. (1996) 'La nuptialité à son niveau le plus bas avant une reprise?' *Insee première*, 438, Paris: INSEE.

Lavertu, J. (1996) 'La famille dans l'espace français', *Données sociales 1996. La société française*, Paris: INSEE, pp. 294–302.

Le Bras, H. (1991) *Marianne et les lapins. L'obsession démographique*, Paris: Olivier Orban.

Legris, B. and Lolliviers, S. (1996) 'Le niveau de vie par génération', *Insee première*, 423, Paris: INSEE.

Lesemann, F. and Martin, C. (eds) (1993) 'Les personnes âgées (dépendance, soins et solidarités familiales – Comparaisons internationales)', *Notes et Etudes documentaires*, 4967–68, Paris: La Documentation française.

Lestaeghe, R. (1995) 'La deuxième transition démographique', in D. Tabotin, T. Eggerix and C. Gourbin (eds) *Transitions démographiques et sociétés*, Louvain-la-Neuve: Academic L'Harmattan, pp. 120–37.

Levy, M.L. (1992) 'De la politique de population', *Populations et sociétés*: 274.

Mension-Rigau, E. (1990) *L'Enfance au château. L'éducation familiale des élites françaises au XXème siècle*, Paris: Rivages.

Nicole-Drancourt, C. (1996) *L'Insertion des jeunes en France*, Paris: PUF, coll. Que Sais-Je?

Pitrou, A. (1978, new edition 1992) *Vivre sans famille? Les solidarités familiales dans le monde d'aujourd'hui*, Toulouse: Privat.

Prioux, F. (1996) 'L'évolution démographique récente', *Population*, 3: 657–74.

Robine, J.-M., Morniche, P. and Cambois, E. (1994), 'L'évolution de l'espérance de vie sans incapacité à 65 ans', *Gérontologie et société*: 65–100.

Segalen, M. (ed.) (1991) *Jeux de famille*, Paris: Presses du CNRS.

Singly, F. de and Commaille, J. (1996) *La Politique familiale*, Paris: La Documentation française, *Problèmes économiques et sociaux*, février 1996: 761.

Spira, A., Bajos, N. et le groupe ACSF (1993) *Le Comportement sexuel en France*, Paris: La Documentation française.

Surault, P. (1992), 'Nuptialité, divortialité et suicide, des ruptures à rapprocher?' *Population*, 4: 1042–4.

—— (1995) 'Variations sur les variations du suicide en France', *Population*, 4–5: 983–1012.

Toulemon, L. (1996) 'La cohabitation hors-mariage s'installe dans la durée', *Population*, 3: 675–716.

Tribalat, M. (1993) 'Attribution et acquisition de la nationalité française', *Population et sociétés*: 281.

Chapter 5

The regions

Patrick Le Galès

The regional issue in France is full of illusions. On the political level, for example, after decades of political campaigning, the 'regions' were created in 1982. This apparent triumph was, however, accompanied by a strengthening of both the *départements*[1] and some cities (the traditional rivals of the regions). Similarly, the political recognition of local and regional economic development achieved during the 1980s was accompanied by increasing regulation and by an accelerated centralization of the economy (including the labour market). Finally, cultural and social initiatives within the regions benefited from European support and recognition, at precisely the time when regionalist movements were themselves on the verge of collapse. In short, the regional issue is no simple one for French society, since the 'long march' from an institutional point of view masks the collapse of economic autonomy; similarly the end of some forms of social and regional identity has disguised the arrival of new ones.

Institutions: The 'long march' of the regions (Mény 1974)

The state versus the provinces

The French State is one of the oldest centralized states of Europe which developed, like the others, through alliances or disputes with the principalities, towns and provinces that were progressively incorporated into the kingdom of France. In 1500, for example, neither Béarn, Savoy, Flanders, Brittany, Alsace nor Franche-Comté were part of the French State, and the difficulties in conquering Burgundy or Aquitaine encountered by more than one king are well known.

Once integrated into the kingdom of France, the majority of provinces kept their parliaments and individual rights, while French administration worked towards standardization and tax collecting, especially through its intendants.

It was without doubt the post-revolutionary Jacobin state which pushed the project of the nation state the furthest. The French State – probably more than any other in Europe – used all available modern methods to forge a nation. Historians point on the one hand to the determination of the French State to succeed, and on the other to the diversity represented by the old provinces. The revolutionaries knew what they were about as they dismantled the provinces in favour of the more rational *départements*, a hundred or so which formed a grid across the territory. Each *département* had its own prefect and sub-prefects. Regional parliaments and privileges were abolished. The prosperous capitals of the *ancien régime*, the rivals of Paris, were reduced to the rank of prefecture; they lost the economic, political and intellectual influence they exercised within their own provinces, within France, and for some cities – such as Lyon – within Europe. The Jacobin state controlled its own borders and rationalized the administrative organization; such centralization was reinforced by the organization of infrastructures and transport. The next step was the contribution made to the nation and to French citizenship by the development of institutions such as the education system and the army – often at the cost of cultural and social differences. The State building project was remarkably successful, but never completed. The paradox is well-known in France: a centralized State able to recognize, accommodate, and even to permit the colonization of itself by the local (Grémion 1976).

Regionalism did not, indeed, disappear. The old Catholic right – nostalgic for the *ancien régime* – created a myth out of the regions; a myth of an older France, of traditional values and the countryside mocked by the Revolution. Regionalism became a right-wing phenomenon in France, at least until the Second World War; associated with the enemies of the State, of the Revolution and of the left. Extreme right-wing sympathies, including collaboration with the Germans by certain extremists in Alsace or Brittany (against the common enemy – the French State), finally discredited such movements.

The State and the regions work together for modernization

After the Second World War, things were different. Following the pattern of other European countries, French regions were 're-invented', while the provinces and provincialism were left firmly in the past. The stabilization of borders and the growing peace in Europe rendered the idea of a sacred nation redundant, thus permitting the development of 'region' as a concept. All these changes were relevant in France, added to which the end of colonization (at the beginning of the 1960s) saw the return of an élite ready to concern themselves with the development of metropolitan France. The political and administrative élite (that is the Gaullist regime and the upper ranks of the Government) prioritized the reorganization of the state in an attempt to modernize the country – regional development played a central part in this. The recognition of the region became part of the modernization initiative (the regional economic élite opposed the 'notables') and of improved planning efficiency, especially the planning of facilities. The whole undertaking became known as administrative regionalism. The divisions (dating back to the War) utilized for such actions demonstrate this logic well: the old provinces (such as Brittany) were cut up, while new regions (Centre or Pays de Loire) were created from nothing. In the face of hostility from local dignitaries, the Gaullist regime launched a project for the creation of regions at the time of the 1969 referendum, allowing the more pro-modern and enterprising sections of French society (trade union leaders, those working in agriculture, associations, managers, heads of businesses, universities) to raise their voices. The failure of this referendum left the regions without power.

During the 1960s and 1970s, an upsurge in cultural and political regionalism (Brittany, Corsica, Alsace) was directed against the French State. These movements were full of young people from the public sector – left wing and middle class – who put pressure on the centralized government. The left, and in particular ecologists and a section of the new Socialist Party, promoted themselves as the defenders of decentralization reforms – reforms which were introduced in 1982 after the arrival of the left in power. Regionalism, formerly an issue of the right representing tradition, had by now become a left-wing phenomenon, representing social, political and economic modernization.

Towards a regionalized republic? (Faure 1994)

These decentralizing reforms, and the creation of regions as local collectivities in the full sense of the term, were welcomed as the beginning of a new era. French society was about to liberate itself from the guardianship of the state: public services and 'big' decisions would be brought nearer to the citizen; local and regional economic development offered pleasant prospects; and regional cultures were recognized for their richness and not merely opposed by the state. At this point I wish to discuss these elements from political and institutional viewpoints; the cultural and economic aspects will be dealt with in subsequent sections.

Contrary to expectations, the regions had great difficulties in establishing themselves as a level of government (CURAPP 1993, Balme 1997, John and Le Galès 1997). In practice, despite the legal status, expertise, elected bodies and budgets of the twenty-two metropolitan regions, the dynamics of decentralization not only presented the most active of players in the French system (the cities) with additional room for manoeuvre, it reinforced the powers of the *départements* – in other words the heart of the Jacobin state. Despite an initial dynamism – strongly supported by public opinion – regional councils had great problems establishing themselves in the face of the older, deep-rooted and richer powers-that-be. Notwithstanding the progress made, regional budgets remained fairly small (except in the case of Ile-de-France). Moreover, given the choice, most politicians preferred national, departmental or local posts rather than regional ones, with a few exceptions (for example Charles Millon in the Rhône-Alpes region). The regional political élite was therefore an intermediary élite, with no real focus either on the political level or in terms of party support (regionalist parties hardly existed, except in Corsica).

Finally, regions as institutions had to contend with the absence of interests organized on a regional level. For the majority of large institutions (trade unions, professional organizations, chambers of commerce and industry, employers, family organizations, associations of war veterans or political parties) the regional level was either non-existent, or at best was a level for co-ordinating local or departmental structures – with certain exceptions, such as Alsace. If the regions constituted a meeting place for political and social networks, they did not provide an effective level for articulating social and economic interests.

The weakness of the regions as a level of government also clashed with the preservation of a centralized state, even if the latter was becoming more and more fragmented. The restructuring of the state has not taken the radical forms that it has in the United Kingdom. France today is characterized by an abundance of plans and policies, of fragmented rationales for public action both within the framework of the State and its various sectors, and within that of local authorities – remembering the importance of diversity between one region or town and another. Generally speaking the State has lost its prerogatives and its means of action: key areas have been taken over by local authorities and the private sector (financial organizations and enterprises). In certain towns and regions, elected bodies are able to develop stable systems of co-operation between public and private companies, to insist that national and international organizations take local issues into account, and to organize both the internal structures and the external representation of these areas.

The structural weaknesses of the French regions are difficult to overcome, especially the absence of a hierarchy. Many function simply as a federation of *départements*. It seems, however, that politicians are becoming more and more interested. In terms of public policy – even if the impact of regional councils has remained limited especially with regard to economic development (with the exception of sectoral policies relating, for example, to the environment and professional training) – the effect of European policies and a tendency towards the regionalization of government adminis-tration have created new conditions. As in other countries, the French regions have tried to use both existing structures and specific programmes (INTERREG, PIM, ARC ATLANTIQUE); on the one hand to reinforce their political role, and on the other to forge alliances with other European regions and to launch a number of innovative programmes.

Some regions (mainly Nord-Pas-de-Calais, Rhône-Alpes and certain southern regions), constitute political arenas; places of inter-dependence between public players on different levels. It is clear that the very long and slow march of the French regions is still contin-uing.

The economy and the regions: An ambiguous model[2]

Heritage, hierarchy and industrial de-concentration: the unification of the French economy under Parisian command

French economic development, tardier than that of other European countries, followed a hierarchical logic, reflecting the country's political structure. Industrial development in France occurred mainly in the region around Paris, and north of a diagonal running from Le Havre to Geneva. The only industrial regions, apart from Paris and Lyon, are the conurbation of Lille-Roubaix-Tourcoing, the northern mining area, Saint-Etienne, Le Creusot and ports such as Le Havre and, to a lesser degree, Marseilles. Essentially, therefore, industry is concentrated in a few areas in the north and east. France very quickly became characterized by strong economic centralization, concentrating business, capital and qualifications in the Paris region, which benefited fully (as did London and Berlin) from the transport revolution. Throughout the twentieth century, the French economy followed the trajectory of Taylorization, which gave rise to the centre-periphery model. After the Second World War, the large labour-intensive companies abandoned manufacturing sites in the Paris region and set themselves up in rural regions with well-educated, cheaper labour. This movement – the industrial devolution of unskilled labour during the 1960s – contributed to the beginnings of industrialization in the west of France, especially Brittany and to a lesser extent, the south-west; areas which began quickly to catch up with the rest of France. Employment dynamics reveal a marked geographical polarization: unskilled workers in the rural west, and in Paris the activities of command and conception where the majority of *grandes écoles*[3] producing the French administrative and economic élite are to be found.

The period of the *Trente Glorieuses*[4] marked the unification of the French economy under the command of the Paris region. In fact, this evolution – in the sense of a hierarchical pyramid (Paris, followed by the regional capitals) – went hand in hand with the collapse of local and regional economies, of what are known today as the industrial districts, or regional forms of economic life. Within this process of disappearance, both of local economies and the small- and medium-sized businesses which supported them, it is necessary to consider (a) the strategy of big business, and (b) the role of the government in supporting the concentration of big business and its devolution at the expense of smaller firms (Ganne 1994). As Veltz (1996) states, there are two exceptions to the disappearance of local and regional economic systems: the survival of a certain number of industrial districts containing small- and medium-sized businesses (Cholet, Oyannax, Vallée de l'Arve), and more especially the case of Paris:

> the survival in the Paris region of a complex mixture of big business and small and medium-sized businesses in the high-tech aeronautical and military electronics industries, substantially and continually privileged by the economy of 'large-scale projects', and by the public financing of research development is an exception ... these companies give weight to the Ile-de-France as the technological centre of the national economy.
>
> (Veltz 1996: 32)

This movement towards industrial devolution was accompanied by an increase in government intervention in social and technological matters. Thus, the Gaullist government of the 1960s invested massively in public services (hospitals, universities, schools, centres for research and *grandes écoles*) and in the modernization of towns experiencing a growth in population levels, particularly in the west and south of France. This development on two fronts, together with economic growth, permitted these regions more or less to catch up financially (for example, the inequality of salaries became progressively smaller, even when compared with Ile-de-France), and in terms of employment opportunities – this, not in relation to the Ile-de-France but to the north-eastern industrial regions, which were themselves experiencing difficulties. Those regional capitals sufficiently far removed from Paris (that is, not those in the Parisian basin), profited most from this period of development (notably Grenoble, Nice, Toulouse, Montpellier, Bordeaux, Nantes, Rennes and Strasbourg), a fact which had repercussions for their regions. The 1970s witnessed the growth of medium-sized towns, while recession appeared to interrupt growth in Paris. The regionalist movements were able to nurture hope.

The rupture of the 1980s: metropolitanization and the segmentation of the periphery

The French economy, as with all western economies, has had to face major ruptures since the mid-1970s, ruptures which provided the context for, and sometimes the cause of, profound transformations in French society. These transformations (de-industrialization, the growth of the tertiary sector, the process of globalization especially with regard to companies, the government's growing incapacity for regulation, the liberalization of exchange rates, unemployment, new conditions for competition, and the telecommunications, financial and transport revolutions) will not be discussed here. But the consequences for towns and regions have been radical.

Cities versus regions?

In France, as elsewhere, metropolitanization has been a major phenomenon. During the 1980s, the Paris region absorbed most of the economic growth, especially with regard to employment. Paris, and the region surrounding it benefited fully from the opening up of the French economy and from the logic of the free market. So, just as some kind of political decentralization was finally being drawn up, economic centralization was again on the increase. In addition to Paris, the Rhône-Alpes region, Alsace, the southern cities, Grenoble, Montpellier, Toulouse, Nantes and Rennes were the major beneficiaries of these economic developments.

This metropolitanization went hand in hand with the disconnection of the metropolitan areas from their regions. Thus, in this new competitive arena, the development of regional capitals no longer meant that the regions benefited; on the contrary, the growth of the regional capitals was accompanied by the economic decline or stagnation of the region. This phenomenon was particularly marked in the west and south-west of France. The metropolitanization of jobs was even more marked than that of population movement; that of production was the most striking of all.

The third major fact was the rapid development of wealth inequalities between different areas, and in particular the appearance of a 'diagonal of recession and desertification', which included the crisis-stricken industrial regions in the north, the mining basin in the centre, the Massif Central and part of the south-west, characterized by the phrase: 'a rural zone in deep decline'. In contrast, the creation of employment and of wealth was growing in the richer and more dynamic areas – Paris, Alsace, the south, and in certain regional capitals which had hedged their bets successfully.

This economic evolution had very selective effects: the concentration of economic activity in the Paris region was accompanied by a disproportionate growth in certain sectors, such as new technology, the media, company services and management. Although the gap in employment levels between Paris and the rest of the country seemed to narrow at this time, Paris continued to dominate all growing sectors and was responsible for job creation and for the most highly qualified section of the labour market. The GNP levels for the Ile-de-France, for example, represented almost 30 per cent of the national GNP. (If the Rhône-Alpes and Provence-Alpes-Côte d'Azur were included this rises to 45 per cent – the other nineteen regions share the rest between them). The gaps in income per person vary from one to five.

Finally, studies repeatedly demonstrate the collapse of the periphery and of the regions as a homogenous economic area; striking differences appeared between them. The rupture between towns, urban regions and the other regional areas has already been underlined. To this must be added the fact that even at the heart of the regions, the integration of the local into the European and world economies was experienced in very different ways. Certain regions possessed particular capacities to organize their economic development, which equipped them to cope with the transformation of the market, whereas others went into rapid decline. Such differences could be found even within one agglomeration. During the 1970s, for example, it was possible to speak of a Breton or Burgundy economy able to stand its ground in face of the dominance of Paris or other similar developments; by the 1980s the idea of a regional economy had lost most of its meaning. In the context of competition between areas, the regions collapsed economically; the expression 'regional economies' now made sense only if referring to urban regions or localities. Despite the efforts of regional councils, regional economies were no longer anything but a fiction.

The French regions could not cope with these economic developments without government support. In fact, the government continued to operate a huge programme of geographical redistribution of wealth. However – and here lay the novelty – the size of this redistribution (notably via social security and public employment) could no longer contain the growth of geographical inequalities, which provoked tensions. The State, guarantor of social and geographical cohesion, was caught between a logic of decentralization, encouraging the economic development of more dynamic regions, and an older logic of management and redistribution. The arrangements in terms of regional financial standardization no longer satisfied anyone.

The picture painted above needs to be developed in more detail. First, as has been pointed out, recent developments are not limited to the domination of Paris in the French economy at the expense of the provinces. Alsace, Rhône-Alpes, and to a lesser extent, the regions in the south-east of France are also experiencing healthy economic growth, especially in the urban area of Lyon, or Strasbourg, Nice, Montpellier and Grenoble. Second, the regional capitals of the south and west have successfully hedged their bets, but they are the exceptions. For reasons connected to the displacement of the economic centre of gravity in Europe as a whole, a diagonal is re-emerging drawn from Nantes to the south-east. The centre, the south-west and the west are either stagnating or experiencing difficulties, whereas the north of the country is experiencing a profound process of restructuring.

Finally, beyond all these developments, the process of globalization and the reconstruction of the role of the state have opened the way for numerous local and regional initiatives. For a good ten years now, France has been characterized by the voluntary sector – political and social organizations attempting to develop the territory. At a more profound level, local and regional authorities, groups of employers, universities, representatives of the devolved state are forming more and more coalitions with the aim of creating the conditions necessary for economic development; in the form, that is, of industrial or technological districts, of all kinds of networks, and large-scale long-term projects. Beyond the impressive rhetoric which accompanies a multitude of small successes, the mobilization of the regions towards economic development has begun. These towns and regions (the élite) often have at their disposal a solid base of public activity and high quality equipment; they are engaged in medium and long-term plans which are starting to bear fruit. It is important to remember that the growth of regional capitals in the 1980s owed much to government investment during the 1960s. The cultural, social and political support for towns during the 1980s was spectacular. Towns and regions lost their inferiority complexes with regard to Paris and the French

Government, who, for its part, showed little interest in the matter. These led to some spectacularly successful economic development; but it was not universal.

The support for and interest in regional and local economies thus constitutes a new and recent phenomenon; it is none the less deep-rooted and treated as such by the media, which would have been unthinkable fifteen years ago. Such support is apparent, for example, in marketing strategies and the production of goods connected specifically with an area, a region or a locality; according to consumer specialists, this is an important tendency (in particular in the south-west, in Brittany, and of course in Provence).

Local and regional societies

The sociologist understands the limited possibilities of political projects such as the nation state or of categories based on economic structures, such as social class. The attempt by the government and the élite to create a nation, though successful in many ways, has reinforced the resistance of certain groups or cultural minorities in the regions and in particular localities. The government (as in other European countries) has had to face up to a regional diversity which has not disappeared, and which has adopted very different forms at different times – for example, political organizations, habits, social and religious practices or economic development (as in the Vendée). It is necessary, therefore, to consider France as both a social and political construction: the result of unification, but also of persistent diversity.

The resistance of regional societies

There was a time in the recent past (above all in the 1960s) when French society seemed finally to correspond more or less to the designs which the governmental élite had been attempting to implement for centuries; that is, organized around the large institutions of state (the nation, classes, unions, the Church, the family and political parties), with an increasing cultural homogeneity encouraged by a century of education, the army, television and the triumph of the nuclear family. Modernists of the 1960s regarded the preservation of regional peculiarities as an archaism bound to disappear, unless these were used for an improvement in the country's resource management. Thirty years later, this vision was seriously questioned, alongside that of the nation state, attitudes which shook France more than other countries considering the structuring role of the state within French society. Economic recession, the globalization of the economy, European integration – all these processes have deeply affected a French society ready to question 'the idea of French society itself'. Forgotten differences re-emerged; a variety of local and regional variations which served as a reminder that if the nation state constituted a valid category in terms of social sciences, and particularly in France, it was high time to take into account the endurance and strategies of groups and areas which offered another vision of French society.

In fact, as Mendras points out, the French constantly like to remind themselves 'that France is known for its diversity' (Braudel 1990). The force of this theme becomes understandable as a counterpoint to the theme of national unity: the two reinforce each other. The goal which guided the national élite to forge the notion of a France belonging to French citizens came up against strong resistance:

> The extraordinary slowness of this amalgamation is stupefying. Despite a desire for centralization which has never weakened, despite sharing national institutions and history, despite religious unity and the power of the Church, despite political and administrative institutions, despite the civil code, despite the single currency and market, despite the roads, followed by railways, despite the wars.... The regional diversity of France gave way only very recently.
>
> (Mendras 1994: 214–5)

As a result:

> The delicate and complex mechanisms of fitting local interests and habits in with national rules provide an explanation for the contradictions of a country which has been highly centralized for four centuries and yet which has managed to conserve marked regional differences.
>
> (ibid.)

Any analysis of French society needs to take into account this tension between the formation of French society and the forces opposed to it. An analysis from the bottom up is indispensable in order to understand what is going on. In a country so little affected by the industrial revolution (at least in its first phase), the class structure has combined with the tenacity of the peasantry (until the 1960s) and with the weight of government and its employees – and all of this within a political entity which has remained remarkably heterogeneous.

Thus, in spite of Jacobin ideology, French sociologists (such as André Siegfried in political sociology or Gabriel Bras in religious sociology) have demonstrated the surprising stability in patterns of behaviour in a large number of localities and regions. Demographers have also shown regional differences with regard to marriage and the birth rate, differences which have been maintained for centuries. Historians and sociologists of the family have demonstrated the stability of different family structures. The map of religious practice is even more surprising: the preservation of Catholic regions in the north or in Brittany in opposition to the areas south of the Massif Central, and to the largely de-Christianized peasants of the Limousin region. Studies of electoral sociology reveal the stability – or extremely slow evolution – of voting patterns; the left-wing vote in the south-west, as opposed to communists in Limousin and the right wing in Alsace.

Family structures, political organization, religious practice and property type are all factors in the production of local and regional societies which have been able to survive by evolving with the times. From this perspective, French society should consider itself the result of opposing, combined or well-balanced forces; combinations which vary according to the area, and which have created a lasting structure for collective behaviour. This analysis can be applied on a large or small scale – that of regions or communes. In a certain *département*, since the time of the Revolution, and therefore independently – or almost – of economic structures, one group of communes voted for the left, did not go to Mass and possessed a democratic system of power, whereas ten kilometres away, another group elected the lord of the manor as mayor (one hears talk of an elected monarchy), went to Mass, did not (or very rarely) get divorced and constituted a micro-society with extremely different demographic, family and political regulations. This is not so surprising in the long term, for if the early establishment of a French state allowed the rapid development of a French language in the Paris basin – a prelude to the cultural unification of the nation – the French language only became current everywhere at the end of the nineteenth century, with the development of a compulsory and secular school system. In between times, on the borders of the country, people still spoke Flemish, Alsatian or German, Occitan, Italian and Basque.

The most persuasive interpretation from this perspective is perhaps that of the demographer and sociologist H. Le Bras, who has identified three structuring influences in the formation of France: the family, regional or local strength very often associated with religion, and the force of national unification:

> In fact, their confrontation has given rise to three stable combi-
> nations, three particular societies of which the self-regulation or
> deregulation takes into account the social and industrial trajec-
> tory of each French region since the Revolution. In the Paris
> basin national strength is absolutely dominant; since the nine-
> teenth century families are small, individuals more mobile than
> elsewhere and neither religion nor political parties wield any
> particular power over them. This region, and only this region,
> corresponds fairly well to the idea of a homogenous France.
> Beyond this, regional or local strength begins to make itself felt,
> in Brittany, in the east, to the south of the Massif Central and
> in the Basque country; ... this has been progressively associated
> with Catholicism. In these already peripheral regions, a
> different style of society has persisted up until the present. In
> the rest of the territory, the south-west, the south-east and the
> centre, the family has long opposed its two rivals, but has now
> almost completely given way to national strength, as it could
> not cope with modern transformations.
>
> (Le Bras 1986: 16)

These analyses reveal the force of traditional family structures and their long-term effects in terms of the local management of social and economic change, of political behaviour, of emigration and of attempts to fit in with the integrationist forces of the State. The family, the locality (the Church) and the State; these are the institutions which have provided the structure for this country.

In this analysis, culture in itself does not appear as a determining factor if considered in isolation. The Breton culture derives its strength from its links with a model of social regulation, which associates the Catholic Church (parishes, schools, guilds and various organizations) with particular forms of the family (variations exist) and with a region possessing a specific history and a social structure, which has evolved slowly without the shock of industrialization (at least until the 1960s). In the Catholic west (barring exceptions), the goals of the nation state have reinforced particularities and the preservation of traditional social and cultural structures without hindering the remarkable economic modernization of the 1950s – but always within a tense and ambiguous relationship with the State. In the east of France, Alsace has also emerged as a regional society, bearing in mind its turbulent political history. Here moderate, pro- gressive social Christianity expresses a strategy of resistance with respect to the great national political forces – a desire for progressive modernization and consensus *vis-à-vis* the Centre.

The beginning or the end of regional specificity?

Since the publication of these classic studies of the local, the regional and the national, a certain confusion reigns. On the one hand, social and cultural tendencies have finally carried the day at the expense of local and regional peculiarities. On the other, the questioning of French society as a national society, and the uncertainties linked to economic transformations and to relations between groups and individuals are prompting a re-examination of the notions of local and regional.

First, the 1960s and following years were marked by increased individual mobility, which contrasted with the extreme parochialism of French society (for example in the choice of spouse). A whole host of factors support this conclusion: the arrival of women on the labour market, the development of higher education, the rapid growth of the middle classes (in the private and public – and espe- cially the tertiary – sectors), the decline of the peasant class, opportunities for social mobility, the nationalization of political life, the end of the urbanization drive of regional capitals and of the Paris agglomeration, the influence of television – all these things have contributed to the structuring of a more homogenous French society.

However, almost simultaneously, regionalist movements experi- enced a resurgence, in defence of their individual cultural identities. Whilst the traditional structures of social organization in Brittany had, for example, been called into question, and just as the region was entering a period of accelerated economic modernization, the political regionalist movement revived (this was also true of Corsica and the Basque country). The triumph of the nation state was called into question by social movements, the middle classes and economic difficulties. In the 1960s, a strong social movement emerged demanding the re-evaluation of the local and the regional, a movement which gained support in the following years. After the more ideological 'small is beautiful' period (post-1968), growth, innovation and the vitality of French society became most apparent on a local level. What is more, the middle classes played a decisive role in this development (*Sociologie du Travail* 1982, OCS 1987, Mendras 1994). On the one hand locality and region, which had long been essential elements in the building of identities, seemed to recede in importance. On the other, the adopted or chosen place became increasingly significant for individuals and the formation of social groups; a shift which illustrates a reversal in the relationships between groups, institutions and individuals. Region and locality (but also religion and family) were no longer imposed on the individual (or considerably less so), but this did not imply that they had disappeared. Indeed exactly the same factors were reformed, re-interpreted and chosen by individuals. The loosening of the link between the individual and his or her place of origin (or family of origin) modified the possibilities. Just like the family, region or locality could become the centre of cultural or social affinity, of invented or re-invented solidarities and could function as a motivating myth. The symbolic dimension of locality or region was particularly strong in the 1970s, when the rejection of society went together with the idea of locality as a refuge (Garden *et al.* 1986).

In brief, the nature of this return to the local and regional changed in the 1980s. Without resorting to determinism, it is clear that territory which is considered as a political and social construction can constitute a significant mediating factor in the lives of individuals, groups and institutions. Attempts to reveal innovative social and political formations in certain areas do not require too much imagination. National symbols lose their significance in the face of uncertainties and the variability of economic relations. Regional and local cultures become once again effective codes for self-expression and identity. This permitted the renewal of towns and regions as local societies, a hypothesis expressed in the following quote:

> if the State plays a less central role and national societies are
> called into question, it is possible for towns (and some regions)

to constitute one of the places where sub-cultures of place and/or social groups are reinforced in particular combinations.
(Bagnasco and Le Galès 1997: 15)

A brief tour of the regions

To give an account of what is happening in the French regions it is, therefore, necessary to take into account both the heritage, still very much present, of the social forces and policies identified above and the transformations which have been briefly outlined. Another difficulty lies in the absence of any sociological reference to the regions (in the institutional sense); similarly the disconnection of local and regional transformations renders the designation of regional boundaries extremely artificial when it comes to comparing statistics. The regions do not constitute a clear level of social structuring, while the defence and reinforcement of local societies is stronger (as is the case in Italy). The reconstitution of spatial and social coherence is underway, but the contours remain hazy. As a result, work dealing with the French regions tends to emphasize political evolutions and economic transformations (as well as various individual strategies), rather than the recomposition of groups and social structures.

Some regional examples illustrate this point. For most French regions – notably those which were created from nothing – the big regional stakes are more or less the same. From one perspective, regional ways of life and customs have lost their significance, but from another attempts are being made to invent or re-invent new identities and to motivate interest in long-term projects. In the majority of cases, these strategies have difficulty overcoming a reality which resembles a mosaic of micro-regions and an acute contrast between the regional capital and the rest, notably the exodus from the periphery and the economic concerns hidden by the developments in transport (with the aim of better European integration). All of this tends to revive tensions within the regions, weakening certain areas and strengthening others.

With this in mind, it is particularly interesting to look at some of the more structured regions: Alsace, Brittany, Corsica, Nord-Pas-de-Calais, Provence-Côte d'Azur and Aquitaine.

The history of Alsace is complicated by successive annexations by France and by Germany. This history has contributed to the preservation of a strong identity, as well as a dialect and different institutions. Alsace has never been completely integrated into France; it is nevertheless remarkably prosperous economically – following the example of the Baden-Württemberg region. Such prosperity has been solidly rooted in the local bourgeoisie for a long time. The question of Alsatian identity has brutally reappeared – since 1988, the Front National has been regularly obtaining 20 per cent of the votes in Alsace, despite the almost total absence of immigrants. This vote has provoked lively debate about the Alsatian identity in a rich, economically prosperous region which has always been open to Europe. The 'Alsatian malaise' is particularly marked in the rural regions of the lower Rhine (whereas the large towns of Strasbourg and Mulhouse have elected left-wing mayors for the first time in many years). The blame has been variously attached to the decline of Catholicism, the loss of local control over the economy, a nostalgia for the past, environmental threats, the beginnings of economic fragility and dependence on external factors. Considered as a French Switzerland, Alsace has existed as a European border region; it is, however, protected by the French State. Indeed Alsace provides an example of a neo-regionalist movement where the safe-guarding of economic prosperity is articulated by a strong local identity and culture (as in the Northern League in Bavaria). The real question for the 're-invention' of Alsatian identity can be put as follows: how will Alsace retain its specificity in an open market and an integrated Europe?

Brittany, too, is experiencing a difficult time; this though is not reflected by a protest vote. Whole sectors of the economy are progressively crumbling (fishing, agriculture, defence, even the electronic industry is drying up), except in the Saint-Malo/Rennes/ Vannes zone, which stretches as far as Nantes. The changes in the labour market mentioned above, allied with the fact that Brittany produces a large number of highly qualified young people, has led to a new exodus of young people leaving for the region around Paris. The region is ageing and so is the élite. On the other hand, the culture is doing well. Attracting tourism, and with a healthy farm produce industry, Breton culture is recognized and encouraged by the political élite up to and including the highest authorities of the French State. Breton cultural practices are growing in popularity and attracting more and more people. The decline in Catholicism is offset by a renewal of traditional practices; the decline of fishing and marine industries are counterbalanced by the success of festivals linked to these activities, and the same is true for agriculture. The weakened region of Brittany, right on the margins of Europe, has become one of the firmest supports of the French State. This is a middle-class region of small businesses which depend on State employment to a large extent. These middle classes have supported the election of left-wing authorities in the towns, and have accelerated the relaxation of traditional morals: Brittany currently has one of the highest birth rates outside marriage in France. Will the culture (and the farm produce) be enough to save Brittany, or is Breton regionalism no longer anything more than a brand image?

The situation in Corsica is difficult to describe in a few words other than to say 'plus ça change plus c'est pareil'. A society dominated by clans and by a clientelism organized by large families, by economic failure, widespread fraud, a workforce lacking in qualifications, endemic violence (400 terrorist attacks alone in 1995), poverty, a black-market economy, dependence on social security and public employment – all this paints a grim picture. In the medium term, the multiple strategies of the French government have done little more than exacerbate the situation. The vicious circle in which Corsican society is trapped seems to offer no means of escape other than continental exile for those who want and can afford it.

The Nord-Pas-de-Calais is in the process of promoting itself as a Euro-region. Beneath the industrial crisis, this region is attempting to set itself up as a European cross-roads, a role based on European transport schemes and which takes advantage of the presence of developed and well-structured interests (Christian Democrat employers, trade unions, political parties, a strong network of associations) and a rapidly diversifying economy. This growth, apparent in workforce training policies for example, aims to start a new chapter in the history of the Industrial Revolution. This has not yet been achieved, but when it is, it will be at the expense of most of the northern working classes. Their concerns have been made clear by an anti-European pro-Front National vote.

Provence-Côte d'Azur is a microcosm of the component parts of French society. A Mediterranean region, with a high proportion of Italians, it has also received a large intake of French people repatriated from North Africa in the 1960s, as well as many immigrants from these countries. The wealth and prosperity of Nice and of the large 'silicon valley' city of Sophia-Antipolis exist side by side with the industrial crisis in Marseilles and its suburbs. This recession, and a notable population increase, have re-opened the debate about

Provençal identity (dormant in the Provence-Côte d'Azur region); a debate championed by the Front National which has enjoyed its greatest success in this region, even gaining control of four municipalities: Vitrolles, Orange, Marignane and Toulon. This Mediterranean region is closing in on itself, accentuating the contradictions present in French society.

Finally, Aquitaine is a region deeply divided between Bordeaux and the rest, taking into account the weight of strong local societies (notably in the Basque country). Strong infra-regional tensions go hand in hand with a powerful homogenization in lifestyle. The region is deeply divided, and its agriculture has suffered from the integration of Spain and Portugal. Governed by people of note, Aquitaine is searching for an identity; an identity which is currently expressed through protest. The more conservative peasant organizations (*Coordination Paysanne*), together with the political movement '*Chasse, pêche et traditions*'[5] have enjoyed remarkable success in their defence of traditional structures against urban groups (especially the ecologists), and against a Europe which wants to impose regulations, for example on hunting and fishing.

Conclusion

In contemporary France, as elsewhere in Europe, culture has become once again the subject of lively debate. As in the other European nation states, the idea of a national culture – imposed by the élite and the institutions which helped to diffuse it (schools, the army, to a certain extent religion) – has been called into question. Some scholars are predicting the end of national society (notably the important group of sociologists who take their lead from Touraine, Dubet, Wieviorka and Lapeyronnie); these people are inviting the French to take greater note of minorities and individual communities. Others, on the other hand, are calling for the reinforcement of the Republican model of integration (for example, Dominique Schnapper). This issue lies at the centre of French social and political debate.

The question of identity and culture goes to the heart of French society, especially in the regions. The regional question in France is linked to that of the State and its component parts. The growing pressure of economic theories and the withdrawal/recomposition of the State has given rise to all kinds of reactions/movements on local and regional levels, signs of the vitality of local and regional society.

This vitality is accompanied by a rise in economic inequalities and, probably, new forms of social and geographical segregation within the frame of the European Union; tendencies which pose profound problems for French society and regions used either to giving in to or to opposing the State.

Notes

1 France is divided into ninety-five administrative areas known as *départements*.
2 For the following points see Veltz 1996, especially the first section on France.
3 Centres of higher education often focusing on professional training (for engineers, lawyers, etc.). There is fierce competition to enter these establishments.
4 A period of relatively sustained economic growth from 1945–1975.
5 'Hunting, Fishing and Tradition'.

Bibliography

Bagnasco, A. and Le Galès, P. (eds) (1997) *Villes en Europe*, Paris: La Découverte.

Benoit-Guilbot, O. and A. (1986) *L'Esprit des lieux*, Paris: CNRS.

Balme, R. (ed.) (1996) *Les Politiques du néo régionalisme*, Paris: Economica.

——— (1997) ' La région française comme espace d'action publique', in A. Bagnasco, P. Le Galès (eds) *Les Paradoxes des régions en Europe*, Paris: La Découverte.

Braudel, F. (1990, new edition) *L'Identité de la France*, Paris: Flammarion.

CURAPP (1993) *Les Politiques régionales*, Paris: PUF.

Ganne, B. (1994) 'Les PME dans le système français, heurts et malheurs d'un mode de gouvernance', in A. Bagnasco and C. Sabel (eds) *PME et développement économique en Europe*, Paris: La Découverte.

Garden, M., Guillaume, P. and Lacave, M. (1986) 'Introduction historique', in *L'Esprit des Lieux*.

Grémion, P. (1976) *Le Pouvoir périphérique*, Paris: Le Seuil.

Faure, A. (1994) 'Vers une république régionale?', in *Pouvoirs Locaux*, 26: 21–4.

INSEE (1997) *La France des régions*, Paris: La Documentation française.

John, P. and Le Galès, P. (1997) 'Is grass greener on the other side? What went wrong with French regions', in *Policy and Politics*, 25 (1): 51–60.

Le Bras, H. (1986) *Les trois France*, Paris: Le Seuil.

Mazey, D. and Loughlin, J. (eds) (1994) *The End of the Unitary State? Ten Years of Decentralisation*, London: Frank Cass.

Mendras, H. (1994) *La Seconde Révolution française, 1965–1985*, Paris: Gallimard.

Mény, Y. (1974) *Centralisation et décentralisation dans le débat politique français (1945–1969)*, Paris: LGJD.

Schmidt, V. (1990) *Decentralising France*, Cambridge: Cambridge University Press.

Sociologie du Travail (1982) 'Le Retour du local' (special issue).

Savy, M. and Veltz, P. (1994) (eds) *Les Nouveaux Espaces de l'entreprise*, La Tour d'Aigues: Editions de l'Aube, 1993.

Veltz, P. (1996) *Mondialisation, villes et territoires*, Paris: PUF.

Part II

Areas of enquiry

Chapter 6

Paid and unpaid work

Linda Hantrais

In France, as in other advanced western societies, the nature of work, the size and composition of the workforce and the character-istics of the workplace have undergone far-reaching changes during the second half of the twentieth century. Early in the period, the agriculture and manufacturing industries were overtaken by the service sector as the main employer of labour. The length of time spent in paid work over the life span has been substantially reduced for men, while women have increasingly entered and remained in employment outside the home. Technological advances have trans-formed the workplace, while working conditions have become more highly regulated. This chapter examines developing forms and patterns of work in French society and looks at their impact on everyday life both at the workplace and in the home; it then goes on to examine some of the policy responses implemented by governments in their attempts to manage the social problems generated by structural and technological change.

The changing nature of work and the workforce

In comparison with its north European neighbours – particularly Germany and the United Kingdom – the shift from a rural and industrial society to a service economy occurred much later in France. The proportion of the French population employed in agri-culture was still almost a third in the 1930s, as shown in Table 6.1, and the service sector did not provide employment for more than half the population until the 1970s. By the mid-1990s, the propor-tion of the working population employed in agriculture in France had fallen to below 5 per cent. As illustrated by Table 6.2, the level for agriculture in France remained above that in Germany and in the United Kingdom, which recorded the lowest percentage in the European Union. Over the same period, the industrial sector maintained a one-third share of the workforce until the mid-1980s. By the mid-1990s, the proportion of the labour force working in industry in France had fallen to a level similar to that in the United Kingdom, while Germany recorded the highest percentage figure for the European Union. If European countries follow the pattern recorded in North America, the decline in the proportion of the population employed in industry might be expected to continue into the twenty-first century. The service sector has been the only net contributor to job creation over the post-war period, accounting for a larger proportion of the labour force in France than in Germany, but remaining below the level in the United Kingdom, which was in fourth place in 1995 after the Netherlands, Sweden and Luxembourg (Eurostat 1996a: Table 1).

As the distribution of the working population by economic sector has changed, the time spent in paid work has undergone a steady decline. Legislation has been implemented to reduce the length of the working day, week and year, and of working life: the

Table 6.1 Distribution of the working population in France by economic sector as a percentage of total working population (1936–95)

	1936	1974	1995
Agriculture	32.9	10.6	4.9
Industry	32.5	38.5	27.0
Services	34.6	50.9	68.1

Sources: Eurostat (1996a), Table 1; Marchand and Thélot (1991), Table 3t.

Table 6.2 Distribution of the working population in France, Germany and the UK by economic sector in percentages (1995)

	France	Germany	UK
Agriculture	4.9	3.2	2.1
Industry	27.0	36.0	27.4
Services	68.1	60.8	70.5

Sources: Eurostat (1996a), Table 1; Eurostat (1996b), Table 041.

forty-hour working week and two weeks paid annual holidays were instituted in France in 1936, and the thirty-nine hour working week was introduced in 1982 by the left-wing government, with the promise, which did not materialize, of a further reduction to thirty-five hours by 1985 (Barou and Rigaudiat 1983). The effect has been to reduce the length of the working day, a trend accelerated by the shortening of the lunch break (Volkoff 1990). Paid annual leave was extended by law to four weeks in 1969 and, in 1982, employees were granted an additional week to be used at another time in the year, bringing total paid leave to thirty working days, of which a maximum of twenty-four could be taken at any one time.

Over the same period, the length of working life has been reduced by later labour market entry and earlier labour market exit. The beginning of working life has been delayed due to longer schooling and compulsory further education and training (see Chapter 9). In 1985, the left-wing Minister for Education, Jean-Pierre Chevènement, set the target of enabling 80 per cent of a generation to reach the level of the *baccalauréat* by the year 2000. By 1995, 63 per cent of the relevant generation had achieved the target level, and half of these were entering universities (Canceill 1996). By the mid-1990s, as shown in Table 6.3, only 10 per cent of 15–19 year olds in France were economically active, the lowest rate in the European Union after Belgium (Eurostat 1996b: Table 003). Although the number of young people in the 15–25 age group in France and the United Kingdom is similar, their activity patterns are very different. In 1995, after Denmark, France recorded the highest rate for the proportion of non-economically active under 25 year olds in education, while the United Kingdom displayed the lowest level in the European Union (Eurostat

Table 6.3 Economic activity rates by age groups and proportion of non-active young people aged under 25 in education in France, Germany and the UK in percentages (1995)

	France	Germany	UK
15–19 years	10.2	31.5	47.5
55–9 years	52.5	60.0	64.7
60–4 years	10.8	19.3	37.2
Aged under 25 years and in education	93.6	89.7	78.3

Sources: Eurostat (1996a), Table 4; Eurostat (1996b), Table 003.

1996a: Table 4). In addition, as a result of the attention given to continuing education, by the early 1990s almost a third of adult wage earners and over half of all job seekers were recorded as undergoing some form of training or re-training (Sauvageot 1993).

The average length of working life has also been reduced as the legal requirement for older workers to leave employment at a specified age has been implemented. Since April 1983, both men and women can legally retire in France at the age of 60. In a number of occupations a lower retirement age applies, for example for miners, lorry drivers or primary school teachers. The trend towards a shorter working life has been further exacerbated by schemes encouraging workers to take early retirement. By the mid-1990s, France was thus the European Union member state with the smallest proportion of men aged 60–4 still in the labour force (Eurostat 1996b: Table 003).

These changes in the working life cycle have contributed to the slowing down of growth in the workforce. From the mid-1960s, the working population was increasing by an average of 200,000 workers a year, as the generations of post-war baby boomers entered the labour market but, since the end of the 1970s, growth has been due almost solely to the influx of women. Overall, by comparison with the United Kingdom, France records smaller proportions of its population, both men and women, as economically active (Eurostat 1996b: Table 3). By the year 2006, the size of the French workforce is expected to attain a steady state when the baby boomers begin reaching retirement age (Brondel *et al.* 1996).

As more women have entered paid employment outside the home and, from the 1970s, developed more continuous full-time working patterns, the composition of the workforce has been transformed. As shown in Table 6.4, by the mid-1990s, about half of women of working age were economically active. The gap between male and female economic activity rates had narrowed to fifteen points in France, compared to nineteen points in the United Kingdom and twenty-one points in Germany. Women constituted over 45 per cent of the total population in employment in France, a higher figure than in Germany or the United Kingdom. In addition, a larger proportion of French women were engaged in full-time work. In the mid-1990s, women across the European Union were less likely to leave the labour force to raise children than in the 1960s. In France, activity rates peaked for the 25–9 age group, fell slightly between 30–4 years, before rising again after the age of 40, whereas in Germany and the United Kingdom they peaked only for the later age group (Eurostat 1996b: Table 003).

The expansion of the services and of public sector employment and the introduction of new technologies have been propitious for women. As illustrated by Table 6.5, in all three countries, by the mid-1990s, women were more likely than men to be working in the service sector. Women have tended to be concentrated in certain areas of employment. They are, for example, over-represented in clerical jobs, in retailing outlets and in caring and supportive roles in the health sector, education and social services, where levels of pay are often poor. Despite lower pay, compared to the private sector, public sector employment in France has proved attractive to women because it offers working conditions and arrangements that are more conducive to combining paid work with family life.

Table 6.4 Female economic activity in France, Germany and the UK in percentages (1995)

	France	Germany	UK
Of female working population	48.2	47.7	52.4
Of total labour force	45.5	42.9	43.8
Full-time as % of female employment	71.1	66.2	55.7
25–9 years	79.7	73.7	73.3
30–4 years	78.5	72.4	70.1
35–9 years	78.1	74.2	74.4
40–4 years	80.0	77.2	77.9

Sources: Eurostat (1996a), Tables 1 and 3; Eurostat (1996b), Table 003.

Table 6.5 Male and female economic activity rates by sector in France, Germany and the UK in percentages (1995)

	France		Germany		UK	
	Men	Women	Men	Women	Men	Women
Agriculture	5.8	3.7	3.3	3.0	2.7	1.2
Industry	36.4	15.1	47.5	20.2	38.3	14.0
Services	57.8	81.1	49.2	76.7	59.0	84.8

Sources: Eurostat (1996a), Tables 2, 3; Eurostat (1996b), Table 041.

As the time spent in the workforce has been concentrated into a shorter period of the life span, and as the economy has become locked into recession, the trend has been towards greater flexibility of working arrangements. A variety of schemes has been introduced to stimulate job creation by giving employers the capacity to adapt their workforce in response to fluctuations in the demand for products and services (Bisault *et al.* 1996). Thus, temporary and fixed-term contracts have replaced more permanent forms of employment, and opportunities have been extended for instituting part-time working schedules.

Since the early 1980s, part-time working arrangements have been actively encouraged by French governments, with the result that part-time rates for women almost doubled between 1980 and 1995. Between 1983–92, the growth in female part-time employment accounted for three-quarters of all new jobs (Rubery *et al.* 1996: Figure 3). However, the level recorded in France in 1995, shown in Table 6.6, remained below that found in most of the other northern European Union member states: the Netherlands reached a particularly high rate with 67.2 per cent, followed by the United Kingdom with 44.4 per cent and Sweden with 41.2 per cent (Eurostat 1996a: Table 3). Labour force surveys suggest, however, that a larger proportion of women working part-time in France than in other EU member states, with the exception of Finland, are doing so because they cannot find full-time work (Eurostat 1996b: Table 059). A form of part-time work that is more popular with women was instituted in the public sector in 1982: working time can be reduced, for example, by 20 per cent, to give mothers the opportunity to be available on Wednesdays to look after young children when they are not at school (Belloc 1987).

The growth in part-time work in France is explained, to a large extent, by the recruitment of younger and older workers to this form of employment. Employers have been offered financial incentives, such as the entitlement to reductions in social insurance contributions, to encourage them to recruit younger workers on a part-time basis. For older workers, part-time arrangements may constitute a form of semi-retirement. Most part-time work is in lower paid and lower status jobs and in the public sector. Where opportunities exist for promoted part-time positions, they are found almost solely in the feminized public sector occupations (Bisault *et al.* 1996).

Since the early 1970s and the end of the *Trente Glorieuses*, which will be remembered as a period of unprecedented and sustained

Table 6.6 Male and female working patterns in France, Germany and the UK in percentages (1995)

	France		Germany		UK	
	Men	Women	Men	Women	Men	Women
Part-time	5.1	28.9	3.6	33.8	7.8	44.3
Involuntary part-time	53.4	36.3	12.9	9.4	26.4	10.6
Unemployment	10.07	14.1	7.1	9.6	10.1	6.9
Unemployed aged under 25 years	23.7	30.7	8.7	8.2	17.9	12.5

Sources: Eurostat (1996a), Tables 2 and 3; Eurostat (1996b), Tables 002 and 059.

economic growth, patterns of working life have become less stable and predictable. Increasing numbers of workers have experienced unemployment and under-employment as the economy became locked into a prolonged recession in the wake of the oil crises. By 1995, as illustrated in Table 6.6, unemployment had reached the 3 million mark, representing nearly 12 per cent of the workforce, a level above the European average, and which compared unfavourably with Germany (8.2 per cent) and the United Kingdom (8.7 per cent) (Eurostat 1996a: Table 1).

Despite the fact that increasing numbers of young people are achieving higher levels of qualifications, and notwithstanding the massive expansion of higher education, intensive efforts on the vocational training front, and the proliferation of new forms of qualification, young people have been particularly affected by unemployment. In the mid-1990s, the unemployment rate for 15–24 year olds was more than twice the level for the working population as a whole, representing the highest figure for the countries in the geographical centre of the European Union (Eurostat 1996a: Table 4). The relative advantage for young men, compared with young women, shown in Table 6.6, was expected to decrease with the phasing out of compulsory military service and the creation of voluntary service for both young women and men, as proposed by President Jacques Chirac in December 1996.

The picture which emerges from this overview of the characteristics of work and the labour force in France by the middle of the last decade of the twentieth century is one of growing uncertainty: relatively few young people will leave the educational system for good at the end of the compulsory period of secondary schooling; fewer still will enter employment directly; an even smaller number will enjoy the security of a full-time job until retirement; and economic activity will be concentrated over a shorter part of the life span. More women will spend a longer period of their lives in paid employment outside the home, most probably in service sector jobs, coinciding with the time when they are also raising young children. They too will experience insecurity, often combined with low pay in a segregated and segmented labour market.

The implications of changes in the nature of work

The trends recorded in the changing nature and patterning of work have had far-reaching effects on the place of paid work within society and on attitudes towards work as a central social value and source of identity. The impact of these changes has been extensively analysed by philosophers, economists and sociologists in France. From the 1970s, the growing interest in more flexible approaches to work in the context of economic recession, technological innovation, the advent of new information systems and the globalization of economies resulted in a number of seminal publications announcing the end of work as it had been known during the *Trente Glorieuses*. They included radical proposals such as the reduction of work time to only two hours a day (ADRET 1977), the idea that everybody should work part-time (Aznar 1980), or the carefully argued social project by the group *Échange et Projets* (1980), designed to enable individuals to gain control over their own use of time as a fundamental citizenship right. With the approach of the new millennium, the longer term impact of new technologies on productive labour has been reassessed, and the debate has intensified over the fragmentation of work, the instrumental role it plays as the main force structuring people's lives and the links between long-term unemployment and social exclusion (Gorz 1988, Castel 1995, Morin 1995, Friot and Rose 1996).

The organization and use of time have been recognized as critical factors in understanding the place of employment in people's lives. Paid work has become increasingly polarized and socially divisive, with an expanding proportion of the workforce employed on short-term contracts, or in casual or part-time work (M da 1996). At one extreme is the highly paid private sector manager, expected to work extremely long hours, in return for which swift career progression is assured, or the well-qualified senior civil servant with the guarantee of a job for life. Both enjoy job satisfaction and can, in principle, look forward to receiving a generous pension. At the other end of the spectrum are the poorly qualified, unemployed or never employed, young people dependent on family or state support and with little prospect of finding a stable job. They are joined by the older beneficiaries of the minimum income, and by workers who have been made redundant and are not entitled to receive full pension rights. Between the two extremes are those currently in work, with a dwindling core possessing the advantage of a permanent contract, a stable number of working hours and access to full social insurance rights, while a growing pool of self-employed workers are subcontracted to firms to carry out specific time-limited tasks.

For an ever larger proportion of the labour force, job security and social security, in the broadest sense, have become illusory, as employers and the State are increasingly entrenched in an era of restructuring and cost containment. Since the cost of labour is frequently the largest component in the budgets of firms, particularly in the service sector, restructuring more often than not means slimming down the workforce and reducing the number of employees on long-term contracts, thereby swelling the ranks of the unemployed or under-employed. The workplace has, consequently, become increasingly stressful, not only due to the greater insecurity of employment but also because the changes in the nature of the employment contract have been accompanied by a growing emphasis on performance indicators, quality control and competitiveness, which has placed greater demands on workers if they want to avoid redundancy and aspire to promoted positions. While technological and organizational innovations have combined to create the demand for a more flexible, multi-skilled, slimmer and autonomous labour force, tighter controls have been introduced to monitor quality, delivery and individual performance. Despite attempts to regulate the new post-Fordist forms of work organization, the cumulative effect for workers is that the working environment has become more constraining (Coutrot 1996).

The dwindling size of the permanent or core workforce also has important implications for the funding of social security in France, since the system is heavily dependent on employer and employee contributions, as a consequence of the insurance principle on which it is based. In international terms, the French system is characterized by the relatively large proportion of funding derived from employment-related contributions, rather than from taxation as in the United Kingdom (Hantrais 1995). The result is that the social cost of labour is proportionately higher, causing employers to be reluctant to create full-time permanent jobs and explaining why incentives in the form of exemption from social security contributions are being offered to employers who take on unemployed people.

Another of the outcomes of the reduction in the time spent in paid work is an important shift in the dependency ratio, which measures the number of workers in employment in relation to the dependent population. By the early 1990s, the proportion of the population aged over 60 was still relatively small in France (19.7 per cent), compared with most other northern EU member states (Eurostat 1993: Table 2). The disparity for France can be attributed to the combined effect of the low birth rates prior to and during the First World War, the number of deaths in the two World Wars, and then the baby boom which lasted well into the mid-1960s. The imbalance between the population aged 60 and over and that aged 20–59 was such that, by the mid-1990s, every individual of working age was supporting one retired person. It is anticipated that by the year 2020, the ratio will be one to two, a higher proportion than in the United Kingdom but a lower level than in Germany (Joshi 1996). Since pension schemes were originally organized in accordance with the occupational pay-as-you-go principle, rather than on a funding basis as in the United Kingdom, in agriculture and in industries which have seen a steep decline in the number of workers, the labour force has long been unable to cover the cost of pensions for the corresponding dependent population. Pensions have, thus, become a major issue in the debate over the future of social protection in France in a context where instability of employment poses a growing threat to occupational pension entitlements.

Since most of the jobs lost through restructuring have been in heavy industry, employing mainly men, and most of the jobs created have been in the services, often employing women, the effect has been that a larger number of men are experiencing longer periods without employment, while a growing number of women are spending more hours in paid work, often at a time in their lives when they are also likely to be engaged in childrearing. As indicated above, compared with their neighbours in Germany and the United Kingdom, French women are more likely to be in employment when they have young children or ageing parents in need of care. Economic activity rates are, in fact, higher in France for women aged 20–59 with one child than for women without children, whereas the reverse is the case in Germany and the United Kingdom. With two children, women in France also achieve a level of economic activity above that for women with no children. The rate then falls steeply for mothers of three children. With offspring under the age of 7, women in France sustain consistently higher levels of economic activity than in either Germany or the United Kingdom (Rubery and Fagan 1992).

The strong commitment of French women to full-time employment at a stage in their lives when they also have family responsibilities might have been expected to result in a more equitable distribution of unpaid work between men and women and greater access to more free time for both sexes. Time-budget surveys suggest that this has not been the case. On average women spend less time than men in paid employment, but they do not enjoy more free time than men. Even if they are in full-time employment, women continue to devote more hours than do men to domestic tasks, particularly the routine unpaid work associated with rearing children. According to a Eurobarometer study in the early 1990s, nearly 60 per cent of married French men admitted to never doing any domestic chores. Among those who did contribute, about half looked after the shopping or driving of children, and a quarter did cooking or housework (Kempeneers and Leli vre 1991: Tables 54 and 55). Although French women have been producing a smaller number of children, the division of labour is such that mothers of young children suffer from overload and time famine, even if they are in a financial position to subcontract tasks by employing domestic labour and childminders during after-school hours (Hantrais 1993). Their traditional role as carers has been placed in competition with paid work.

The reduction in the amount of time spent in paid work over the life span and its concentration at a stage in life which coincides with a peak in reproductive activity for women have occurred during a period when life expectancy has been extended, particularly among French women. France is the country in the European Union with the greatest female life expectancy: the average French woman can expect to live almost to the age of 82 years, compared with 80 years in Germany and 79 years in the United Kingdom (data for 1996 supplied by Eurostat). Because of their high life expectancy, French women are over-represented among the older generations: after the age of 75 years, they outnumber men by two to one. Whereas generous provision has been made by the state to accommodate the children of working mothers, less attention has been paid to arrangements for older people. Demographic predictions have given rise to the concern that, in the twenty-first century, the number of older people requiring care will present an intolerable burden on welfare resources. Since female life expectancy is much greater than that of men, a large proportion of these older people will be women who have not accumulated full pension rights due to the more fragmented nature of their employment. But a growing number of men will also be in the position of having experienced interrupted and curtailed employment careers, thereby reducing their pension rights and their ability to purchase good quality care.

Policy responses

Like other EU member states, France is faced with a number of social problems arising from changes in the nature of work, the size and composition of the workforce and the characteristics of the workplace. Attention is given in this section to the policy responses developed by French governments to deal with the problems of old age, unemployment and social exclusion and the need to reconcile paid work and family life.

By the early 1980s, old age was already the area of social security accounting for the largest share of social spending. Although the relative cost of health care was stabilizing, older people were big consumers of medical care, and the health budget was, therefore, expected to rise (Charraud et al. 1984). Pension insurance schemes have been progressively extended to the whole population, but they continue to offer different benefits from one occupational group to another, resulting in greater disparities in old age than during working life. In addition, complementary and supplementary pension schemes have been maintained, further emphasizing the inequities between different categories of pensioners, particularly since the value of these additional pensions has been increasing more rapidly than that of basic pensions. Because pensions have been financed essentially on a pay-as-you-go basis, the result has been that contributors in occupations where the number of workers has fallen steeply, for example in mining, agriculture or the railways, are supporting a larger number of beneficiaries. Transfers have, therefore, been required from the more balanced funds to offset deficits.

In an effort to find a solution to the growing problem of care for the elderly, in 1995, the French government decided to experiment with a new caring allowance (*prestation de dépendance*) for older people. It was to be funded from the *contribution sociale généralisée* (CSG), which has operated since 1990 as a tax levy of 2.4 per cent on all sources of income, supplemented since 1 February 1996 by an additional levy of 0.5 per cent (*contribution pour le remboursement de la dette sociale*), designed to help pay off the cumulative deficit incurred by the social security system. The allowance was intended for people aged over 60 on low incomes, and it was to be used to pay for care either at the person's home or in an institution, although the expectation was that the need for institutional care would be postponed as more older people would be able to remain longer in their own homes. Although the experiment was deemed to have been successful, the scheme was modified in 1997 in response to the need to contain costs and to ensure equity of treatment. Rather than being paid to the care-receiver, the allowance was to be handled by an association charged with looking after assistance for older people in their own homes.

The caring allowance can also be seen as one of the many measures implemented by Alain Juppé's Government in the mid-1990s to tackle the endemic problem of unemployment, in that it created several thousands of jobs. The same logic underpinned proposals for extending the *chèque service*, a voucher system first introduced in December 1994. The voucher was intended to simplify administrative procedures for individuals wanting to employ workers in their homes to carry out domestic and caring tasks, but not nursing care, initially for less than eight hours a week. The vouchers can be used to pay carers at a rate which does not fall below the minimum guaranteed wage. Employers purchase the vouchers from a bank or post office and use them to pay their employees who can, in turn, cash them at a bank or post office. In 1996, the scheme was extended to employment of more than eight hours a week. Firms offering financial support to employees wanting to resort to this type of service for childminding and elder care are exempted from social insurance payments on any contributions they make to the scheme, and employers are entitled to income tax deductions.

These measures, like schemes to encourage firms to take on young people by offering exemption from social insurance contributions, have developed as a supplement to the standard income-related unemployment benefit, which has progressively been concentrated on the population aged 25–50, in line with the reduction in the effective length of working life. Alternatives to social assistance have also been sought to meet the needs of the growing number of long-term unemployed and those not entitled to receive statutory benefits. In 1988, the Socialist Government introduced the *revenu minimum d'insertion* (RMI), a minimum income for unemployed people aged over 25 who agreed to undertake some form of training or work placement designed to help them re-enter the job market on a longer term basis. The scheme is funded primarily by central government, but with a contribution from the *d partements*. Evaluation of the RMI after it had been in operation for three years showed that nearly 2 million people, including dependants, had benefited from the scheme, but it had been taken up by a larger proportion of young single people than anticipated, and less than half the recipients were found to have succeeded in finding longer term jobs (Poubelle and Simonin 1993).

The RMI was not intended for people aged below 25, yet the group displaying the highest unemployment rates were young women under the age of 25, shown in Table 6.6. As women have confirmed their ability to achieve in the educational system, their expectations have been raised in the labour market. They have been the main beneficiaries of many of the new jobs created, but at the expense of job security, stability and status. For several decades, French governments have sought to introduce measures designed to help women combine paid work outside the home with family life. Within the European Union, France is among the member states which have been leaders in the State provision of childcare facilities, support for childminding, parental leave and other family-friendly policies (European Commission Network on Childcare 1996, Hantrais and Letablier 1996). These measures have not been without their critics, as demonstrated by the debate at the National Assembly and in the media in 1994 over proposals to extend paid parental leave (*allocation parentale d'éducation*, APE) to families from the second child, whereas previously it applied only to parents with three children. Feminist groups interpreted the proposal as an attempt by politicians to remove mothers from the labour market in the belief that this would create more jobs for unemployed men. Analysis of the take-up of the APE by women on the arrival of their second child showed that the immediate effect of the change in the eligibility criteria was to encourage an unexpectedly large number of women to leave the labour market, particularly if they were unemployed or in low-income family units, thereby reducing the unemployment count but increasing the amount paid out in benefits (Afsa 1996).

The much contested reforms of the French social security system in the mid-1990s were prompted by the on-going concern of French governments about the problems resulting from structural changes in the labour force and from population ageing (Hantrais 1996). They were exacerbated by the prolonged economic recession, which coincided with the growing pressure on France to be among the countries able to meet the criteria for European Monetary Union by the end of the decade. Issues which had moved up the policy agenda in the 1970s and 1980s, such as equality of opportunity and the reconciliation of paid and unpaid work, had lost their salience. Unemployment, the top priority of the 1980s, was far from being resolved and was being used to justify shifts in policy. Many of the measures introduced to relieve unemployment were, however, contributing to the development of less secure and less stable forms of employment. The flexible working patterns required by employers to encourage them to take on labour and to enable them to maximize productive capacity were creating the need for more individualized support services to cater for non-standard working schedules. The unpaid work of mothers as homemakers was being replaced by paid work supplied by non-family members, and larger numbers of the women who took a break in employment to look after their own children were being paid to do so. From being reproductive units supported by public provision of services, families were becoming privatized consumers of casualized services in a secondary labour market, indirectly supported by the State. The boundaries were thus being blurred between the public and private spheres, reflecting the changing nature of the relationship between paid and unpaid work.

References

Afsa, C. (1996) 'L'activité féminine à l'épreuve de l'allocation parentale d'éducation', *Recherches et prévisions*, 46: 1–8.

ADRET (1977) *Travailler deux heures par jour*, Paris: Seuil.

Aznar, G. (1980) *Tous à mi-temps ou le scénario bleu*, Paris: Seuil.

Barou, Y. and Rigaudiat, J. (1983) *Les 35 heures et l'emploi*, Paris: La Documentation française.

Belloc, B. (1987) 'Le travail à temps partiel', *Données sociales 1987*, Paris: INSEE, pp. 112–19.

Bisault, L., Bloch-London, C., Lagarde, S. and Le Corre, V. (1996) 'Le développement du travail à temps partiel', *Données sociales 1996. La société française*, Paris: INSEE, pp. 225–33.

Brondel, D., Guillemot, D. and Marioni, P. (1996) 'La population active: facteurs d'évolution et perspectives', *Données sociales 1996. La société française*, Paris: INSEE, pp. 110–16.

Canceill, G. (1996) 'La première année à l'université', *Données sociales 1996. La Société française*, Paris: INSEE, pp. 80–5.

Castel, R. (1995) *Les Métamorphoses de la question sociale*, Paris: Fayard.

Charraud, A., Devouassoux, J. and Morel, B. (1984) 'La consommation médicale: évolution et disparités', *Données sociales*, 5th edn., Paris: INSEE, pp. 359–87.

Coutrot, T. (1996) 'Les nouveaux modes d'organisation de la production: quels effets sur l'emploi, la formation, l'organisation du travail?', *Données sociales 1996. La société française*, Paris: INSEE, pp. 209–16.

Échange et Projets (1980) *La Révolution du temps choisi*, Paris: Albin Michel.

European Commission Network on Childcare and other Measures to Reconcile Employment and Family Responsibilities (1996) 'A review of services for young children in the European Union, 1990–1995', Brussels: European Commission Directorate General V, Equal Opportunities Unit.

Eurostat (1993) 'Older people in the European Community', *Rapid Reports, Population and Employment*, 1.

Eurostat (1996a) 'Labour Force Survey. Principal results 1995', *Statistics in Focus. Population and Social Conditions*, 3.

Eurostat (1996b) *Labour Force Survey. Results 1995*, Luxembourg: Office for Official Publications of the European Communities.

Friot, B. and Rose, J. (eds) (1996) *La Construction sociale de l'emploi en France: les années soixante à aujourd'hui*, Paris, L'Harmattan.

Gorz, A. (1988) *Métamorphoses du travail. Quête du sens: critique de la raison économique*, Paris: Galilée.

Hantrais, L. (1993) 'Women, work and welfare in France', in J. Lewis (ed.) *Women and Social Policies in Europe: Work, Family and the State*, Aldershot and Vermont: Edward Elgar, pp. 116–37.

—— (1995) *Social Policy in the European Union*, London and New York: Macmillan.

—— (1996) 'France: squaring the welfare triangle', in V. George and P. Taylor-Gooby (eds) *European Welfare Policy: Squaring the Welfare Circle*, London: Macmillan, pp. 51–71.

Hantrais, L. and Letablier, M-T. (1996) *Families and Family Policies in the European Union*, London and New York: Longman.

Joshi, H. (1996) 'Projections of European population decline: Serious demography or false alarm?', in D. Coleman (ed.) *Europe's Population in the 1990s*, Oxford: Oxford University Press, pp. 222–66.

Kempeneers, M. and Lelièvre, E. (1991) *Employment and Family within the Twelve*, Brussels: Commission of the European Communities, V/383/ 92-EN.

Marchand, O. and Thélot, C. (1991) *Deux siècles de travail en France: Population active et structure sociale, durée et productivité du travail*, Paris, INSEE.

Méda, D. (1996) 'Travail, emploi, activité: De quoi parle-t-on?', *Données sociales 1996. La Société française*, Paris: INSEE, pp. 104–9.

Morin, P. (1995) *La Grande Mutation du travail et de l'emploi: Emploi juste à temps et travail éclaté dans la société post-industrielle*, 2nd edn, Paris: Les Editions d'Organisation.

Poubelle, V. and Simonin, B. (1993) 'Le RMI: Un million d'allocataires en trois ans', *La Société française. Données sociales 1993*, Paris, INSEE, pp. 548–56.

Rubery, J. and Fagan, C. (1992) 'Bulletin on women and employment in the EC', no. 1, Brussels: Commission of the European Communities Directorate General V.

Rubery, J., Smith, M., Parker, J. and Turner, E. (1996) 'Bulletin on women and employment in the EC', no. 8, Brussels: Commission of the European Communities Directorate General V.

Sauvageot, C. (1993) 'L'éducation nationale forme aussi des adultes', *La Société française. Données sociales 1993*, Paris: INSEE, pp. 114–19.

Volkoff, S. (1990) 'Les conditions de travail: une évolution contrastée', *Données sociales*, Paris: INSEE, pp. 109–11.

Chapter 7

Trade unions

Susan Milner

It is tempting to dismiss trade unions as irrelevant to French society: fewer than 10 per cent of the workforce is organized in trade unions, and perhaps only 5 per cent of workers in the private sector. By comparison, British union membership stands at 21 per cent in the private sector, and 61 per cent in the public sector, and this after nearly two decades of anti-union legislation. Yet low union density itself reflects specific characteristics of French society, and the relationship between economy and politics, which are of interest to outside observers. The dramatic decline of union membership since the 1970s is thus symptomatic of wider social change. In this respect, trade unions can be seen as a weathervane, indicating the strength and direction of social trends.

There is no doubting the sheer scale of the problems facing trade unions in France in the 1990s. French trade unions have never organized more than a quarter of the workforce (apart from such exceptional moments as the Popular Front government in 1936 or the Liberation). But the current membership crisis is more than a cyclical trend. Overall, trade unions have lost roughly two-thirds of their membership since 1976, and half since 1981. Labbé (1997) notes that, within one generation, trade unions have virtually disappeared from the workplace. Despite increasing efforts by the major confederations (especially the Confédération Française Démocratique du Travail (CFDT))[1] to boost recruitment, there are few signs of renewal. Throughout the 1980s, membership dropped especially sharply among young people, white-collar workers, private sector workers, right-wing and Socialist Party voters, while it fell less markedly among public sector and manual workers, older employees and Communist Party voters: hardly, as Soubie (1992) notes, an encouraging sign for the future. It is particularly significant that younger generations of workers find little use for trade unions: between 1981 and 1991, the proportion of workers aged between 18 and 24 who were union members dropped from 9 per cent to 1 per cent (Aïdan 1991: 287). Even the groundswell of public sympathy for trade unions following the mass strike movement of November–December 1995 did not translate into membership gains. Rather, it exacerbated splits within the labour movement and revealed the ideological and strategic disarray of the confederations as they struggled to move forward (Mouriaux 1997). In December 1996, 51 per cent of French people surveyed thought the strikes had negative consequences for the unions (Olivennes 1997: 158).

There are some signs of change, but they are few and far between. There appear to be two, quite different, types of grass-roots renewal. The first corresponds to the traditional, conflictual model (*syndicalisme de lutte*) based on antagonistic industrial relations, most often within profitable multinational companies where jobs are threatened by 'downsizing' or moves towards flexible working practices. Here, defensive unionism coupled with strong company identification may recreate some of the elements of the workplace unionism characterized by Labbé (1995) as constituting 'le syndicalisme à la française', but divisions between the 'core' and 'peripheral' workforce and acute job insecurity make this model much less stable than the earlier one, based in the huge car plants of the 1960s.

The second type follows a more utilitarian logic and constitutes a radically new approach for French trade unions. Thus, for example, the success of two CFDT federations in achieving an annual membership growth rate of 7–9 per cent was due to a move away from CFDT values and towards the provision of services, as well as to determined marketing. Activists put the 'real CFDT element' among the new recruits at between 'virtually none' and 10 per cent. According to one observer (admittedly with a pro-management bias), 'The trade union is led into behaving like a business' (*Les Echos*, 5 June 1997). The development of a service-based strategy has long been advocated by academic experts in France, and it has proved its worth in Britain, but it requires a huge leap into the dark for many French trade unionists. If British trade unions have succeeded in stemming decline by providing financial and practical services to members, why have so few French unions been able to develop similar strategies?

The answer lies in the peculiar historical development of the labour movement. However, it will also be argued here that the social values and attitudes underpinning union organization are themselves often contradictory and are reflected in union responses to change. This chapter examines the characteristics of French trade unions and their response to a changing economic, social and political environment.

Unions and employee representation in the workplace

The French system of employee representation is more formalized than the British, but developed in a piecemeal way throughout the twentieth century. Many of its current difficulties result from the lack of a coherent logic or framework (in contrast to, say, the German model). In particular, the link between unions' representative role and statutory workplace bodies is ill-defined and problematic (Le Maître and Tchobanian 1992). The 1981 Auroux laws which aimed to strengthen employee representation made the problem worse in some ways, by increasing the burden on already overstretched activists and by giving employers new opportunities to bypass unions (Bevort and Labbé 1992, Kesselman 1996).

The cornerstone of the employee representation system is the workplace committee (*comité d'entreprise* or *comité d'établissement*, set up in 1945), although the statutory requirement applies only to companies with fifty or more employees, 25,000 workplace committees exist today, with over 100,000 delegates. The compliance rate is relatively high, particularly as a result of pressures and new attributions under the Auroux laws: in 1987, workplace committees existed in nearly three-quarters of companies obliged to set them up. However, this is not so surprising given that larger employers are more likely to comply with social legislation and to tolerate a trade union presence. The functions of the workplace committee are twofold: to act as a forum for dialogue between management and employees, and to organize social and cultural activities for the workforce. In some companies, the committee does little more than organize the Christmas party, but in general the committee's economic role has become more important, thanks to successive laws which gave it rights of information and consultation on company strategy and work organization. Workplace committees must also be consulted before redundancy or redeployment plans are carried out.

Committee members are directly elected by employees every two years, and these elections provide an additional source of information about the strength of support for trade unions. Unions which are legally recognized (at national, sectoral or plant level) determine the field of candidates in the first round of the elections, and any remaining seats are filled in a second, open round. In addition, each union which is recognized within the workplace can designate a non-voting representative on the council.

The striking change in workplace committee elections has been the rise in the proportion of non-union delegates elected. Whereas in 1967–68 14.2 per cent of members were elected at the second round, in 1979–80 the figure was 18.9 per cent and in 1989–90 26.5 per cent (Coffineau 1993). Table 7.1 shows the results of workplace committee elections in 1966–7, 1970–1, 1990–1, and 1992–3. The participation rate fell by only 5.5 points during this period, suggesting a high degree of employee interest in the institution itself. However, the figures indicate a marked drop in the support given to trade union candidates, particularly the Confédéation Générale du Travail (CGT), whose share of the vote halved as the proportion of non-union candidates doubled. Non-union candidates now occupy nearly half of seats on workplace committees (47.8 per cent in 1992–3). In nearly half of the companies with workplace committees, there is no trade union presence at all.

These trends – employee support for representative bodies in the workplace coupled with disaffection with union candidates – are echoed in surveys carried out for the two major confederations, in which employees place a high value on 'dialogue' and criticize the

Table 7.1 Elections to workplace committees (percentage of votes cast)

	1966–7	1970–1	1990–1	1992–3
Participation	71.9	72.1	64.4	66.4
CGT	48.4	44.4	22.7	22.5
CFDT	18.6	19.1	20.2	20.7
CFTC	2.3	2.4	4.0	4.6
FO	7.9	7.4	12.2	11.9
CGC	4.1	5.2	6.5	5.7
Other unions	3.6	7.8	5.6	6.6
Non-union	14.6	13.8	28.7	28.1

Source: Figures supplied by the Ministry of Labour and Social Affairs.

unions for emphasizing conflict at the expense of negotiated solutions (Cayrol 1996). As a result, whilst some large companies remain union strongholds, many are finding ways of involving employees in discussions while leaving unions behind.

Workplace committees concern only medium- and large-sized companies. Personnel delegates (*délégués du personnel*, created in 1936), on the other hand, ensure a wider representation since the law applies to all companies with at least eleven employees. There are some 300,000 personnel delegates today. The delegate's role is essentially representative: he or she carries individual or collective requests, complaints or suggestions to the management, who must listen but need not act. In addition, in companies employing over fifty people but with no workplace committee, the personnel delegate carries out the committee's function. Since 1993, companies with between 50 and 199 employees can amalgamate the personnel delegate and the workplace committee, and in 1994, 60 per cent of companies had such a structure. The rapid prevalence of the new, single delegation structure, particularly among companies at the lower end of the scale, confirms the need already voiced by employers' organizations and identified by researchers for the system to be simplified. In practice, most of the tasks were carried out by the same individuals anyway. Significantly, over half the elected representatives in the 'single delegation' structure in 1994 were non-union.

Compliance with the legal requirement to allow the election of personnel delegates has long been a problem, which the Auroux laws alleviated to some extent. In 1985, 47.6 per cent of workplaces subject to the statutory requirement (covering 73.9 per cent of employees) had personnel delegates; by 1988 the figure had risen to a more respectable 69.7 per cent (Coffineau 1993). However, the compliance rate is much lower in small companies (well under half of those with between eleven and forty-nine employees), where there is also no provision for workplace committees. This means that the majority of companies with fewer than fifty employees have no formal representative body, although some may have 'expression groups' (instituted in 1982 under one of the Auroux laws).

Even in larger companies where personnel delegates exist, the institution is said to be 'in difficulty' (Le Maître and Tchobanian 1993). The personnel delegate function has been closely associated with trade union activism, and herein lies much of the problem. As the number of union activists dwindles, the pressure on those who remain (and who are probably also carrying out the job of personnel delegate, workplace committee member and possibly also health and safety committee member) increases. Many personnel delegates already 'double up' in the sense that they hold several mandates (for example, a company with eighty employees, which statutorily should have three delegates, may in fact have only one person carrying out this task). Furthermore, the personnel delegate's functions overlap with those of the workplace committee and trade union delegates, where these are present. In larger, highly unionized workplaces, the personnel delegate may therefore be superfluous. In small non-unionized plants, it is likely that there will be no delegate at all. In medium-sized companies, there will probably be some kind of representative body but it will be non-union.

The law gives employee representatives protection from dismissal, freedom to move around the workplace to consult colleagues and time off for recognized activities. Recognized trade union delegates also benefit from these legal rights and are paid their normal salary during the hours legally allocated to their union work. In large workplaces, employers must also give the unions office space and allow them to distribute material and hold meetings. There are over 41,000 trade union delegates today: 28.8 per cent of these belong to the CGT, 24.6 per cent to the CFDT, 18.5 per cent to Force Ouvrière (FO), 13.6 per cent to the Confédération Générale des Cadres (CGC), 7.5 per cent to the Confédération Française des Travailleurs Chrétiens (CFTC) and 7 per cent to other organizations. (For a full explanation of these unions, see Appendix, p. 145.) This core of activists is responsible for individual casework, collective demands to management and the organization of campaigns, and for workplace bargaining. As we shall see, collective bargaining has seen a shift towards the company level, adding to the delegates' workload.

It is generally recognized that union strength is a major determinant of the existence and functioning of workplace representation structures. In France, the weakness of trade unions in the workplace has allowed employers to flout or pay lip service to legal provisions. By strengthening legislation and requiring employers to account for their practices, and by boosting collective bargaining, the Auroux laws gave an important fillip to employee representation in the workplace. But the trade unions have been too weak to take advantage of this change, and as a result many of the bodies which were set up fell outside their influence. This was even more true of the new law requiring companies to set up expression groups. Unlike legislation on workplace committees and personnel delegates, which stipulate the mode of election and give priority to recognized unions in fielding candidates, the Auroux law on expression groups allows companies to find their own mode of organization. As a result, trade unions were often at a loss to respond, and in many cases employers quickly took advantage to impose management hierarchies on the new groups.

Unions and the state

The unions' failure to take advantage of the new opportunities offered by the Auroux laws raises fundamental questions about their attitude towards legislation and more generally the State's role in industrial relations in France. Originally created when the state showed little interest for social affairs, the labour movement stressed its autonomy. However, it increasingly looked to the State to force hostile employers to concede demands. It is significant that the State has intervened at several junctures in the twentieth century to boost negotiation between employers and unions, in a way which would be unthinkable in Germany or Britain, with their traditions of free collective bargaining. The idea of *acquis sociaux* (hard-won rights) wrested from the State, or from employers via the State, is central to union thinking, and this is backed up by opinion polls which show that the French public associates the unions' historical role with gains such as pensions and health cover. In this respect unions form part of the 'republican pact' at the heart of French political culture.

The French Constitution guarantees that 'Every man [sic] may protect his rights and interests by trade union action, and belong to the union of his choice', as well as granting the right to employment and to strike. As mentioned earlier, the State grants recognition to union organizations according to criteria defined in the Labour Code (size of membership, independence from political parties, experience and length of existence). Some are recognized only within companies, others within sectors, others nationally; the 'big four', plus CGC and Fédération de l'Education Nationale (FEN) are recognized as having authority beyond their membership. Along with these guarantees come access to state bodies, particularly in the running of the social security system, and a complex system of material benefits such as training subsidies and payment of official delegates. According to some observers (Adam 1983, Rosanvallon 1988, Labbé 1997), the union movement has been cocooned by the state and it is little wonder that it pays more attention to state-sponsored activities than the harsh world of the shop floor. Labbé is particularly scathing: whereas in the 1960s the typical union activist worked alongside his/her colleagues and the union depended on membership dues, he argues, today's unionists are full-time bureaucrats who no longer 'need' members. A vicious circle occurs as the divide between grass-roots and union leadership widens. Certainly, the negative public image of French unions is closely linked with judgements of this type (Cayrol 1996). In other words, to use Streeck's terminology, the logic of 'influence' has prevailed over the logic of 'membership' (Streeck 1992).

This criticism is aimed particularly at the unions' role in the public sector. Thus, Labbé (1997) notes, the State-run electricity company provides 3,000 full-time union posts, and similar subsidies are given in other state companies.

There is also some truth in the argument that the legalistic nature of the French industrial relations system lessens the incentive for employees to join unions, since improvements in working conditions come about by State intervention rather than by bargaining between employers and unions. The 'free rider' problem is thus particularly acute, and helps to explain France's traditionally low union density. The predominance of the State may also encourage the union movement to choose conflict over workplace bargaining, since it could be more cost effective to organize a national strike (covered by the media) than to involve local-level representatives in long-term discussions with employers.

What is of particular interest here is that this model is today under threat, not only because it traps unions in patterns of behaviour which are increasingly rejected by employees and the wider French public, but because the State's own role is evolving. Financial pressures and changing political values mean that the State has withdrawn from some earlier responsibilities. Most obviously, the size of the public sector has shrunk through privatization: in 1991 public sector employment represented 9.1 per cent of the total active population, but by 1994 had been reduced to 6.7 per cent. Public sector jobs were frozen. Within the public sector, a new discourse of managerialism appeared in the 1980s. The various perks associated with civil servants, and the time-honoured tradition of promotion by seniority, came under threat as the government sought to impose new, more flexible classifications. However, the strike movement of Autumn 1995 may have indicated the limits of such policies, and significantly the Socialist Party's successful electoral campaign in 1997 included promises to halt privatization programmes and to increase public sector employment. Right-wing politicians made serious errors of judgement in thinking that public sector workers could be made easy targets of spending cuts, due to their image as *nantis* (privileged): opinion polls show a majority of French people have a positive image of public services, and a clear majority felt that the strikers' demands in 1995 were justified (Olivennes 1997). How long the government can steer between these values (the French 'model' of public service) and the demands of the global economy, or more prosaically the Maastricht convergence criteria, is an open question, however.

Similar dilemmas appear in the state's approach to labour legislation. In the 1980s, labour market flexibility was promoted in a number of ways. Active labour market policies aimed particularly at alleviating the problem of youth unemployment introduced a dual labour market with various employer exemptions and subsidies. Numerical flexibility was facilitated by laws allowing fixed-term contracts and temporary work, although within strictly defined limits. Temporal flexibility was encouraged in a series of laws on working time, although the issue is still contentious and employers are pushing for greater freedom to annualize hours and use overtime, as in the United Kingdom. Furthermore, the thrust of laws on working time was to place responsibility for their practical implementation in the hands of the 'social partners', particularly through the encouragement of workplace (as opposed to sectoral) bargaining. However, although workplace bargaining (notably on working time) has increased significantly (see 'Collective bargaining', p. 141), the State has not felt able to withdraw completely: instead, it has sought to frame bargaining within a series of laws and, as in the 'national summits' of December 1995 and October 1997, to bring employers and unions physically together.

Some commentators attribute the 'malaise' of French social relations to this uneasy mixture of state intervention and a move towards contractualization which internalizes the constraints caused by the unequal power relationship between employer and employee (Supiot 1996). Certainly the continuing state presence makes it difficult for unions to break completely with comfortable old ways and gives them little preparation for a new role as bargaining partner with employers.

Collective bargaining and the regulation of conflict

Collective bargaining in France has traditionally been weak in comparison with other northern European countries. It has undergone many changes since the 1970s, although contrary to some expectations it has not disappeared. Indeed, the number of workers not covered by collective agreements dropped from 3 million to 1 million between 1981 and 1991. With 86 per cent of its workforce covered by collective agreements, France compares well with Germany (90 per cent) and Scandinavian countries, and does rather better than Britain (around half) (Lecher 1994). Rather, the objectives, scope and form of collective bargaining have changed. Its objectives are no longer, as during the *Trente Glorieuses*, for employees to claim their share of productivity-driven rises in profits (in terms of pay rises and improved working conditions), but to set basic rules and then give companies the means to interpret them flexibly. In fact, bargaining of the 'old type' was notoriously weak in France, even after the State intervened in the early 1970s to boost it, and had been grafted on to a culture of 'perpetual guerrilla warfare in the workplace' (Howell 1996). Today, bargaining can often be a means for employers to lessen the rigidity of labour legislation and nationally imposed rates and conditions, although it can also be a vehicle for real innovation. Accordingly, the content of bargaining has changed to include a greater number of agreements on working time, training and technologies, although pay remains the most important subject.

The cornerstone of the industrial system in France has traditionally been sectoral-level bargaining, and it has remained stable, with some fifty new agreements signed each year and usually around 800 updates. However, it is increasingly limited in scope, essentially confined to setting minimum pay levels and classifications. It could be argued that the declining role of sectoral bargaining has been compensated by an upsurge in company bargaining, the main beneficiary of the 1982 Auroux law requiring employers to negotiate annually and of a series of laws on working time and new technology. The number of company agreements rose from 1,477 in 1981 to 5,165 in 1985, 6,750 in 1991 and 7,450 in 1994 (Coffineau 1993, Boulin 1996). In 1996, boosted by the 'De Robien' law giving companies financial help for reducing working time to save or create jobs, 4,001 company agreements were reached on working time alone (up from 3,571 in 1995).

It is difficult to argue, however, that the undoubted rise in company bargaining denotes the emergence of a new consensual culture in French industrial relations. Company-level bargaining takes place overwhelmingly in large companies, leaving employees in smaller companies covered by increasingly minimalistic sectoral agreements and accentuating the 'two-track' nature of the industrial relations system. Howell (1996: 141) observes a 'growing disjunction between highly politicized but weak national trade union federations on the one hand, and more quiescent and autonomous enterprise unions, representing workers inside the firm but not beyond its boundaries, on the other.' Evidence of this 'microcorporatism' within the firm can be seen in the growing number of non-union or 'other' (not belonging to the 'big five' confederations) within the firm. But their bargaining power remains limited. In the 1990s, 'other' unions signed around 14 per cent of collective agreements each year; by way of comparison, the smallest of the 'big five', the CFTC, signed around 20 per cent, and the CGT around 45 per cent. 'Other' unions are not significantly more likely to sign agreements, where they are present, than the major confederations. The most glaring gap remains that between unionized and non-unionized firms.

The number of strikes and strikers has dropped sharply since the 1970s, as in most other western European countries (see Table 7.2). The strike rate more than halved in the early 1980s, and then again in the late 1980s, and today is close to the British rate. The debate about 'union power' in Britain in the 1970s revolved around the legal 'indemnities' enjoyed by strike-leading unions, and subsequent right-wing governments set about dismantling these rights and imposing tough controls on unions wishing to organize strikes. In contrast, there is very little state regulation of private sector strike activity in France, whose Constitution guarantees the individual right to strike (as long as it does not interfere with the even more sacred right to work). Private sector strike action is not generally seen as problematic in France, and employers have not campaigned for legal curbs, although a 1996 survey showed 81 per cent of French people (and 75 per cent of those who took part in the 1995 movement) to be in favour of secret ballots before strike action (Olivennes 1997). On the other hand, employers complain bitterly about the economic effects of public sector strikes, and the French public resent public transport strikes in particular. Public sector actions are already subject to prior warning requirements and to measures aimed at reducing the effect of targeted, limited strikes, but compliance is a problem: a legal ban on air traffic control strikes does not prevent them from happening. The problem appears to be not so much the legal limits on strike action but the role of unions in the public sector.

The decline in the number of strike actions and more generally in worker militancy has been put forward as an explanation for the crisis of unionism in France, which has traditionally set great store by conflict. However, since the mid-1990s the strike has come back into favour among French workers. Interestingly, Mouriaux (1996) points out that, contrary to popular stereotype, support for strike action is strongest not among public sector workers or workers with permanent contracts, but among those facing job insecurity. Also, younger respondents in this survey were more likely to find strike action effective. Renewed support for the strike as a means of action coincides with increased feelings of job insecurity and remoteness from companies' decision-making centres in the 1990s. It is noteworthy that the 1995 strike movement, sparked off by Alain Juppé's clumsy presentation of his reform plans, had been preceded by several months of unrest in the private as well as public sector.

Conclusion

The causes of trade union decline in France are several. Some relate to the economic environment and display similar trends to those seen elsewhere in western Europe. Unemployment is an obvious factor, and the rising curve of unemployment shows a strong inverse correlation with union density. Today, there are twice as many unemployed people as trade unionists in France. Labour market deregulation (see Chapter 6) has also taken its toll on a union movement based, like its counterparts in many other countries, on the 'typical' working pattern of skilled manual (male) workers in large industrial plants. Other factors are more specific to France. Pressures on the social security system, regarded as a union victory and an important source of influence and material support for the unions, and more generally on the role of the traditionally powerful State have eroded the unions' established support bases. Their dependence on State-centred solutions has allowed them to survive as virtual 'unions without members' (Groux and Mouriaux 1996). In this respect, the crisis of trade unions mirrors the more general problems faced by French society as it attempts to redefine the

Table 7.2 Industrial disputes in the European Community – number of days lost due to strikes and lockouts, per 1,000 employees (annual average)

	1975–9	1980–4	1985	1986	1987	1988	1989	1990	1991	1992
Germany	52	55	2	1	2	2	4	14	6	60
France	217	95	41	32	29	69	50	39	34	25
Italy	1,553	938	269	391	278	196	262	298	164	160
UK	517	483	301	89	163	166	183	70	33	24
Spain	1,440	660	423	300	643	1422	422	282	478	650
Netherlands	57	20	19	9	13	2	5	50	17	8
Denmark	86	110	990	39	58	40	20	40	31	30
Greece	700	740	620	711	9,940	3,550	4,950	12,130	n/a	n/a

Source: Lecher 1994, based on International Labour Office and OECD figures.

State's role, the relationship between State and citizens, and the expectations which can realistically be made of the 'French social model' beloved of politicians as diverse as Jacques Chirac and Jacques Delors. Like the unions, French people are attached to many of the social values which underpin this model. In their expectations of the unions, they appear to support defensive action rather than the forward-looking, experimental approach favoured by the CFDT leadership (see Soubie 1992); the CGT is castigated for its ideological rigidity but appreciated above all the other confederations for its defence of workers' rights.

Could rising grass-roots unrest translate into a renewal of defensive unionism? Cayrol (1996) notes that employees continue to expect unions to carry out a function of 'defence'; but 'defence' has given way to 'bargaining and solidarity' as the most important function. The challenge for French trade unions is how to combine fulfilment of their traditional role with a more pragmatic, consensual approach to workplace relations; in other words, to integrate 'microcorporatism' into the mainstream. The evidence suggests that they have an uphill struggle on their hands.

Appendix: Main trade union organizations

Confédération Générale du Travail (CGT)

Founded in 1885, the CGT is the oldest trade union confederation, and for a large part of the twentieth century dominated the union movement. In 1949, the CGT had 4 million members; today, it has around 600,000 members. It recruits mainly among unskilled and manual workers (automobile, shipbuilding, steel, chemical and printing industries). In the post-war period, the CGT had a close relationship with the Parti Communiste Français (PCF), to the extent that its general secretary was traditionally a member of the PCF's executive body. However, this practice was discontinued in 1995 under the leadership of Louis Viannet. Nevertheless, close working links remain and the legacy of 'mass and class' trade unionism persists in the CGT's insistence on 'struggle'. In 1995, the CGT withdrew its long-standing affiliation to the (Communist) World Federation of Trade Unions. It has repeatedly attempted to join the European Trade Union Confederation (ETUC) but met with a veto from Force Ouvrière.

Confédération Générale du Travail-Force Ouvrière (CGT-FO)

Force Ouvrière was set up in 1948 by a minority of CGT members unhappy with their leadership's close ties with the PCF. Today FO has between 350,000 and 400,000 members, mainly in the public sector (white-collar workers, technical and professional groups). In the mid-1980s, it claimed to be the second-largest confederation, with nearly a million members, but considerable doubt existed over the real figure. With its apolitical stance and emphasis on collective bargaining, FO undoubtedly gained from the perceived politicization of the CGT and CFDT in the 1970s. However, membership gains in the early 1980s did not last. Politically, FO members are the most heterogeneous, spanning the Gaullist right and the Trotskyite left and anarchists, with more recently a significant level of support for the far-right Front National. This has created internal divisions and problems for the leadership as it sought to steer between, and sometimes forge alliances with other confederations. FO is affiliated to the International Confederation of Free Trade Unions (ICFTU) and the ETUC.

Confédération Française Démocratique du Travail (CFDT)

The CFDT was created in 1964 when a majority of the Confédération Française des Travailleurs Chrétiens voted to change the confederation's name to mark its secularization. Today it has over 600,000 members. It is strongest in engineering, the health sector, the oil and chemicals industries, and banking and insurance. In the late 1960s and early 1970s, the CFDT became associated with the 'second' (non-Communist) left. Although in 1978 it 'recentred' its policies, the CFDT was closely identified with socialist governments in office after 1981. Under the leadership of Nicole Notat in the 1990s, it sought to distance itself further from the political left and to portray itself as the champion of innovation and reform. Several left-wing federations (especially in the public sector) left or were expelled, and some became autonomous unions. Notat's approval of Prime Minister Alain Juppé's controversial health reform plan in 1995 exacerbated the splits and the CFDT's role in the 1995 strike movement was ambivalent. The CFDT is a member of the ICFTU and the ETUC.

Confédération Française des Travailleurs Chrétiens (CFTC)

Although it has at most 100,000 members today, the CFTC is the fourth 'representative' union recognized by the state as having the authority to take part in national-level bargaining. This recognition reflects its historic role as representative of Christian (Catholic) unionism. The CFTC was founded in 1919 and a minority of its members carried on under the old name following the majority's 1964 decision to become the CFDT. The CFTC's power base includes miners, schoolteachers, health workers and banking employees. It is affiliated to the International Confederation of Christian Trade Unions (ICCTU).

Confédération Française de l'Encadrement-Confédération Générale des Cadres (CFE-CGC, often referred to as CGC)

Established in 1944, the CGC is the only nationally representative body for lower management, technical and supervisory staff. It has over 100,000 members, who are mainly engineers, supervisors, technicians and sales representatives. In workplace elections, a special electoral college is formed for these categories of employee, and the CGC usually wins most of these seats. The CGC is strongest in the engineering and chemical industries and among sales representatives. It has campaigned for recognition of the special status of its member groups and to maximize pay differentials. The CGC is the fifth 'representative' union recognized by the state in national bargaining.

Fédération de l'Education Nationale (FEN)

Founded as an independent union in 1948 when it broke away from the CGT. It is an umbrella organization rather than a true confederation, since many of its fifty-plus member unions are also affiliated to one or other of the three main confederations. Accordingly, it has fallen prey to internal divisions. It is committed to the principle of secular education. During the demographic boom of the 1970s, the FEN boasted half a million members. The FEN today has some 120,000 members, and is particularly strong in primary education.

It is recognized as a representative union in its dealings with the State (as employer).

Fédération Syndicale Unitaire (FSU)

Formed after a split within the FEN in 1993, it has around 180,000 members today, half of whom work in secondary education, and it has made gains in the further education sector. The FSU came first in workplace elections in December 1993, slightly ahead of the FEN. During the Autumn 1995 protest movement against Juppé's health plans, the FSU participated in demonstrations alongside the CGT and FO.

Union Nationale des Syndicats Autonomes (UNSA)

Formed in 1993. Its seven member unions belong mainly to the civil service, the biggest being the FEN. Its total membership stands at nearly 300,000. It has been recognized as having representative status for public sector bargaining.

Other autonomous unions:

Fédération Générale Autonome des Fonctionnaires (FGAF)

Recognized in civil service bargaining and elections to civil service committees.

Solidaires, Unitaires et Démocratiques (SUD)

Civil service (for example, postal, tax workers), set up by (usually left-wing) activists expelled from or having left the CFDT.

Groupe des Dix (Group of Ten)

Formed in 1981, with originally ten, now twenty-three autonomous unions (including some SUD). In 1997, they claimed a total membership of 60,000 and announced plans to seek recognition as a representative federation.

Note

1 See Appendix. Note that there is disagreement over whether the CFDT or the CGT is the largest confederation. For many years, official membership claims were grossly inflated, and it was difficult to estimate actual figures. The confederations collect and count membership dues in different ways, and as collection is done centrally this made it difficult to relate aggregate figures to local practices. More recently, however, the confederations have been more willing to reveal the truth about their membership and finances. Indeed, in 1995 the CGT leader went so far as to concede that the CFDT, which it had always outstripped, had overtaken it slightly. Labbé (1997), however, gives the CGT the edge, with 630,00 members (against the CFDT's 515,000). Note that the combined membership of the major confederations is below 2 million, less than the number of trade unionists in Belgium.

References

Adam, G. (1983) *Le Pouvoir syndical en France*, Paris: Dunod.

Aïdan, G. (1991) 'Abécédaire de l'opinion', in SOFRES, *L'état de l'opinion 1991*, Paris: Seuil, pp.251–88.

Ambassade de France (1996) *Trade Unions in France* (leaflet), December, London.

Bevort, A. and Labbé, D. (1992) *La CFDT: Organisation et audience depuis 1945*, Paris: La Documentation française.

Boulin, J.-Y. (1996) 'Trade union modernisation in France: Is there still time?', *Transfer*, 1: 129–45.

Cayrol, R. (1996) 'Les syndicats dans l'opinion publique française', *French Politics and Society*, 14(4): 459.

Coffineau, M. (1993) *Les Lois Auroux, dix ans après*, Paris: La Documentation française.

Groux, G. and Mouriaux, R. (1996) 'The dilemma of unions without members', in A. Daley (ed.), *The Mitterrand Era: Policy Alternatives and Political Mobilization in France*, New York: Macmillan, pp. 172–85.

Howell, C. (1996) 'French socialism and the transformation of industrial relations since 1981', in A. Daley (ed.) *The Mitterrand Era: Policy Alternatives and Political Mobilization in France*, New York: Macmillan, pp. 141–60.

Kesselman, M. (1996) 'French labor confronts technological change: Reform that never was?' in A. Daley (ed.) *The Mitterrand Era: Policy Alternatives and Political Mobilization in France*, New York: Macmillan, pp. 161–71.

Labbé, D. (1995) 'La crise du syndicalisme français', *La Revue de l'IRES*, 16, Autumn: 75–101.

—— (1997) *Syndicats et syndiqués en France depuis 1945*, Paris: L'Harmattan.

Lecher, W. (ed.) (1994) *Trade Unions in the European Union. A Handbook*, London: Lawrence & Wishart.

Le Maître, A. and Tchobanian, R. (1992) *Les Institutions représentatives du personnel dans l'entreprise*, Paris: La Documentation française.

Milner, S. (1998) 'Industrial relations in France: towards a new social pact?' in M. Maclean (ed.) *The Mitterrand Years*, Basingstoke: Macmillan, pp. 168–84.

Mouriaux, R. (1996) 'Syndicalisme faible et revendications urgentes', in G. La Chaise, *Crise de l'emploi et fractures politiques*, Presses de la Fondation Nationale des Sciences Politiques.

Olivennes, D. (1997) 'Les Français et l'État', in SOFRES, *L'état de l'opinion 1997*, Paris: Seuil.

Rosanvallon, P. (1988) *La Question syndicale*, Paris: Calmann-Lévy.

Soubie, R. (1992) 'La crise des syndicats', in SOFRES, *L'état de l'opinion 1992*, Paris: Seuil, pp.37–55.

Streeck, W. (1992) 'Interest heterogeneity and organizing capacity: two class logics of collective action?', in *Social Institutions and Economic Performance: Studies of Industrial Relations in Advanced Capitalist Economies* (London: Sage).

Supiot, A. (1996) 'Malaise dans le social', *Droit Social*, 2 (February): 115–20.

Chapter 8

French politics 1981–97

Stability and malaise

Cécile Laborde

On 1 June 1997, the left secured an unexpected and resounding victory in the legislative election imprudently called by President Chirac a few weeks earlier. As the French political world is slowly taking the measure of such a spectacular change of government, it is a good time, perhaps, to reflect on the achievements and failures of the French political system in the last fifteen years. Even a cursory glance at recent French political history reveals something of a paradox. Never have French institutions been the object of such widespread acceptance, and yet, never has French political life been subject to such scepticism and disillusion. The themes of institutional entrenchment and political malaise may thus conveniently be dealt with in two distinct sections.

Institutional entrenchment

The Mitterrand years and the mutations of semi-presidentialism

On 10 May 1981, François Mitterrand became the first socialist president of the Fifth Republic. The event itself, while the predictable reward of the left's patient march towards power, had both an ironic and a momentous significance. For Mitterrand was, at one and the same time, a long-time critic of the Gaullist-type presidency, and the leader of a left-wing coalition committed to 'changer la vie' – and perhaps, the Constitution, too. While some hoped that president Mitterrand would succeed in democratizing the regime, others worried that a socialist-inspired institutional revolution would undermine the authority of the Gaullist republic.

Such fears, and such hopes, were soon to be dissipated. The 1981 *alternance* (the first-time accession to power of the Opposition) was successfully absorbed by the Fifth Republic. As Mitterrand put it, 'the institutions were not designed with me in mind but they suit me' (*Le Monde*, 2 July 1981). Characteristically, the new president's interpretation of presidential functions was hardly less extensive than that of his predecessors. The Mitterrand years set the stage for the near-universal acceptance which the president has acquired as the dominant figure in the French State. In the 1980s and early 1990s, the institutional entrenchment of the Fifth Republic was further confirmed by the successful test of *cohabitation*, the co-existence at the pinnacle of the State of a socialist president and a conservative prime minister backed by parliament. Lastly, semi-presidentialism *à la française* was altered but not, it seems, threatened by the rehabilitation of parliament in the late 1980s and the accession to power of Jacques Chirac in 1995. Whether the events of spring 1997 (the ill-fated dissolution of parliament ushering into power a socialist-dominated coalition) will inaugurate a new constitutional practice remains to be seen.

Semi-presidentialism à la française

It is *faute de mieux* that the Fifth Republic has been labelled 'semi-presidential' by political scientists. The concept refers to a hybrid between a US-type presidential system (where there is a strict separation between presidential and parliamentary powers) and a British-style parliamentary system (where the prime minister-led cabinet is responsible to its majority in parliament). Semi-presidentialism in France was the outcome both of explicit constitutional provisions and incremental institutional practice.

In 1958, the constitution of the new regime was set up under the impulse of Charles de Gaulle to remedy the weakness of the parliamentary system of the Fourth Republic, whose fate was sealed by the advent of the Algerian war, when institutions were virtually brought to a standstill. In keeping with the Gaullist concern to restore the authority of the state, key constitutional provisions included the creation of a respected president, guardian of the Constitution and supreme, non-partisan arbitrator (article 5), and the restriction of parliamentary powers. Parliamentarism was, to use the infelicitous French word, *rationalisé*. This meant that the authority of the government over parliament was enhanced by a number of constitutional weapons which, in essence, drastically constrained the exercise of the two main functions of parliament, passing laws and the control and censure of government. Besides, it seemed clear that the government, not the president, was the major actor in domestic decision-making (article 20). None the less, this constitutional synthesis, best described, perhaps, as a parliamentary regime without parliamentary sovereignty, did not escape ambiguities. How the dual executive (president-prime minister) would function in practice was, in 1958, open to question.

More than the Constitution itself, it is, therefore, to subsequent institutional practice that we should turn to trace the development of semi-presidentialism in France. The rise of the president to unchallenged predominance is related to a combination of political and personal factors. Among these was de Gaulle's own charismatic leadership, his undisguised dislike of parliament, the popular prestige and institutional autonomy he acquired during the Algerian crisis, the (then controversial) introduction of the election of the president by universal suffrage in 1962 and, above all, unanticipated changes in the party system in the 1960s. With the emergence of strong, disciplined and dominant parties (the Gaullist UNR in the 1960s, the Socialist Party in the 1980s), in a position successfully to form stable coalitions in parliament, Fifth Republic presidents were able to rely on an unprecedented degree of parliamentary subservience and partisan support (albeit at the cost of relinquishing their non-partisan image).

As a result, the prestige and authority of the office grew, surpassing even its inspirer's dreams. There is no clearer symbol of the 'presidentialization' of the regime than the centrality of presidential elections in French political life. Not only do they attract the highest level of public interest and media coverage, they also structure partisan and personal strategies. Mitterrand's victory in 1981 was made possible by his patient work of coalition-building and support-gathering for his successive presidential candidacies. The presidency is still the disputed prize of party competition.

Of course, presidential office does not only promise prestige, it also offers real powers, although these have mainly developed at the margins of the Constitution. From 1958 onwards, presidential decision-making powers have increased, apparently in irreversible fashion. While de Gaulle (1958–69) appropriated the now famous *domaine réservé* (foreign policy and defence), subsequent right-wing presidents, Georges Pompidou (1969–74) and Valéry Giscard d'Estaing (1974–81), added economic, social and cultural policies to the 'presidential domain'. By the time Mitterrand (1981–95) began his second term in office (in 1988), potentially every field of public action could be overseen by the president. In parallel, typically 'presidentialist' prerogatives, such as the exertion of influence over the government's composition, or the discretionary dismissal of prime ministers (a right which does not appear in the Constitution), became accepted features of the new balance of power.

The irresistible extension of the president's 'potential' domain did not necessarily imply that the president felt inclined to use to the full and at all times the resources put at his disposal. Nor was it the case that the relationship between prime minister and president was always one of subordination between a democratically elected president and an appointed, 'rubber-stamp' prime minister. Rather, subordination, conflict, symbiosis and partnership should be seen as the features of an essentially shifting and ambiguous pattern of relations (Wright 1993). Not until 1986, however, was the centrality of the president challenged, even if personalities and, above all, the balance of party power have been crucial variables in the varying resources of presidents. Observers have identified phases of 'hyper-presidentialism' (when the president's autonomy is enhanced by the support of a solid majority in parliament, as under De Gaulle, Pompidou, and Mitterrand between 1981 and 1986) and phases of 'tempered presidentialism' (when the prime minister derives power from his own parliamentary basis or from the need to accommodate fragile majorities, as under Giscard, and Mitterrand between 1988–93) (Keeler and Schain 1996: 23–52).

Cohabitation: The recent rehabilitation of parliamentary government and its limits

In 1986, semi-presidentialism *à la française* was put to the test. Because of the non-coincidence between presidential mandate (seven years) and legislative mandate (five years), the possibility had ever been present, in the Fifth Republic, that legislative elections might produce a majority hostile to the incumbent president. Such a configuration emerged with the victory of the right-wing RPR–UDF coalition in 1986. President Mitterrand was forced to appoint as prime minister his political foe, the Gaullist Jacques Chirac. Thus began *cohabitation*, the sharing of the regime's dual executive between the left and the right. It lasted two years, and occurred again in 1993–5, when Mitterrand 'cohabited' with another Gaullist prime minister, Edouard Balladur. In June 1997, the third *cohabitation* began, this time between a Gaullist president (Chirac) and a socialist prime minister (Lionel Jospin).

There is no question that the balance of powers shifted towards the prime minister and the government, backed by their majority in parliament. The Fifth Republic came, under *cohabitation*, close to a parliamentary regime. Article 20 of the Constitution regained its full significance, as the government was given free rein to implement its economic and social programme. Yet *cohabitation* eroded but did not undermine the status of the president in the French system (Bigaut 1995a).

On the one hand, at least during the period 1986–8, Mitterrand succeeded in preserving the integrity of the presidential *domaine réservé*, exercised his power to veto *ordonnances* (legislative acts taken by the government), and did not hesitate to appeal to public opinion to raise principled objections against the most radical of the ultra-liberal measures of the Chirac government. Bitter confrontations at the top of the State were not infrequent under the first *cohabitation* (dubbed by some 'cohabitension') while, in turn, the second *cohabitation* put face-to-face a weakened president and a courteous but powerful prime minister. On the other hand, the aura of the presidency paradoxically benefited from its temporary (and perhaps illusory) 'aloofness' from partisan politics under *cohabitation*, a not insignificant factor in Mitterrand's triumphant re-election in 1988, and a lesson learned by President Chirac between 1995 and May 1997 (he shrewdly sought to shift the burden of responsibility – and unpopularity – for economic and social setbacks to his premier, Alain Juppé).

Two lessons may be drawn from the episode of *cohabitation*. First, it has contributed further to entrench the Fifth Republic, proving surprisingly popular among the electorate. Second, it has not substantially threatened the institutional dominance of the presidency. After the parenthesis of *cohabitation*, the *logique des institutions* took over. In 1988, Mitterrand championed a less regal exercise of power, but his influence over the government's composition, his interference with governmental action (as during the *lycées* crisis of 1990), and his dismissal of premiers Michel Rocard and Edith Cresson (in 1991 and 1992) suggested that the weapons of semi-presidentialism were still at hand. In 1995, Chirac committed himself to a restrained, modest presidency, but his choice of a loyal lieutenant (Alain Juppé) as premier, his own activist style, coupled with a power position reminiscent of that of the Gaullists in the

1960s (the RPR–UDF coalition until the last election controlled the National Assembly, the Senate, and most regional and local assemblies) hardly pointed to an attenuation of the semi-presidentialist system. However, 1997 might have signalled a major change here. The disastrous outcome of Chirac's decision to call elections has seriously undermined his personal position, perhaps irremediably, as the left prepares to govern for a full five years in conjunction with a weakened president. Whether the president can recover from this novel position of vulnerability remains to be seen.

For all the legitimacy secured by the Fifth Republic institutions in recent years, they have not been immune from recurrent criticism. Critics have stigmatized both the 'monarchical drift' inherent in the concentration of power in the hands of the president (in 'normal' periods), and the lack of effective control of executive action by parliament. Both phenomena are not unrelated, though the former also refers to a cluster of pathological practices at the top of the French State (stemming notably from the importance of patronage in the administration and from a traditionally secretive exercise of power). Yet recent reforms have sought primarily to address the latter issue, and the theme of the rehabilitation of parliament has become a leitmotiv, notably under the combined influence of the socialist-inspired Comité Vedel and of the president of the National Assembly, Philippe Seguin (1993–7). On 4 August 1995, what was perhaps the most important constitutional reform since 1962 was passed (Albert 1996: 257–62; Bigaut 1995b). It created a single annual parliamentary session (giving more time to MPs to discuss and amend bills), and reinforced parliamentary control of the legislative timetable and of governmental action. The *déficit démocratique* was further addressed through the extension of the domains in which the president could call a referendum – a somewhat pyrrhic victory for critics of the regime's presidentialization.

In sum, the last fifteen years have seen both indisputable mutations and a remarkable survival of the semi-presidentialism which characterizes the Fifth Republic. The Constitution has proved its flexibility and enjoys near-universal support. Or does it? Recent events have, quite unexpectedly, revealed a number of fault-lines in the French semi-presidential system. In the spring of 1997, Chirac's *dissolution tactique* turned out to be a *dissolution tragique*, and this unprecedented political 'blunder' has stimulated public debate on French institutions. First, the non-coincidence between presidential and parliamentary mandates is increasingly perceived as a liability.

In the last sixteen years, France has seen no less than five *alternances* and three *cohabitations*. As a result, few governments have benefited from a full five years in office. One suggested solution would be to reduce the presidential mandate to five years, which would have the additional advantage of attenuating the 'monarchical drift' of French institutions. Recent proposals for the democratization of French politics (such as those spelled out in *Le Monde* of 7 May 1997, by five prominent constitutionalists) included such *quinquennat*, together with the much-needed prohibition of *cumul des mandats* (the existing right of French politicians to hold several elected positions at one time) and further extensions of parliamentary and direct democracy. Some of these reforms are explicitly on the agenda of the new socialist-led government.

Second, many were disturbed by the fact that the president could call general elections for purely opportunistic reasons and yet remain in power in the event of defeat, against all principles of democratic accountability. Significantly though, few in France were prepared to contemplate the only obvious solution to this French anomaly, the transition towards either a pure presidentialist or (more sensibly) a pure parliamentary regime. The 'Sixth Republic' still has very few supporters, a clear indication, in a time of reformist activism on the part of the governing left, of the popularity of France's current constitution.

The 'pacification' of politics?

Other, less palpable, factors have played their part in the entrenchment of the French political system. In the late 1980s, it became fashionable to herald the 'normalization' of French politics. France, it was asserted, had moved away from the pathologically conflictual mode of politics inherited from the Revolution of 1789, towards a pacified, de-ideologized, modest and consensual political life. While such a diagnosis was perhaps premature and at any rate imprudently sanguine in its conclusions, there is no doubt that the emergence of 'consensus' as a new political value has contributed to the stabilization of the Fifth Republic. Three facets of the 'république du centre' (Furet *et al.* 1988) will be considered: the development of a cross-party agreement on policy, the (eventually abortive) emergence of a political centre, and the regulative role played by the Constitutional Council.

The development of a broad policy consensus is perhaps the

single most significant event of the 1980s. It emerged from the failure of socialist economic policy. In 1981, the socialists and their communist allies came to power armed with an ambitious programme of reform. Significant cultural, political and social changes were successfully carried through (abolition of the death penalty, promotion of minority rights, democratization of industrial relations, liberalization of the media, decentralization of power to local authorities). By contrast, the left's attempts to promote growth and reduce economic inequalities via a programme of budgetary expansion were soon thwarted by a stifling economic climate. The failure of the 'socialist experiment' prompted Mitterrand to initiate a decisive volte-face in March 1983. The French left operated a swift conversion to the virtues of a strong currency, low inflation, budgetary austerity, competitiveness and entrepreneurial values. Paradoxically, the key achievements of Mitterrand were in areas where his action had been least expected: European integration, the modernization of French industry and financial capitalism, and the de-ideologization of the left (Cole 1995: 329).

This trend was pursued and accentuated under the neo-liberal Chirac government, which explicitly drew its inspiration from the 'Thatcherite revolution'. The experiment in *laissez-faire* radicalism, however, was received with only lukewarm approval by a wary electorate. By the late 1980s, as a result, all major parties had embraced the moderate ideal of the mixed economy, a combination of free enterprise and state intervention (the welfare state and the public service state). The French have presumably learnt to live with a more low-key, less heroic style of leadership, but whether they have been able to live with limited expectations is more doubtful, as recent developments have shown (see below, pp. 166–8).

It is, however, not surprising that this process of de-ideologization and consensus-building has contributed to the blurring of the differences between left and right. Such a distinction, born out of two centuries of ideological conflict, was crystallized under the Fifth Republic with the 'bipolarization' of the party system (the emergence of two cohesive right-wing and left-wing coalitions, confronting one another around distinctive ideological platforms). While such confrontations had long shaped the political culture of the Fifth Republic, it was found that by 1988, most voters thought left-right differences were irrelevant (Eatwell 1988: 467).

On his re-election, Mitterrand was quick to grasp the political significance of this. He had campaigned as the consensual candidate of the *France unie*, and appointed a centre-left prime minister, Michel Rocard, who experimented with centrist politics and *ouverture* (the opening up of the majority to the centrists, the Greens, and non-political personalities). Although the much talked about emergence of an independent centre group in French politics was a non-starter (as shown by the disappointing results obtained by the centrist Simone Veil in the European elections of 1989) and *ouverture* itself was put to an end by 1991 (Borella 1993: 236), the motto of *France unie* proved a mobilizing slogan. True, the presidential election of 1995 saw a classic left–right, bipolar contest in the second round; nevertheless, Chirac's (temporarily) successful appeal to a non-partisan, progressive, 'republican' platform capitalized on the apparent disgust of the electorate for 'ideological' politics.

Undeniably, there seemed to be few fundamental ideological divergences between the mainstream French parties in the late 1980s, notably on economic management, Europe, foreign policy, the welfare state, education, even immigration. For all its pernicious side effects, there is little doubt that such a consensualization of politics has been a major factor in the entrenchment of the system. Both the Socialist Party (PS) and the RPR–UDF coalition are now seen as responsible *partis de gouvernement*; and neither *alternance* nor *cohabitation* are likely to be perceived as disturbing leaps into the dark.

One institution is sometimes said to have helped this 'pacification': the Constitutional Council. The Council, created in 1958, was originally designed to keep parliament in check. In one of those ironic twists of history, it developed a life of its own, slowly emerging as a rigorous censor of government-initiated laws and a protector of rights. In 1971, the Council extended its control by examining the conformity of the content of the laws to the preamble of the Constitution (which includes the Declaration of Human Rights of 1789). In 1974, the right to refer cases to the Council was opened to groups of sixty deputies or senators, thus giving the Opposition an additional opportunity to challenge the government (though on legal not political grounds). The Council has been said to function as a 'Third Chamber' (Stone 1992).

In some ways, the Council has contributed to the consensualization of French politics by 'judicializing' the policy-making process. It has progressively elaborated a coherent body of constitutional case-law acting as a set of constraining (and legitimizing) principles for governmental action. When the Council annuls, validates, or amends laws on sensitive subjects such as privatization and nationalization, immigration or abortion, political debate gives way to 'neutral', dispassionate, legal adjudication. *L'Etat de droit* transcends parliamentary conflict. According to the constitutionalist Louis Favoreu, the Council has played a positive role, regulating the change of parties in office, pacifying ideological conflict, defining rules that narrow reform options, in short, creating the conditions for centrist politics (Harrison 1990: 618).

The 1980s thus witnessed major mutations which have, in part, contributed to the institutional entrenchment of the Fifth Republic. The institutions have been strengthened by the successful tests of *alternance* and *cohabitation*, and political life has been characterized by consensus and pacification. There is, however, a less sanguine side to the story.

Political malaise

Traditional parties in crisis

The Communist Party

In 1946, the Parti Communiste (PCF) was the single largest French party. By the early 1990s, it seemed to have dwindled into electoral insignificance and become a 'marginalized and decaying institution' (Hazareesingh 1994: 300), resigning itself in 1995 to the relatively 'satisfactory' score of 8.64 per cent obtained by its candidate Robert Hue in the presidential election. Between 1978 and 1988, the PCF's share of the votes in legislative elections fell from 20.6 to 11.3 per cent (10 per cent voting intentions last BVA poll, 16 April 1997). The PCF has fallen victim to a number of political and sociological mutations (Baudouin 1993). First, the party has long suffered from its incestuous association with Soviet communism, and a fatal blow was given to its ideological coherence by the implosion of the Eastern Bloc in 1987–90. Second, with the disintegration of the working class, the party has lost much of its traditional militant and electoral base, and has been unable to renew it. Third, the bipolar logic and presidentialization of the Fifth Republic seemed ineluctably to condemn the party to political marginalization.

Hence the realistic strategy of the union of the left (PS–PCF). This, however, proved a self-destructive move for the communists, as the PS, emerging in the 1970s as the dominant party of the left, in effect drove communist electors away from the PCF. Ever since its inglorious participation in a socialist-led government (1981–4), the PCF sought desperately, and with some success, to re-activate what political scientists call its *fonction tribunicienne*, articulating at the margins of the system expressions of protest and aspirations for change. In the 1990s, the new leader of the Communists, Robert Hue, has toned down the maximalist programme of the PCF and has shown himself prepared to participate in a left-wing government. This evolution, combined with the reasonable score of 9.91 per cent (37 seats) obtained in the 1997 elections, has secured the 'new' communists three posts in the Jospin-led government.

The Socialist Party

The 1980s was the decade of the Parti Socialiste. By 1981, socialists and their allies controlled the presidency and the National Assembly, and they remained in power for fourteen years, with the exception of the four *cohabitation* years. From a marginal position in the 1960s, the party had been thoroughly transformed, under the leadership of François Mitterrand (who took over the party during the 1971 Congrès d'Epinay), into a cohesive and domineering political force. By 1988–91, the Socialist Party had achieved the enviable status of being the first party of France, a typically 'catch-all' party appealing to large sections of the electorate. To other socialist parties of Europe it offered a model for the successful transformation of old-fashioned socialism into a modern, social-democratic movement (Bell and Criddle 1988), able to woo a new electorate sensitive to 'post-materialist' values, such as environmentalism and feminism.

The fall was perhaps as spectacular as the rise. Following the legislative elections of March 1993, when the PS obtained a humiliating 17.6 per cent, the headline of *Le Monde* read: 'L'effondrement socialiste' ('the fall of the socialists') (Portelli 1993). In a nauseating atmosphere of financial scandals and revelations about Mitterrand's past, the socialists were punished for their complacent, at times secretive and 'monarchical' exercise of power, and for their inability to give an economic and social content to the vacuous mottoes of human rights, republicanism and *France unie*. After the years of hope, these were the years of disillusion (Yonnet 1995).

The PS then set out to reverse its political and ideological exhaustion, notably under the leadership of Lionel Jospin, who in the first round of the 1995 presidential election obtained a surprising 23 per cent of the votes. Jospin's medium-term strategy involved a (cautious) *aggiornamento* of Mitterrand's legacy, the patient elaboration of an *alternative de gauche*, and the building up of alliances with the Greens and the Communists. He did not expect to have to fight early elections, nor did he expect to win them. With 245 MPs in the 1997 elected assembly (against 56 in 1993), the PS is again the first party of France, faced with the formidable challenge of meeting the aspirations for change expressed during the election.

The right: Gaullists, liberals and centrists

The moderate French right is made up of two parties, usually united politically and electorally: the Gaullist RPR (Rassemblement pour la République, founded by Chirac in 1976) and the liberal and centrist coalition of the UDF (Union pour la Démocratie Française, created by Giscard in 1978). Between 1993 and 1995, when it successively conquered the presidency and the National Assembly, the right regained the hegemony it had lost in the 1980s. Yet it has not completely surmounted the problems of internal coherence which have plagued the coalition in the last decade (Baudouin 1990, Dreyfus 1990, Ysmal 1990, Knapp 1994, Daley 1996), and indeed, as of June 1997, seems on the verge of implosion.

The right in the 1980s was faced with the double challenge of responding to the rise to pre-eminence of the Socialist party on its left and to the competition of the Front National (see below, pp. 165–6) on its right. Both challenges combined to push the RPR towards the right in the mid-1980s, thus threatening the hegemony of neo-Gaullism within the coalition, and alienating more moderate fractions of the right. The Christian-Democrat CDS (Centre des Démocrates Sociaux), a component of the UDF, attempted to achieve greater autonomy, backing the candidacy of centrist candidates, such as Raymond Barre in the first round of the 1988 election. The RPR has also faced recurrent internal divisions, both with the 'dissidence' of Seguin and Pasqua (prompting a deep fissure in the party on European issues during the referendum on the Maastricht Treaty in 1992) and with the fratricidal contest between Chirac and the *cohabitation* prime minister Balladur in the first round of the 1995 presidential elections. Nevertheless, in the

1990s, the right emerged in a dominant position, winning the legislative elections of 1993 and the presidential election of 1995. With the UDF reduced to a shadow of its former self by persistent divisions (the coalition had no candidate in the first round of the 1995 presidential election), the RPR achieved an enviable position of dominance.

As with the PS earlier, however, such a hegemony was built on shakier foundations than Chirac and Juppé thought. Undeterred by rising unpopularity, and underestimating the growing mood for political change, they decided in 1997 to dissolve the National Assembly, seeking a 'convincing' majority able to steer France through the dangerous waters of European monetary union during the next five years. This, it turned out, was a reckless move. In the aftermath of the second round of 1 June, the moderate right found itself at a historical low (with only 30 per cent of votes cast) and vulnerable to fatal internal divisions, as bitter leadership contests threaten to undermine the authority of Chirac over an increasingly polarized right.

Today there is little doubt that the traditional party system is in crisis. The first indicator of this is the fact that, in the last fifteen years, no governing coalition has managed to secure its re-election to office. Parties from the right and from the left have in turn been brought to power and then have been severely sanctioned at the next election. Such a high level of electoral volatility reveals a deep-seated dissatisfaction with the achievements of mainstream politicians. The second indicator is the fragmentation of the political landscape. In the 1970s, the PCF, PS, RPR and UDF formed a smoothly functioning four-party, two-bloc (bipolar) system. In the last decade, this system was seriously undermined (Machin 1989). The 1980s witnessed both the emergence of fringe parties (see below, p. 164) and a significant erosion of support for established parties (Appleton 1995). Most spectacular was the European election of June 1994, when the combined scores of the *partis de gouvernement* barely reached 40 per cent (Portelli 1994, Todd 1995). In the first round of the presidential election of 1995, the fragmentation of the political landscape was such that five political families each occupied one-sixth to one-quarter of the electoral space (Cole 1995: 335). Electoral abstention also significantly increased during the period, reaching its peak in 1988–9. In the legislative election of 1997, 32 per cent of voters abstained. It is these factors, combined with a palpable sense of widespread social malaise, which have led some observers to refer to a crisis of representation in France (Portelli 1995), understood in the widest sense, as a growing (and dangerous) gap between masses and élites.

Crisis of representation?

The emergence of anti-system parties

The French party system in 1997 is singularly fragmented. No less than nine significant parties (PCF, Mouvement des Citoyens, PS, Radical, Verts, Génération Ecologie, UDF, RPR, Mouvement pour la France, Front National) compete for the votes of the electorate. Fragmentation, of course, is not *per se* a sign of crisis. However, on the one hand the development of dissident groups (within established parties or breaking away from them) is one indicator of the weakness of the traditional party system. The careers of such mavericks as Bernard Tapie (a flamboyant businessman who became a minister before taking over the Radical Party and ending an infamous career in prison) and Philippe de Villiers (a Vendée notable who left the UDF to create the rightist and Euro-sceptic Mouvement pour la France) bear testimony to the attractiveness of a diluted form of anti-élitist populism at the margins of traditional parties. On the other hand, some parties have developed an explicit anti-system rhetoric.

The Greens are a successful 'new' party (Ladrech 1989, Appleton 1995, Daley 1996). In 1992, ecologists obtained a surprising 14 per cent at the regional election, winning the presidency of the regional Council of the Nord. They set a new ideological agenda for the left (on the environment, but also on issues such as work-sharing, lifestyle concerns and participatory democracy), while adroitly tapping the disgust of the electorate for traditional politics with their 'neither left nor right' slogan. Soon, however, ecologists fell victim of their own divisions and indecision. Against the timid neutralism and radical autonomism of Waechter's Verts, Brice Lalonde created Génération Ecologie in 1990, whose determination to work 'with the system' sometimes veered towards opportunism. Persistent electoral weakness prompted the new leader of the Verts, Dominique Voynet, to seek an electoral alliance with receptive socialists. The strategy paid off in the 1997 legislative elections. Although barely securing 3.5 per cent of the votes in the first ballot, ecologists benefited from transfers of votes in the second ballot, and obtained (eight) parliamentary seats for the first time. With two ministers in the Jospin government, the Greens have entered the official political scene and turned their back on purely oppositional politics.

The worrying symptom of the malaise of French democracy is the rise of an extreme right, populist, racist and nationalist party, the Front National (FN), in the 1980s and 1990s (Fysh and Wolfreys 1992, Milza 1992, Wolfreys 1993, Marcus 1995, Simmons 1996). Founded in 1972 by Jean-Marie Le Pen, the FN went through a decade in the political wilderness, before breaking through in the European election of 1984. In 1986, owing in part to the introduction of proportional representation, thirty-five FN candidates were elected to the Assembly, and Le Pen obtained 14.4 per cent in the 1988 presidential elections. After a deceptive decline in the early 1990s, the party's fortunes surged again, with 15.1 per cent of voters choosing Le Pen in 1995, and four large southern towns (Orange, Toulon, Marignane and recently Vitrolles) electing Frontist mayors. Most strikingly, over a quarter of the French electorate have voted FN at least once.

The Front's themes – immigration, national identity, crime, the family, populist anti-élitism – have seduced not only traditionally right-wing voters (anti-socialist upper middle class, artisans, shop-keepers) but also, in recent years, the young, the unemployed, and the working class at large (28 per cent of industrial workers vote FN). The Front has also been successful in setting the political agenda over a number of issues, notably immigration and crime (Daley 1996). Cynically jumping on the anti-immigrant bandwagon, the right (notably Minister of the Interior Charles Pasqua) and, to a lesser extent, the left have in turn toughened immigration and nationality laws. Despite the occasional movement of protest (in the winter 1996–7, massive demonstrations against the repressive *Loi Debré*, named after the RPR Minister of the Interior, stigmatized the *lépénisation des esprits*), there is no doubt that Le Pen's rhetoric is tapping a vein of discontent within French society.

The legislative election of 1997 was yet another landmark in the rise of the FN. With just over 15 per cent of the votes (yet only one MP in the new assembly, because of the FN's inability to secure electoral alliances with the moderate right), the FN could legitimately boast to be the third party of France. No wonder some RPR and UDF members have recently been floating the (hitherto taboo) idea of alliances with Le Pen. Just as the PCF in the 1950s and

1960s 'froze' a substantial fraction of the left-wing electorate, so – some suggest – the FN is today an obstacle to the victory of the right (which, as a whole, obtained an 'arithmetic' victory in the last election). While allying with the FN has become tempting for some on the right, an alternative, if more arduous, strategy for *partis de gouvernement* would be to address the social problems that are at the root of the FN's success.

Political, economic and social malaise

Le Pen's populist appeal against the 'gang of four' (the four established parties) plays on a deep-rooted discontent with the state of politics, economy and society. The *république du centre*, heralded in the late 1980s as the symbol of the consensualization of political life, has ushered in a wide political space at both ends of the political spectrum, rapidly filled by an anti-consensus, anti-élite discourse. Elite consensus has clearly produced a feeling of mass exclusion, as the apparent exhaustion of political alternatives, the stubborn persistence of serious social and economic difficulties, and the growing discredit of established politicians have widened the gap between the political élites and a disillusioned citizenry.

The climax of this process was the referendum on the Maastricht Treaty of 20 September 1992 (Criddle 1993, Appleton 1996). Although established parties, on the right and on the left, campaigned in favour of Treaty ratification, the 'Yes' vote only secured an underwhelming 51 per cent, with 49 per cent of the electorate endorsing the Euro-scepticism of the PCF, the FN, and a collection of dissidents from left and right. The outcome appeared to reveal a number of fault-lines in French political life. Instead of a traditional left–right, bipolar cleavage, observers detected the emergence of a fundamental gap between the mass public and the political class, itself a reflection of the widening gulf between the 'haves' and the 'have-nots'. Although the European issue was important, it was above all symbolic of a number of concerns which seemed to separate a confident France (the France of 'Yes') and an insecure and worried France (the France of 'No'). The result came as a warning at the incapacity of political élites to address the concerns of the majority of the populace.

In truth, the political élite had been discredited by a number of scandals, ranging from the distribution of tainted blood, insider trading, to the misuse of public funds. The problem of corrupt financing of elections, which led to leading party personalities being condemned in court, was partially addressed by legislation which prohibited the funding of parties by private business (Dolez 1993, 1995). Yet the feeling that politicians were primarily motivated by self-interest persisted, aggravated by their seeming incapacity to solve the problem of unemployment. High levels of unemployment (currently standing at 12.8 per cent), especially among the youth (25 per cent), are the black hole of an otherwise healthy economy.

It was on the mobilizing theme of the fight against soaring unemployment and the eradication of the *fracture sociale* (the growing number of socially excluded) that Chirac won the presidency of 1995. There was, of course, some irony in the fact it was the right which was challenging the fiscal orthodoxy of the previous decade and taking the measure of mass discontent. Yet Chirac and the Juppé-led government swiftly reneged on the RPR campaign programme, notably in order to allow France to meet the convergence criteria (in particular the 3 per cent limit on budgetary deficit) required to join the European common currency. Initiating a risky volte-face in the autumn of 1995, Juppé announced significant austerity measures, including tax rises, a freeze on public sector wages, and reduced retirement benefits for civil servants. In such a context, the government's arrogant policy-making style and its refusal to consult with union leaders seemed to add insult to injury. In November–December 1995, France saw the most extensive movement of social protest since 1968. Strikes paralysed the country, and on 7 December, over a million people joined in street demonstrations (Kesselman 1996; see also Chapter 7 of this volume).

Both popular discontent with deteriorating economic conditions and the close results of the Maastricht referendum have revealed the European source of the French malaise. As governments strive to reduce deficits and maintain a strong currency, thus compromising the reflation indispensable for job creation, an increasing number of people doubt whether the European promise is worth the sacrifice. While in the 1980s, France was at the forefront of European integration on the basis that what was good for Europe was good for France, the compatibility between domestic goals and a deepened commitment to Europe (particularly to a common currency by 1999) now appears radically problematic (Cameron 1996). The clearest sign of this sea-change is perhaps Jospin's commitment to put growth and jobs at the centre of his European strategy, thus adding a crucial 'social' dimension to the dominant, 'monetarist' approach to economic integration.

The left's victory of 1997 may hold other promises, and other dangers, too. On the one hand, there is some scope for a much-needed rehabilitation of the political process. The left has sought to put an end to the perceived exhaustion of political alternatives, and inspired hopes that change was, after all, possible. Image mattered, too, and Jospin's government, young, feminized, ideologically pluralist, and committed to a modest, even austere policy-making style, attracted much initial public sympathy. On the other hand, today perhaps even more than before, failure to live up to expectations may well have catastrophic effects. If it turns out that the left does not succeed in giving substance to its (still tentative) economic programme and in bringing unemployment down, even more voters may be tempted to take at face value Le Pen's claim that the Front National offers the only genuine alternative to traditional politics. The left, in a word, is condemned to succeed – a daunting, if exhilarating, task at a time of economic sluggishness, social malaise and political scepticism.

Table 8.1 French presidents and prime ministers – 1981–97

	President	Prime Minister
1981	F. Mitterrand (PS)	P. Mauroy (PS)
1984		L. Fabius (PS)
1986	*Cohabitation*	*J. Chirac (RPR)*
1988	F. Mitterrand (re-elected)	M. Rocard (PS)
1991		E. Cresson (PS)
1992		P. Bérégovoy (PS)
1993	*Cohabitation*	*E. Balladur (RPR)*
1995	J. Chirac (RPR)	A. Juppé (RPR)
1997	*Cohabitation*	*L. Jospin (PS)*

Key:
PS = Parti Socialiste
RPR = Rassemblement pour la République

Acknowledgement

I would like to thank Sandrine Jarry and Nadine Kanhonou for their help in the preparation of this chapter.

Bibliography

Albert, J.L. (1996) *Vingt ans de vie politique en France*, Paris: Les Editions d'organisation.

Appleton, A. (1995) 'Parties under Pressure: Challenges to "Established" French Parties', *West European Politics*, 18(1): 52–67.

——(1996) 'The Maastricht referendum and the party system', in J.T.S. Keeler and M.A. Schain (eds) *Chirac's Challenge, Liberalization, Europeanization and Malaise in France*, London: Macmillan, pp. 301–24.

Baudouin, J. (1990) 'Le 'moment' néolibéral du RPR: Essai d'interprétation', *Revue Française de Science Politique*, 40(6): 830–44.

——(1993) 'Le parti communiste', in D. Chagnollaud (ed.) (1993) *La Vie politique en France*, Paris: Seuil, pp. 292–309

Bell, D.S. and Criddle, B. (1988) *The French Socialist Party, The Emergence of a Party of Government*, Oxford: Clarendon Press (2nd edn).

Berstein, S. (1996) 'Les deux septennats de François Mitterrand: Esquisse d'un bilan', *Modern and Contemporary France*, 1: 3–14.

Bigaut, C. (1995a) 'Les cohabitations institutionnelles de 1986–93', *Regards sur l'Actualité*, May: 3–29.

——(1995b) 'La révision constitutionnelle du 4 août 1995', *Regards sur l'Actualité*, Sept–Oct: 3–92.

Borella, F. (1993) 'Le système des partis' in D. Chagnollaud (ed.) *La vie politique en France*, Paris: Seuil, pp. 223–42

Cameron, D. (1996) 'National interest, the dilemmas of economic integration and malaise', in J.T.S. Keeler and M.A. Schain (eds) *Chirac's Challenge. Liberalization, Europeanization and Malaise in France*, London: Macmillan, pp. 325–82

Cole, A. (1994) *François Mitterrand, A Study in Political Leadership*, London and New York: Routledge.

——(1995) 'La France pour tous? The French Presidential élections of 23 April and 7 May 1995', *Parliamentary Affairs*, 30: 327–46.

Criddle, B. (1992) 'Electoral Systems in France', *Parliamentary Affairs*, 45: 108–16.

——(1993) 'The French Referendum on the Maastricht Treaty. September 1992', *Parliamentary Affairs*, 46: 228–38.

Daley, A. (ed) (1996) *The Mitterrand Era. Policy Alternatives and Political Mobilization in France*, London: Macmillan.

Dolez, B. (1993) 'La loi anti-corruption du 29 janvier 1993', *Regards sur l'Actualité*, June: 33–43.

—— (1995) 'Financement de la vie politique: Les lois anti-corruption de 1995', *Regards sur l'Actualité*, May: 31–41.

Dreyfus, F.G. (1990) 'Place et poids de la démocratie chrétienne', *Revue Française de Science Politique*, 40(6): 845–65.

Eatwell, R. (1988) 'Plus ça change? The French Presidential and National Assembly Elections', April, June 1988', *Political Quarterly*, 54: 462–72.

Favier, P. and Rolland, M.M. (1990) *La Décennie Mitterrand*, Paris: Seuil.

Frears, J. (1991) *Parties and Voters in France*, London: Hurst & Co.

Furet, F. (1995) 'Chronique d'une décomposition', *Le Débat*, 83, January–February.

Furet, F., Julliard, J., and Rosanvallon, P. (1988) *La République du Centre. La fin de l'exception française*, Paris: Calmann-Lévy.

Fysh P. and Wolfreys, J. (1992) 'Le Pen, the National Front and the Extreme Right in France', *Parliamentary Affairs*, 45: 309–25.

Gildea, R. (1996) *France since 1945*, Oxford: Oxford University Press.

Hall, P.A., Hayward, J.E.S. and Machin, H. (1990) *Developments in French Politics*, London: Macmillan.

Harrison, M. (1990) 'The French Constitutional Council: A Study in Institutional Change', *Political Studies*, 38: 603–19.

Hazareesingh, S. (1994) *Political Traditions in Modern France*, Oxford: Oxford University Press.

Hollifield, J.F. and Ross, G. (eds) (1991) *Searching for the New France*, New York and London: Routledge.

Keeler, J.T.S. (1993) 'Executive Power and Policy-Making Patterns in France: Gauging the Impact of Fifth Republic Institutions', *West European Politics*, 16(4): 518–44.

Keeler, J.T.S. and Schain, M.A. (eds) (1996) *Chirac's Challenge. Liberalization, Europeanization and Malaise in France*, London: Macmillan.

Kesselman, M. (1996) 'Does the French labour movement have a future?', in J.T.S. Keeler and M.A. Schain (eds) *Chirac's Challenge. Liberalization, Europeanization and Malaise in France*, London: Macmillan, pp. 143–67.

Knapp, A. (1994) *Gaullism since de Gaulle*, Dartmouth: Aldershot.

Ladrech, R. (1989) 'New Movements and Party Systems: The French Socialist Party and New Social Movements', *West European Politics*, 12: 262–79.

Laudet, C. and Cox, R. (eds) (1995) *La Vie politique en France aujourd'hui*, Manchester: Manchester University Press.

Laughland, J. (1994) *The Death of Politics. France under Mitterrand*, London: Michael Joseph.

Maclean, M. (1995) 'Privatisation in France 1993–4; New Departures, or a Case of *plus ça change?*', *West European Politics*, 18(2): 273–90.

Machin, H. (1989) 'Stages and Dynamics in the Evolution of the French Party System', *West European Politics*, 12(4): 59–81.

Marcus, J. (1995) *The National Front and French Politics. The Resistible Rise of Jean-Marie Le Pen*, London: Macmillan.

Milza, P. (1992) 'Le Front National: Droite extrême ou national-populisme?', in Sirinelli, J.F. (ed.) *Histoire des droites en France*, Paris: Gallimard.

Portelli, H. (1993) 'Les élections législatives de mars 1993', *Regards sur l'Actualité*, April: 23–31.

——(1994) 'L'élection européenne des 9 et 12 juin 1994', *Regards sur l'Actualité*, June–August: 3–13.

——(1995) 'Le débat sur la crise de la représentation politique', *Regards sur l'Actualité*, March–April: 43–50.

Schain, M. (1996) 'The immigration debate and the National Front', in J.T.S. Keeler and M.A. Schain (eds) *Chirac's Challenge. Liberalization, Europeanization and Malaise in France*, London: Macmillan, pp. 169–97.

Simmons, H.G. (1996) *The French National Front. The Extremist Challenge to Democracy*, Boulder and Oxford: Westview Press.

Stone, A. (1992) 'Where Judicial Politics are Legislative Politics: The French Constitutional Council', *West European Politics*, 15: 28–49.

Todd, E. (1991) *The Making of Modern France. Politics, Ideology and Culture*, Oxford: Basil Blackwell.

——(1995) 'Aux origines du malaise politique français. Les classes sociales et leur représentation', *Le Débat*, January–February: 98–130.

Tuppen, J. (1991) *Chirac's France, 1986–88. Contemporary Issues in French Society*, London: Macmillan.

Wolfreys, J. (1993) 'An Iron Hand in a Velvet Glove: The Programme of the French National Front', *Parliamentary Affairs*, 46: 415–29

Wright, V. (1993) 'The President and the Prime Minister: Subordination, conflict, symbiosis or reciprocal parasitism?', in J.E.S. Hayward (ed.) *De Gaulle to Mitterrand, Presidential Power in France*, London: Hurst & Co, pp. 101–19.

Yonnet, P. (1995) 'L'entrée en désillusion', *Le Débat*, January–February: 121–30.

Ysmal, C. (1990) 'La crise électorale de l'UDF et du RPR', *Revue Française de Science Politique*, 40(6): 810–29.

Chapter 9

Education and training

Ted Neather

French schools

'Our school, closely bound up with the idea of the Republic, is the place where our national identity is formed and constantly renewed.' (Fauroux 1996: 55). This ringing declaration from the Fauroux report reminds us without any possible ambiguity of the republican roots and principles from which French education grows. But the report, the latest in a long series instigated by ministers in an effort to find solutions to the problems of adapting and modernising education, has some grim statistics on the current state of affairs. It reports that:

> one child in seven does not really know how to read and write on entry to secondary school; one child in four is weak, at the same age, in arithmetic; many secondary school pupils have problems when they enter the sixth form.
>
> (Fauroux 1996: 50)

Views from other authors are similarly negative: 'Our school is subject to pressures which weaken it and leave it badly placed to fulfil its most essential aims' (Soubré 1995: 8). And yet, an extensive SOFRES survey carried out by *Le Monde* and teachers' unions reported that 'a majority of French people believe that the education system is operating successfully' (*Le Monde*, 19 November 1996). The satisfaction rating is higher (52 per cent against 37 per cent) than in similar surveys in 1984 and 1988. A total of 74 per cent judged that the work of teachers was 'quite satisfactory' or 'very satisfactory'. How can one make sense of these apparently contradictory findings?

The problems for education in France, as in all contemporary developed societies, spring from the need to modernize the system so as to match the rapidity of social change, and to cope with the explosion of educational demand: 'there is hardly any public institution or private firm which has undergone such an expansion of its activity in such a short time' (Fauroux 1996: 14). Fauroux draws attention to the growing gap between, on the one hand, the successful education of élites, the growing popularity of institutions such as the *grandes écoles* and the advantages of social position and wealth in gaining an educational lead; on the other hand, there are the young people of the *banlieues*, deprived and destined to fail. 'The gap has grown wider over recent decades. If we have to speak of the failure of the Republic in dealing with its schools, this is where the failure lies.' (ibid.: 16)

Fauroux's reference to the link between the Republic and its schools is a reminder of the underlying principles which influence all concerns about the French education system and its development. The republican tradition in education, with its origins in the works of Condorcet and its strengthening and confirmation in the reforms of Jules Ferry and the Third Republic, requires education to be public, secular (*laïque*) and compulsory. *Laïcité* is the central feature, since, in banning all promotion of religion within schools, it confirms that schools are open to all without discrimination, and are therefore public and egalitarian. *Laïcité* remains a central issue, as has been indicated in recent years by conflicts over the wearing of Islamic scarves (the *affaire du foulard*). For Bayrou, Minister of Education until the elections of May 1997, *laïcité* is 'the keystone of living together in society' (Bayrou 1996: 133). The affirmation of these principles in the laws of 1881 and 1882 played a major part in unifying French society around a moral order based on republican values (see also Chapter 5).

It follows from the central principles outlined that the State has a pre-eminent role in education, as in other aspects of French society. The reforms which allowed English schools to opt out of local authority control and assume a quasi-independent status under the direction of a headteacher and board of governors cannot be imagined in France. Nevertheless, the crude view of French education as totally controlled from the centre is far from the truth. A major concern of educational reform in recent years, seen above all in the decentralization reforms of 1982 and 1985, has been to achieve a balance of central and local control: on the one hand, a degree of decentralization and autonomy throughout the system which allows individual institutions to adapt and innovate; on the other, a concern not to increase social inequalities or prejudice the coherence of the system as a whole.

Since the early 1970s, France has faced the same challenges as other advanced nations in adapting its educational system to the enormously increased demand for education and qualifications and in responding to the pressures of social and technological change. In a series of reforms, the system has attempted to meet the challenges while holding to the republican principles of public, secular and egalitarian education. The Background report prepared for the OECD examiners by the French Ministry of Education (OECD 1996: 17–18) lists four main orientations of French policy since 1970.

- promoting equal opportunity and avoiding the exclusion of a minority (the primary goal);
- improving quality and effectiveness in the context of mass education and unavoidable public spending restrictions;
- achieving a better match between the types of training available and employment prospects;
- steering an increasingly decentralized education system while promoting innovation and supporting change in a fast-moving environment.

In describing the current state of French education following the most recent reforms, this chapter will return constantly to these four orientations, and to the guiding principles of the republican school set out above. The fourth point is specific to France and the modernization of its centralized system. But the first three of these points could certainly stand for the objectives of education in England in recent years, or in any modern society.

Primary schools

Until the Berthouin reforms of 1959, French primary and secondary schools effectively operated as separate and parallel systems, and not as a unified concept. Primary education grew from the parish schools of the *ancien régime*, and was made compulsory in the laws of 1881 and 1882. These laws, inseparably linked to the name of the Minister, Jules Ferry, established the republican elementary school, 'free, secular and compulsory'. Elementary schools had their own corps of teachers, trained in *écoles normales*. The schools were closely associated with their local communes and developed their own sections, known as *cours complémentaires*, to cater for the secondary age range. Secondary education in the *lycées* grew from a different tradition. They were founded by Napoleon in 1802 and administered centrally by the state. The corps of teachers was trained at university, and the pupils, drawn largely from the middle classes, followed a strict instructional regime to reach the level of the *baccalauréat* examination. There was little chance for pupils to enter secondary schools on merit alone, and many bright children from poor families gained access to the *baccalauréat* by completing elementary school and *cours complémentaires*, and then gaining entry to a teacher training college, there to prepare the *bac* and to become, themselves, elementary school teachers.

The most recent major reforms of primary education (this includes pre-elementary plus elementary schools) came into force at the beginning of the school year in 1991, following the Education Act (*Loi d'Orientation*) of 10 July 1989. With the objective of responding more flexibly to the differing rhythms of children's learning, and to avoid any sharp break between the pre-elementary school and elementary school, the primary phase of education was reorganized into three stages (see Table 9.1). The early learning stage covers the nursery age range from 2–5 years old. (99 per cent of French 3 year olds have places in pre-elementary school). The basic learning stage, 5–8, includes the upper-end of the nursery school and the first two classes of primary school. The development stage, 8–11, covers the last three years of the primary school. The recommended three years of each stage can be varied to two or four years to match the individual child's learning pattern, but such a variation can only occur once in the child's primary school career. Decisions on each child's progress are taken by the teachers responsible for the stage, the headteacher and members of the local advisers on educational psychology. Parents may appeal against this decision. The word *redoublement* (staying down to repeat a year's work) disappears from the vocabulary of the primary school, as the stages are intended to avoid repetition of an identical year's work. The curriculum and the learning objectives for each stage are laid down centrally. Great stress is laid on the curriculum as child-centred (a relatively new concept in French education) and coherent. Coherence is given to the programme of subject studies (French, history, geography, civic education, maths, science and technology, physical and artistic education) by a stress on cross-curricular life-skills: use of reference materials; interpretation of images; information technology (Programme de l'école primaire 1996). Maximum and minimum hours per week are laid down, but within this range teachers may adapt their programmes week by week and year by year. The weekly teaching time totals twenty-six hours, releasing one hour per week (thirty-six hours per year) for the 'school project' and for staff meetings and meetings scheduled to discuss children's work and progress. The teaching of a foreign language to primary school children is gradually being extended. *Le Monde* (31 August 1996) reported that 500,000 children aged 7–8 years were now involved in foreign language classes. (These figures should be seen in the context of some 6 million pupils in primary schools.)

Table 9.1 Outline structure of the French education system

Age					
23					
22					
21			GE		
20					
19	Univ	IUT	CPGE	STS	
18					
17	Terminale		LG and LT	LP	
16	Ire		**Lycée**		CFA
15	2e	*Decision stage*			
14	3e	*Orientation stage*			
13	4e	*Development*			
12	5e	*stage*	**Lower Secondary Comprehensive**		
11	6e	*Observation stage*		**(Collège)**	
10	CM2				
9	CMI	*Development stage (8–11)*			
8	CE2	**Primary School (Ecole élémentaire)**			
7	CEI				
6	CP	*Basic learning stage (5–7)*			
2–5	**Pre-elementary School (Ecole maternelle)**				

Key: GE = Grandes écoles; IUT = Instituts universitaires de technologie; CPGE = Classes préparatoires; STS = Sections de technicien supérieur; LG = Lycée général; LT= Lycée technologique; LP = Lycée professionnel; CFA = Centre de formation d'apprentis; CM = Cours moyen; CE = Cours élémentaire; CP = Cours préparatoire.

Each school is free to choose the organization of classes which suits its local conditions; for example, the same teacher might follow a class for all three years of the stage; or children might be grouped by stage and not by age. All possibilities are accepted within the main objective, 'to ensure the continuity of learning without pointless repetition or interruption'. There is also a move, supported by the Sports Minister as well as by the Minister of Education, to restructure the primary school day so that afternoons can be devoted to sporting activities. Although only around 100,000 children are so far involved, a pilot scheme involving two *départements* was planned to start in September 1997.

The school's individual strategy for meeting local needs is the school project. This is a sort of contract defined for a fixed period, usually three years. The project is drawn up as a precise plan of action by the school's educational team co-ordinated by the headteacher, and with the co-operation and collaboration of parent representatives. The novelty of the idea, within the French system, is the conviction that education is not limited to the school premises.

Secondary schools

The reform of primary education introduced in September 1992 was the first really significant change this century, apart from the hiving off of *cours complémentaires* in 1959 ('For almost 100 years the primary school has not moved', *Le Monde de l'Education*, September 1991: 23). But secondary schools have undergone a continuous series of major reforms starting with the Berthouin reform of 1959, which raised the school leaving age to 16, introduced secondary schools for all from the age of 11, and established the idea of the *lycée* as a kind of sixth form college. Subsequent strengthening of the comprehensive principle followed, notably in the Haby reforms of 1975, which established the comprehensive *collège unique* for the age range 11–15 years. The *collège*, though much criticized and since subject to further reforms, was a key element in establishing equality of opportunity and access to further and higher education.

These reforms built up a single path of development from primary schools, through the *collège* and on to sixth form and further education in one of three types of *lycée* as appropriate to aptitudes and ability. (See Table 9.1). Whereas it was always the case that primary schools were closely associated with their communities, secondary schools had no such local link until given a degree of local autonomy by the decentralization laws of 1982 and 1983. The *collège* then came under the administrative supervision of the *département*, and the *lycée* under that of the region. 1982 also saw the establishment of educational priority areas, a major effort to improve the working of the *collège* in deprived urban areas. Following the Legrand report of 1982, moves were made during the 1980s to buildup active educational projects where schools developed program-mes bringing them closer to their local population, and established links with firms and cultural organizations. The then Education Minister Lionel Jospin's *Loi d'Orientation* of 1989 made this school project compulsory for all schools, guiding teachers towards working in teams, individualizing the learning path for pupils, giving responsibilities to the school and involving parents. Despite doubts and uncertainties on the part of teachers and others, these moves can be seen as major steps towards the objectives of combating failure and aiding social integration.

A second aspect of recent developments aimed at involving the community and, in particular, parents in school developments has been the school contract (*Contrat pour l'école*) of François Bayrou. The text of the contract was published in June 1994, after wide-ranging consultation. Its 158 paragraphs cover the entire field of the French school system, setting dates for fulfilling key objectives. A shortened version of the document groups the paragraphs under a series of headings which recall the main orientations of policy set out earlier in this chapter:

- clarify aims and increase social cohesion;
- give absolute priority to the fight against inequality;
- welcome and encourage diversity;
- a new management policy; have confidence in local manage-ment.

(Le Nouveau Contrat 1994)

The bulletin of the Ministry of Education for November 1996 reports that all 158 paragraphs are now being applied in some form throughout the country. The closer involvement of parents in the work of schools is a feature of the Contract as it is of the School Project described on p. 177. Parental involvement in schools is another development which France has in common with other countries, for example, all English schools must now have parents as members of their governing body.

The reform of the baccalauréat

The French do not like anyone touching their *bac*, claimed *Le Monde de l'Education* in an article which appeared in January 1995. But the *bac* was the subject of a rolling reform which began with the reorganization of the teaching programme in 1992 and was completed by the first examinations in 1995. The reform must be seen within the context of growth of the *lycée*, which had been an élite and selective institution until the reforms of the Fifth Republic. Between 1960 and 1996 the numbers of students at this stage of the educational process grew from 805,000 to 2,200,000 (Repères et Références Statistiques 1996: 192). At the same time, the percentage of the age group entering for the *bac* grew from 10 per cent at the end of the 1950s to 30 per cent in 1970 and 62.7 per cent in 1996. According to the aims set out in Jospin's orientation law, 80 per cent of the age group should gain the *bac* (either general, technical or vocational) by the year 2000. The *lycée* now offers a three-year course, from age 15, as set out in Table 9.2. The general plan of studies follows certain clear principles:

- a common core of studies in the first year of the course (*seconde*) for all students whatever their specialisms;
- a sequence of options which are intended to open up a coherent path of studies and not to close doors irrevocably. The students are encouraged to see the progress through the three years to the *bac* as part of a strategy of making choices.

In *seconde*, seven subjects form the common curriculum for all students, providing a balance between humanities, science, mathematics, languages and physical education. There are three hours of compulsory modules for extended or support studies in French, maths, foreign language and history/geography. In addition, two options must be chosen from a list of fifteen possibilities (some of these are relatively rare, and not all *lycées* can offer a full list). Pupils are encouraged to choose their options as part of their long-term plan. A second foreign language is urged for all pupils, and the other option might be seen as a support for the likely choice of *bac* (literary, scientific, technological or social scientific bias). In *première* decisions are made about which of the main routes of the *bac* to follow; in *terminale* specialisms and the specific, individual 'profile' of each student are developed.

Table 9.2 Paths to the *baccalauréat* (table to be read from left to right)

General studies path

	Première L, ES, S	Terminale L, ES, S	**Bac Général**	Higher Education
Seconde Générale et Technologique	**Technological path**			

	Première Technological options	Terminale Technological options	**Bac Techno- logique**	HE
Seconde Spécifique	Première spécifique Bac Hôtellerie	Terminale spécifique	**Brevet de Technicien**	Work/HE
	Première d'adaptation			

Vocational path

	Terminale BEP	**BEP**	Première/ Terminale Professionale	**Bac Profess- ional**	Work
Seconde					
Preparation for CAP		**Certificat d'Aptitude Professionnel**		Work	

Note: The Diplomas of Vocational Education, BT, BEP and CAP, can also be prepared via apprenticeships in a *Centre de formation des apprentis* (CFA).

Key: L= Literary; ES = Social Sciences; S = Natural Sciences.

The analysis by contributors to *Le Monde de l'Education* in its January 1995 survey claims that the *bac* is still too overloaded and overly rigid in the paths it lays down, but it is perhaps too early to make a fair judgement.

Private education

Some 14 per cent of primary age children and 20 per cent of secondary age children are in private schools, which are for the most part Catholic institutions. The Falloux law of 1850 restricted local authority funding of private schools, and established the role of the Church in running educational institutions. Any attempt to change the balance leads very easily to confrontation, as has happened twice in recent years (see also Chapter 11). In 1984, the Savary plan, which proposed a single, secular public service, was shelved after mass rallies in the streets. In 1993, despite demonstrations, Bayrou pushed through a vote amending the Falloux law and allowing local authorities to exceed the 10 per cent limit on funding to private schools. The current legal framework for relations between the state and private schools was laid down by the Debré law of 1959. The law states that, on the one hand the state should not interfere with the freedom and independence of private schools; on the other, it should monitor the quality of education and ensure that republican values are maintained. Contracts ensure that teachers are paid by the State, and certain other running costs may be met as long as the schools meet teaching quality criteria and comply with the national curricula. In general, day pupils are educated free of charge except for a contribution towards maintenance costs and religious instruction.

Technical and vocational education

The OECD Examiners' report of 1971 was unusually critical of contradictions in the French education system:

> which rests on the idea of equality but in which failure is the lot of most people, which teaches fraternity but stresses competition and which celebrates liberty but offers most individuals only limited options.
>
> (OECD 1971: 27)

A series of measure in the 1970s and 80s sought to address these criticisms. Among these measures was the development of technical and vocational training (see Table 9.3). The culmination of this process was the goal included in the 1989 reform of bringing one hundred per cent of a school generation to a recognized level of qualification by the year 2000 and the statutory right for all pupils to vocational training. The progress of French education in this field is shown by the figures reported by Green and Steedman (1993):

4.2.2 Stocks of skills in the labour force: Britain and France

In the 1960s, stocks of recognized vocational qualifications held by the French labour force were below British levels. Since the 1960s France has made continued efforts to remedy the situation and overtook Britain in the early 1970s. Of particular interest is the much more rapid growth in craft-level qualifications achieved by France in the 10-year period 1979–89. During this period, the stock of craft-level qualifications in the labour force in Britain grew by only three percentage points. In France, stocks increased by 25 per cent from a higher base.

4.2.3 Growth in skills attributed to educational planning

A National Institute study attributes the more rapid French growth rate to the more systematic planning and management of educational provision in France offering all young people full-time training and education within the education system leading to a recognized craft-qualification.

(Green and Steedman 1993: 29)

French post-compulsory education and training is predominantly school-based. For most pupils the final year of compulsory secondary education is the fourth year of *collège*, but some students may transfer to a *lycée professionnel* (LP) after two years of *collège*. Students following a technical track at LP prepare for the *Brevet d'Etudes Professionnelles* (BEP) or the *Certificat d'Aptitude Professionnelle* (CAP) at the age of 16. The CAP is considered to be at the same level as the BEP but is more closely linked to specific occupations, particularly skilled manual occupations. With the increasing popularity of the BEP and the *baccalauréat professionnel* (*bac pro*) enrolments on the CAP are declining (OECD 1996: 81). The *bac pro* was introduced in 1985, and after a period when it had low esteem, has gained in status recently because of its value on the jobs market. The course for the *bac pro* lasts two years in the LP and covers twenty-six different vocational programmes of study, each relating to broadly based occupational areas, and all sharing an extensive common core curriculum of general studies. For full-time students, depending on the subject, there is a requirement for sixteen weeks of work experience:

> normally comprising eight weeks for each year of the course, arranged into two blocks of four weeks. Employers are expected to organize realistic programmes of work which enable the students to gain skills using equipment which is not always available in the *lycée*.

(HMSO 1993: 5)

Over 70 per cent of 16–18 year olds are in full-time education and only 15 per cent in apprenticeships. In their report to the OECD examiners (OECD 1996: 81) the French authorities refer to 'the constant efforts to bring vocational training out of the educational ghetto and to increase the internal fluidity of the training system'. They point out how this fluidity has been gained by introducing possibilities for crossing over between general and vocational streams at key orientation points in the system, for example between *collège* and *lycée*. In approaches to vocational education, as in perhaps no other area, national educational policies converge. The need for a highly educated and professionally competent workforce has, in all societies, led to a need to achieve parity of esteem for vocational qualifications. Achieving German levels of vocational qualification and labour productivity has been seen as an objective by both France and the UK. French achievements in this area, as documented by Green and Steedman (1993) are impressive, though it must be doubted, as in the UK, whether parity of esteem has yet been achieved. (But see the comments above on the changing valuation of the *bac pro*.)

The next major reform of vocational education is scheduled for 1999, when the quinquennial law on employment of 1993 finally

Table 9.3 The vocational education system in France

Age			
	First stage of university studies:		
20	BTS = Brevet de Technicien Supérieur;		
19	DUT = Diplôme Universitaire de Technologie		
18			
17	Bac Professional	Brevet de Technicien	
16		CAP BEP	
15	LP	Seconde de détermination (Decision stage)	CFA (Apprentice training)
14		4th year of *collège*	

Note: Over 70 per cent of 16–18 year olds are in full-time education, and only 15 per cent are in apprenticeships.

comes into force, making regional councils directly responsible for vocational training and guidance into employment. By January 1996, fifteen of the twenty-two metropolitan regions had already moved to take on this responsibility. The outcome of this transfer of power is still difficult to predict.

Careers guidance and the job market

Orientation is a word much used in French education, with a general meaning of guidance through the system, from class to class and from school to school, and a more specific meaning of advice about careers and future job and study prospects. In the case of careers education, this is organized and operated by regional centres. Jospin's orientation law sought to place the pupil at the centre of the whole process. The new school contract also suggests a list of measures affecting guidance and orientation, and the same theme is taken up in advice to parents, for example, on the subject of guidance at the end of each year of secondary school:

> Guidance is a matter of consensus and working together. As long as a dialogue is established between teachers and families…[teachers] appreciate parents who regularly ask, once a term, to meet the head of department and check on the achievements of their child at school. […] so we are a long way from the time when the class council debated these issues in strict privacy.
>
> (ONISEP July 1996: 17)

The HMSO report on vocational education in France draws attention to the high priority given to careers education and guidance in French schools, and to the improvements brought in by the 1989 law:

> One aspect of this made teachers as well as career specialists responsible for careers guidance. All careers advisers are trained educational psychologists. They spend approximately one day a week in school working closely with class teachers. This provision is available from the age of 11 and takes place on an individual, small group or class basis. The main focus, however, is on those about to leave school or enter vocational education.
>
> (HMSO 1993: 7–8)

But a more negative note on the problems of careers guidance in a shrinking jobs market for young people is expressed in the following extract from an interview with the Director of a regional centre for careers guidance:

> It seems that since last year [1995] the attitude of young people to work has changed somewhat. From 1985 there was the idea that if you couldn't find a job, it was because you didn't have qualifications...so there was a considerable demand for more education and training. Over the last year, numbers have been dropping in training courses. We put on a lot of courses for those aged 16–25, and many of these courses are empty. The other solution was apprenticeships with firms, but we are noticing that many young people are abandoning apprenticeships; and many young people say that it's not worth investing the effort, because whether you have qualifications or not, vocational training or not, it's all the same when it comes to getting a job.

Higher education

The reform of teacher training

One of the proposals in Jospin's *Loi d'Orientation* of 1989 was to offer training at university level for all teachers. The plan was to complete a process begun in 1979 (and which itself goes back to a proposal in Edgar Faure's law of 1968). French universities have not previously been involved with the training of all teachers. Departments of Educational Sciences are newcomers to the universities, having been established first in 1967, and being concerned solely with the theory of educational research. The divide between the training of elementary school teachers and teachers in *lycées* had always been strongly marked. The university and the *école normale*, where elementary school teachers were trained represented two different worlds, each of which had always jealously defended its own territory. For the duality of training was a reflection of the division between the elementary school for the children of workers and peasants and the *lycée* for children from professional and well-to-do families. From the *lycée* the way led directly to university or a *grande école*. From the elementary school the way led to work or, at the age of 14, directly into the *école normale*, firstly to receive a secondary education leading to the *baccalauréat* and then to qualify as an *instituteur*. Jules Ferry pushed through his school reforms in the laws of 1881 and 1882, but first he had to train the teachers who would carry through his campaign. In 1879 he established an *école normale* in each *département*, and it was teachers from these training colleges who between 1880 and 1914 went out to every village in the land to disseminate the principles and beliefs of the Third Republic. Only after the Second World War did the nature of the *école normale* gradually change. With the school reforms of 1959 and 1963, all children were given the chance of a secondary education. The traditional bond between village school and *école normale* was broken. Pupils now prepared their *bac* in secondary schools, and the rise of comprehensive education led to the need to create a more unified teaching profession. The social conditions which had given the *école normale* its quite distinct character were also rapidly changing. Not only were students older, many of them entering at age 23 and with a university degree, but they came from the bourgeoisie as well as from workers' families (Berger 1979).

The period 1968–79 saw a number of developments which indicated the move towards university participation in teacher education, but the time was not yet ripe for such a fundamental change. An important factor was the tradition of the elementary school teacher, the *instituteur*. Prost (1991) points out that in 1968 the union of *instituteurs* did not wish to fight for university education for its members, fearing the loss of 'democratic recruitment'. But changes came gradually. In 1969 the training time was extended from one to two years, and in 1971 a start was made in closing down the preparatory class for the *bac*. In 1979 the training period was extended to three years and the first efforts at collaboration between *école normale* and university led to shared course units and the joint preparation of the first general diploma of university studies (DEUG). *Professeurs* of the *lycée*, as in such schools throughout Europe, needed no training beyond their subject competence for many years. Beyond the first degree there was only the highly demanding academic competitive examination offered by the *agrégation* until 1952, when a new qualification was introduced, the *Certificat d'aptitude au professorat de l'enseignment du second degré* (CAPES). The CAPES is also a competitive academic examination, but after 1952 a network of regional centres for pedagogical training was set up to provide training seminars for CAPES candidates during their first year of teaching.

By 1989, the teacher training situation in France was as follows:

all students, in whichever institution, studied for four years before entering the profession. It was within this context that Jospin introduced the new law on teacher education and announced the founding of a new institution, the *Institut universitaire de formation des maîtres* (IUFM). The IUFM brings together, for the first time, the training of all teachers within an institution of university rank. Students are recruited after three years or more of university studies, and follow a two year course. The historical and traditional title of *instituteur* has been dropped (to the chagrin of many commentators) and primary school teachers will in future be known as *professeurs des écoles*. Secondary teachers are now *professeurs des lycées et collèges*. At the end of the first year of study, which is concerned with developing subject competence, students have to enter for the competitive examination of their particular branch, CAPES for secondary school teachers (or more specialized variations for technical and sports teachers), CAPE for primary school teachers (*Certificat d'aptitude au professorat des écoles*). Success in the examination confers civil servant status and allows salaried progress into the second year which includes extended periods of block practice in schools. At the end of the second year the student receives certification from the institution for completing the course, followed by the official recognition of the qualification by the authorities and nomination to a teaching post.

It seems somewhat ironic, to a British observer, that at the moment when teacher education in France has reached university status and a two year course of post-graduate training, the policy of the British government has been to retreat from university education of teachers. The one year course of post-graduate teacher-training in England is increasingly seen as predominantly school-based, following a model which owes more to nineteenth century views of teacher apprenticeship than to a university education of teachers for the twenty-first century. (Parts of the above section are drawn from Neather 1993.)

The universities

In 1985, the then Education Minister, Jean-Pierre Chevènement, set the aim for 80 per cent of the age group to gain the *bac* by the year 2000. This was followed by an explosion of student numbers in the *lycées*. In 1989, ninety-five new *lycées* were built, and the *lycée* was transformed from an élitist establishment to a centre of mass education. With 90 per cent of *bacheliers* (those successful at the *bac*), choosing to go on to university, the growth in numbers hit the universities in the late 1980s. In 1980 there were 1,180,000 students in France; in 1994 there were 2 million:

> Since 1990, the will of the authorities to balance the flow of students between the more or less selective paths such as University Institutes of Technology (IUT), Higher Technician Sections (STS) preparatory classes and *grandes écoles* (all taking 39% of the total) and the university routes (61%) came up against the immovable elements in the French system. The *grandes écoles* refused to increase their levels of entry. The universities started to crack.
>
> (Compagnon and Thévenin 1995: 193)

Despite desperate attempts to adjust to the strains on buildings and resources, the standards of university education have suffered (Fauroux 1996: 26) Many of the students' complaints were forcibly expressed by sit-ins and confrontations during the autumn of 1995. A further bone of contention is the failure rate. Statistics vary, but up to 40 per cent of students fail at the end of their first year (ibid.: 25), and leave university with no qualifications. But any suggestion that there should be a more selective entry than is provided by the *bac* is quickly rejected by the student unions.

To assist the administration in coping with the flow of students, the State voted a law in 1990 which allowed the responsibility for new university building to be taken over by the regions. In the same year the 'University 2000' plan was adopted, which projected the building of ten new universities as well as the renovation of older ones. In addition, universities have been encouraged to form financial links with businesses. Research co-operation is leading more frequently to joint laboratories and the sharing of technological know-how. Business links are also essential for universities to be able to direct their graduates into suitable posts. More and more courses have taken on a vocational direction since the mid-1980s in response to students who see their studies as having specifically vocational outputs. For example, the two year courses leading to the Diploma of Science and Technology (DEUST) respond to local and regional employment needs. The University Institutes of Vocational Studies follow on from the first year of higher education and offer a three year course in such subjects as financial management and sales management. Courses leading to a Master's degree with a vocational bias are also popular, for example the *Maîtrise de sciences et gestion* (MSG) or the *Maîtrise de sciences et techniques* (MST) are run as sandwich courses between the university and business.

Classes préparatoires *and the* grandes écoles

The *grandes écoles* have an unchallenged reputation for preparing the French élite for the top jobs in government, administration or business. Graduates of the *Ecole nationale d'adminstration* or of the *Polytechnique* seem destined to move effortlessly up the ladder of preferment. As the universities have cracked under the strain of increasing numbers and diversification of courses, the *grandes écoles* have remained élitist, selective and relatively small in size. (The *Polytechnique* had a total of 1,146 students in 1991–2.) They have a predominantly scientific, engineering or business bias. The most ancient, the *Ecole nationale des ponts et chaussées* (ENPC) was founded in 1747 for the training of civil engineers. The most famous, the *Ecole Polytechnique*, was founded as the *Ecole centrale de travaux publics* in 1794 and was renamed in 1795. In 1804, Napoleon gave it its status as a military institution, and it is still administered by the Ministry of Defence. The famous *Ecole nationale d'administration* is a newcomer by comparison, founded in 1945 and since then producing many leading members of the government and the top echelons of the adminstration and financial establishment. A study published on the fiftieth anniversary of the founding of ENA revealed that 86 per cent of *énarques* had passed most of their career in public service and only 14 per cent had passed part of their career in the private sector.

Entry to the *grandes écoles* is by fiercely competitive examination taken after two years of further study following the *bac*. These studies are carried out in preparatory classes, usually located in selected *lycées*. The courses of the *classes prépa* were reformed at the beginning of the 1995 school year. *Le Monde de l'Education* (February 1995) summarized the reforms as follows:

> The aim [of the reform] is to provide more variety in the access routes to the élite paths of the educational system. Maths should no longer be the queen of all disciplines, the only criterion for selection and for the reputation of students, lycées and courses.

Inevitably, there is a tendency to group the *grandes écoles* together as if they were a coherent body of like institutions, but there are considerable differences between them. Jean-Pierre Nioche (reported in *Le Monde de l'Education*, December 1995: 31) makes a distinction between, on the one hand, the schools which are market-oriented, such as the business schools and schools of engineering, and, on the other hand, the schools which exercise a monopoly over recruitment into certain high levels of the civil service (for example, *Polytechnique*, ENA, *Ponts et chaussées*, Inspection of Finances, etc.).

The popularity and power of the *grandes écoles* seem unchallenged, but there have been critical voices raised. In certain areas, the universities have offered significant competition, for example in business administration. More generally there are questions asked about the whole élitist nature of these institutions in the current social climate and at a time when businesses are reducing hierarchies and exercising power more collectively. Finally, in an international perspective, there are doubts about the *grandes écoles* and their capacity to adapt to the global economy, to recruit on an international scale or to make their training system more flexible.

Conclusion

There is no denying the scale of changes and reforms in French education during the last forty years. The problems have been formidable. How can the traditional values of the republican school be maintained within a fast changing modern society? How can the claims of democracy and the education of an élite be reconciled? How can an increasingly decentralized system be steered while maintaining coherence and avoiding destabilization? How is it possible to cope with the explosion of demand for further and higher education? How can training and job guidance be offered to the broad range of school leavers? Many parallels could be drawn with other developed societies confronting the pressures of mass education in a period of accelerating social and economic change. But specifically French solutions have to be found for problems which arise when the need for change meets the weight of French tradition. One central and enduring problem remains the move from a centralized to a more devolved system of educational administration and responsibility. The education system may still not be ready to react swiftly enough to opportunities and needs arising in local contexts. The Fauroux report (1996: 32) calls specifically for greater autonomy at the level of the individual institution as a major factor in meeting current problems. The OECD report makes the same point when it states:

> decentralization may be a necessary prerequisite, but it is certainly not the only one, for overcoming the strategic obstacles stemming from a high degree of centralization. It would be a mistake to place too much hope in a simple redistribution of powers, responsibilities and resources. For one thing, it has to be emphasized that the dead weight of a long tradition of centralism still exists.
>
> (OECD 1996: 249)

There are other issues which face the French educational planners in the immediate future; educational failure, particularly among immigrant families and in areas of urban deprivation; the appropriate balance between initial education and lifelong education; the need for the education system to react flexibly to the pace of social change and the individual's need to retrain and readapt to the demands of the job market.

The measure of public support for the major post-war reforms is considerable. The continuing confidence of parents in the school system, was evident from the SOFRES survey quoted at the beginning of this chapter. The high priority accorded to the education system by successive ministers and governments is shown by the budget allocations over the twenty-one years from 1974 to 1995. The total education budget for metropolitan France:

> rose to 563 billion francs in 1995 that is to say a rise of 81.5% since 1974 (growth in real terms) which represents an annual growth of around 2.9%. Over the same period the gross national product rose by 55.2%, that is 2.1% per annum. In 1974 the education budget represented 6.3% of GNP; in 1995 the figure is 7.3%.
>
> (Repères et Références Statistiques 1996: 248)

The Fauroux report placed education at the centre of any debate on the future of French society (1996: 13) and the conclusion of the report stresses the need for a more flexible approach to the individual in an age of shifting work patterns and qualifications which become outdated.

In this report we have [...] pleaded with the school to fight with all its strength to ensure or to re-establish equality of opportunity for all pupils. There will be a point to such a long and difficult path only if business and administration and above all the national education system [...] decide to judge adults by different standards than [...] the qualifications they acquired at the age of twenty.

(ibid.: 247)

Similar questions point to future concerns in the conclusions of the OECD report:

Is it possible permanently to reconcile the principle of equal educational opportunities with job structures and functions that are highly unequal and characterized by the juxtaposition of 'intellectual' and 'manual' tasks, of mental and physical abilities?

How can a situation be reached where the desires and abilities of all youngsters will be globally compatible with the jobs available and necessity for the survival and well-being of society, and in what ways could the education system contribute to this?

What could and should be the proportion of time devoted to education and training activities throughout an individual's life?

(OECD 1996: 245)

The change of government in May 1997 resulted in Lionel Jospin taking over the role of Prime Minister. It is clear from references in the preceding pages that Jospin himself, when Minister of Education, was responsible for launching a number of current initiatives in his law of 1989. It is therefore unlikely that there will be any major change of policy, and this has been confirmed by the new Minister, Claude Allègre, who has already agreed to the continuing application of Bayrou's university reforms. Jospin himself, in his general parliamentary statement of 19 June 1997, underlined the place of the school as 'the cradle of the Republic, which must guarantee the acquisition of civic responsibility'. And so, in the final sentence as in the first sentence of this chapter, education, the republic and French national identity are brought together into a single and indivisible concept: both a political programme and an act of faith.

Bibliography

Bayrou, F. (1996) *Droit au sens*, Paris: Flammarion.

Berger, I. (1979) *Les Instituteurs d'une Génération à l'Autre*, Paris: PUF.

Bourdoncle, R. and Louvet, A. (eds) (1991) *Les Tendances nouvelles dans la formation des enseignants: stratégies françaises et expériences Ètrangères*, Paris: INRP.

Compagnon, B and Thévenin, A. (1995) *L'Ecole et la société française*, Paris: Éditions Complexes.

Dubet, F. and Martuccelli, D. (1996) *A l'Ecole*, Paris: Editions du Seuil.

Fauroux, R.(1996)*Pourl'Ècole*,('RapportFauroux'),Paris:Calmann-Lévy.

Férole, J. and Chevrel, A. (1995) *Transformer l'école – 210 propositions pratiques*, Paris: Hachette Education.

Green, A. and Steedman, H. (1993) *Educational Provision, Educational Attainment and the Needs of Industry*, London: National Institute of Economic Research.

HMSO (1993) *Aspects of Vocational Education in France*, London: HMSO.

Legrand, A. (1994) *Le Système E.*, Paris: Denoël.

Legrand, L. (1983) *Pour un collège démocratique. Rapport au ministre de l'Éducation nationale*, Paris: La Documentation Française.

Lesourne, J. (1987) *Education et société demain. Rapport au ministre de l'éducation nationale*, Paris.

Neather, E. (1993) 'Teacher education and the role of the university: European perspectives', *Research Papers in Education*, 8(1): 33–46.

OECD, (1971) *Reviews of National Policy for Education: France*, Paris: OECD.

——(1996) *Reviews of National Policy for Education: France*, Paris: OECD.

ONISEP (1996) *De la 6e au bac: spécial parents*, July, Paris: ONISEP.

Prost, A. (1991)'Le passé du présent: D'où viennent les IUFM?', in R. Bourdoncle and A. Louvet (eds) *Les tendances nouvelles dans la formation des enseignants: Stratégies françaises et expériences étrangères*, Paris: INRP.

Rafaelli, G. (1996) *L'école en France*, Paris: Hachette.

Soubré, L. (1995) *L'école sous pressions*, Paris: Editions Stock.

Vasconcellos, M. (1993) *Le Système éducatif*, Paris: Editions de la Découverte.

Werrebrouck, J-C., (1995) *Déclaration des droits de l'école – Comprendre la crise de l'institution scolaire*, Paris: L'Harmattan.

Other sources

Press 1984–1997

Éducation
Le Monde
Le Monde de l'Education

*Ministère de l'Education Nationale, de l'Enseignement
Supérieur et de la Recherche*

(1992) Le Projet de l'Ecole, CNDP/Hachette.
(1994) Le Nouveau Contrat pour l'Ecole, Paris.
(1996) Programme de l'école primaire française.
(1996) La Lettre de l'Education Nationale (25 novembre).
(1996) Repères et Références Statistiques.

Chapter 10

Religion and *laïcité*

Grace Davie

This chapter is divided into four sections. The first outlines the facts and figures of religious life in France, underlining the changes that have occurred in the post-war period. The second sets the French situation within the context of western Europe. In many ways France represents a hybrid case: Catholic in culture, its religious indicators display a profile more usually found in the Protestant North. The third section explains in more detail the concept of *laïcité*,[1] an idea more fully developed in France than anywhere else in Europe. The fourth and final section uses a case study to illustrate the persisting tensions within the current situation; it traces the *affaire du foulard* through the early 1990s, with a particular emphasis on what it means to be a truly tolerant and pluralist society within western Europe at the end of the twentieth century.

Facts and figures

France remains a majority Catholic country, though the statistics that support such a statement are considerably less convincing than they were in the immediate post-war period. In the late 1950s, 90 per cent of French people declared themselves Catholic, a figure which has dropped to less than 70 per cent in the 1990s. A public opinion poll in 1994[2] produced a figure of 67 per cent (see Table 10.1), a drop which mirrored the fall in regular practice (now about 10 per cent on a weekly basis) and in the proportion of infants baptized within the Catholic Church. A whole range of other indicators tell the same story, the most striking of which is the fall in the number of vocations to the priesthood. At the beginning of the twentieth century, there were fourteen priests for every 10,000 inhabitants; in 1965 this number had fallen to seven. If the trends continue, there will be one (or less) priest for same number of people as the twentieth century gives way to the twenty-first. A country which ordained close to a thousand priests a year in the immediate post-war period, now ordains just over a hundred (Willaime 1996: 168). A dramatic change has undoubtedly taken place.[3]

There are, however, counter-tendencies. Certain forms of religion flourish in France, as they do elsewhere at the turn of millennium, notably the one-off gatherings for a special occasion (a papal visit or a particular anniversary). One such event took place in the summer of 1997 when more than a million, mostly young, people took part in the Mass at Longchamp racecourse which marked the climax of the twelfth celebration of the biennial World Youth Days. That such numbers were possible in August (essentially a holiday month) and in France, supposedly one of the most secular countries of Europe, astonished the pundits. The event needs, however, to be set in context. It mirrors (a) the growing success of pilgrimage sites (whether old – Lourdes, or new – Taizé) all over France, and indeed Europe, and (b) the widespread appeal of a range of charismatic figures – not only the Pope himself, but the late Mother Teresa and the more specifically French Abbé Pierre. Young people, the group who are most disenchanted with regular churchgoing or with Catholic dogma (Lambert 1994, 1995), are attracted by the emotionality of the large gathering and respond to the charisma of those whose lives embody unworldly values (Hervieu-Léger 1994). Theirs is a spirituality easily missed by the conventional statistics of religious attendance or credal statements; it cuts across conventional denominational boundaries.

How should such changes be interpreted? This question is best considered in light of the growing individualism in French religion, a shift which has equal significance for the religious minorities now present in modern France. Their relative profiles will be outlined before returning to the underlying theme.

Not all religious minorities are recent arrivals: indeed both the Protestant and the Jewish communities have been part of French culture for centuries. Both communities, moreover, though numerically small, have played a highly significant role in French history, not least in the political vicissitudes of the Third Republic (Encrevé 1985; Marrus 1985; Baubérot 1988; Cholvy 1991). Their evolutions in the post-war period have, however, been markedly different.

First the Protestants. The size of this community is difficult to estimate: in 1995, 1.7 million French people (3 per cent of the

Table 10.1 Indices of religious attachment (1986 and 1994), shown in percentages

Religious identity

What is your religion, if you have one?	1994	1986
Catholic	67	81
Protestant	2	—
Jewish	1	—
Muslim	2	—
Orthodox	—	—
Other	3	—
No religion	23	15.5
No answer	2	—

Do you consider yourself to be:		
A convinced believer	24	30
A believer by tradition	24	—
An uncertain believer	17	13
A sceptic	14	—
A non-believer	19	14
No answer	2	—

Indices of religious belief

Does the existence of God seem to you to be:		
Certain	29	—
Probable	32	—
Improbable	17	—
Out of the question	18	—
No answer	4	—

What do you think will happen after death?		
Something, but I am not sure what	38	—
Nothing	25	—
Another life in another realm	22	—
Reincarnation	11	—
No answer	4	—

The Church and individual conscience

In the major decisions of life, do you take notice of your conscience or the teaching of the Church?		
Conscience	83	—
The teaching of the Church	1	—
Both	9	—
Neither	6	—
No answer	1	—

Source: Information taken from the CSA/*Le Monde* poll, published in *Le Monde*, 12 May 1994.

population) declared themselves 'close to Protestantism', though 27 per cent of these were members of the Catholic Church. A figure of 2 per cent is probably closer to the mark. More to the point, the Protestants have lost considerable numbers of those prepared to support their churches financially and regular practice continues to fall (Willaime 1996: 168–9). A vague attraction to the ideals of Protestantism does not count for much when it comes to paying pastors. In this respect, the gradual erosion of the community mirrors the process taking place in the French Catholic Church. Conversely the Protestant constituency still produces disproportionate numbers of individuals who become prominent in French public life (notably, though not exclusively, in the Parti Socialiste) and in the business world. Indeed there is a school of thought that suggests that the real problem for Protestant identity is the 'protestantization' of French culture as a whole. The growing emphasis on individualism and personal freedoms is one such shift, though there is less evidence of a Calvinist austerity. In such circumstances, it becomes increasingly difficult to delineate a Protestant specificity, a necessary element in the formation of identity (Baubérot 1988, Willaime 1992).

The Jewish population, on the other hand, has doubled in size in the post-war period, a shift brought about by the influx of Sephardic Jews from North Africa. (The Jewish population is currently estimated at 5–600,000, and is the largest Jewish community in Europe.) The causes of this immigration are multiple but include the Suez crisis, the decolonization of the Maghreb and the repercussions of the Israeli–Arab conflict, especially in Muslim countries. The new arrivals tend, moreover, to settle in different places from the long-standing Jewish communities; they have also altered profoundly the demographic and cultural profile of French Jewry. Questions of identity are posed with greater urgency and find expression in an increasing number of Jewish schools and places of worship, both of which become centres for the rediscovery of Jewish roots and Jewish history (Azria 1996). Regrettably, anti-Semitism, easily alarmed by signs of Jewish consciousness, cannot be considered entirely a thing of the past.

The Muslim community, however, is by far the largest religious minority in modern France (Etienne 1989, 1991 and Kaltenbach 1991; Kepel 1991). In origin, it is largely an immigrant population from North Africa and very different from its British equivalent. British Muslims come for the most part from the Indian sub-continent and relatively few are Arabs. In France, in contrast, the words Muslim and Arab are almost interchangeable in popular parlance. The patterns of immigration are, however, similar in both countries. Initially a largely male and necessarily rootless population responded to demands for labour in France (as in other west European countries) but assumed a moderately rapid return home. The gradual awareness that residence was likely to be permanent transformed the situation. Wives and families arrived to join their menfolk, at which point the demand for institutional foci for both community and religious life became widespread. The number of mosques on French soil – a visible indicator of permanent presence – grew from a handful in the early 1970s to more than a thousand by 1990 (see Chapter 2).

It is difficult to give a precise figure as to how many Muslims are currently living in France, this is because estimates depend to a large extent on the accuracy of immigration figures. A conservative estimate indicates a community of between 3 and 4 million. The French Muslim community is the largest in west Europe; it remains, none the less, a minority, a situation that is bound to result in tension. The particular nature of this tension is, however, a two-sided affair as the Islamic minority negotiates its position within French society, a nation noted for its emphasis on *laïcité* and the Jacobin tradition. The third and fourth sections of this chapter will explore this tension in some detail.

If we return now to the underlying features of religious life in modern France, it is evident that the traditional churches are losing ground in terms of their institutional presence and capacity to control both the beliefs and practices of most French people. Religion, whatever the affiliation (or lack of affiliation) of the respondent, is becoming increasingly a matter of self-definition rather than a submission to institutional discipline. This is even more true of younger generations. An increasing pluralism has, it seems, encouraged the notion of choice, as French people – like most Europeans – work out their personal destinies, selecting from a growing range of alternatives on offer. Individual conscience is a better guide for most people than the teachings of the historic Church, notably in the area of personal morality.[4] Such a situation should not be exaggerated: the vast majority of French people will return to the fold at death, if not before. Choices, moreover, are framed by history and French history is indisputably Catholic. The parameters of French society cannot be altered that easily: time (public holidays) and space (the presence of a church spire) remain resolutely Catholic. Also enduring are deep-seated regional differences in religious practice or denominational distribution. Despite the mobilities of modern French society, these contrasts remain marked; some of them are illustrated in Chapter 5.

A further point is worth noting. Growing individualism does indeed lead to fragmentation within the religious sphere; a fragmentation that occurs *within* the institutions themselves as well as in the wider belief systems of modern societies. Choices, for example, proliferate within Catholicism as well as between Catholic teaching and the increasing range of alternatives on offer. One choice within this array can, however, manifest itself in a return to basics. In France, as indeed in other western societies, some lines are hardening as a certain type of individual selects religious alternatives with firm parameters. The attraction lies, precisely, in the firmness: in answers rather than questions, in eternities rather than explorations. Hence within Catholicism, the growing identity of the committed 'cathos' and within Protestantism the growing strength, relatively speaking, of evangelicals. Parallel movements can also be found within the minority faiths: within Judaism, encouraged by the attitudes of the new arrivals from North Africa, whose developed sense of identity or belonging stands in marked contrast to the assimilationist tendencies of the older Ashkenazi population; and within the Muslim community as each generation tries to come to terms with what it means to be a Muslim in a western, historically Christian, society.

A complex picture thus emerges: symptoms of weakness and fragmentation alongside the re-affirmation of belonging and identity on the part of certain minorities, whether Catholic, Protestant, Jewish or Muslim. The same combination can be found in many European countries as post-war immigration (mostly for economic reasons) has brought a range of minority faiths into Europe at precisely the moment that the historic faith was beginning to lose its influence. Each situation is, however, different: it is important to place the French case within a comparative perspective before looking more closely at the particularly French concept of *laïcité*.

The European framework: France as a hybrid case

France is a hybrid country in religious as well as geographical terms (Willaime 1998). Its 57 million people straddle Northern and Latin

Europe, incorporating a significant variety of climates and cultures between the English Channel and the Mediterranean. In religious terms, the hybrid takes a rather different form. We have already seen that most French people are Catholic by tradition and up to a point remain nominally attached to their Church. In many ways, however, their religious behaviour reflects the patterns of Northern Europe. Religious practice, for example, at approximately 10 per cent reflects the levels of Britain or Scandinavia rather than the Catholic South; similarly the percentage of the population assenting to 'belief in God' are closer to Calvinist or Lutheran areas than to Catholic populations of Latin Europe (only the Belgians show some similarity to the French).

Tables 10.2 and 10.3 'place' France within the European context in terms of both practice and indices of belief.[5] Those wishing to scrutinize this situation in more detail are referred to the publications of the European Values Study both for Europe as a whole and for more detail about France herself.

Why should France be so different from her Catholic neighbours? One answer to this question lies in the particular evolution of French society since the Revolution, a subject to which we must now turn.

The concept of *laïcité* – a French invention

The second article of the French Constitution describes France as 'une république indivisible, laïque, démocratique et sociale'. *Laïque*, or the noun *laïcité*, is the key concept here. France is a Republic that neither recognizes nor supports financially any particular religion, but which guarantees to all its citizens freedom of conscience and freedom to practise their respective faiths. More specifically it is a concept which denotes the *absence* of religion from public space and public affairs, the consequences of which are considerable in everyday life.

French people, for example, are taken aback to discover that Bishops of the Church of England sit by right in the House of Lords; they are equally bewildered to observe that each parliamentary session in Britain begins with an act of public prayer. Such gestures are unthinkable across the Channel, in a nation in which Church and State have been rigorously separate since 1905.[6] One very visual reminder of separation can be seen in the tomb of the unknown warrior. In France, this symbol of national pride can be found on secular soil; the tomb is placed beneath the Arc de Triomphe in the

Table 10.2 Frequency of church attendance in western Europe (1990), shown in percentages

	At least once a week	Once a month	Christmas, Easter, etc.	Once a year	Never
European average	29	10	8	5	40
Catholic countries					
Belgium	23	8	13	4	52
France	10	7	17	7	59
Ireland	81	7	6	1	5
Italy	40	13	23	4	19
Portugal	33	8	8	4	47
Spain	33	10	15	4	38
Mixed countries					
Great Britain	13	10	12	8	56
West Germany	19	15	16	9	41
Netherlands	21	10	16	5	47
Northern Ireland	49	18	6	7	18
Lutheran countries (attendance once a month or more)					
Denmark	—	11	—	—	—
Finland	—	—	—	—	—
Iceland	—	9	—	—	
Norway	—	10	—	—	—
Sweden	—	10	—	—	—

Source: Table adapted from Ashford and Timms (1992: 46); additional figures for the Lutheran countries from EVSSG data.

heart of the capital city. In Britain, the same symbol lies just inside the main door of Westminster Abbey where institutional Christianity (embodied in Anglican form) meets the secular world or indeed the world of popular belief. The 'burial' of the unknown warrior in Britain in 1920 took the form of a symbolic funeral under the auspices of the State church, at which the king was the chief mourner, a pattern reflected in the annual celebrations of remembrance held at the Cenotaph each November. In France there is no king, no State church and a strictly secular ceremony.

How has this pattern come about? The reasons are theological

Table 10.3 Extent of religious belief in western Europe (1990), shown in percentages

A belief in:	God	A soul	Life after death	Heaven	The devil	Hell	Sin	Resurrection of the dead
European average	70	61	43	41	25	23	57	33
Catholic countries								
Belgium	63	52	37	30	17	15	41	27
France	57	50	38	30	19	16	40	27
Ireland	96	84	77	85	52	50	84	70
Italy	83	67	54	45	35	35	66	44
Portugal	80	58	31	49	24	21	63	31
Spain	81	60	42	50	28	27	57	33
Mixed countries								
Great Britain	71	64	44	53	30	25	68	32
West Germany	63	62	38	31	15	13	55	31
Netherlands	61	63	39	34	17	14	43	27
Northern Ireland	95	86	70	86	72	68	89	71
Lutheran countries								
Denmark	64	47	34	10	8	19	24	23
Finland	76	73	60	31	27	55	66	49
Iceland	85	88	81	19	12	57	70	51
Norway	65	54	45	24	19	44	44	32
Sweden	45	58	38	12	8	31	31	21

Source: Table adapted from Ashford and Timms (1992: 40); additional figures for the Lutheran countries from EVSSG data.

(or, more accurately, ecclesiological) as well as political. Paradoxically the emergence of an effective *laïcité* depends, in the first place, on a developed awareness of clericalism. That is why the notion of *laïcité* exists only in the Catholic cultures of Europe; and, more specifically, only in those where the Catholic Church was sufficiently allied to secular power to provoke a counterbalancing, or counter-Catholic, alternative. Within Protestantism, the opposition between clerical and lay (in ecclesiological terms) is much less sharp, leading to different formulations in church–State relationships. In the Protestant nations of Northern Europe it is more normal to find a greater degree of religious pluralism, with, more often than not, a Protestant State church coexisting with a culture which is secular in content but not oppositional.[7] Protestantism itself declericalized the church; there was no need for an anticlerical alternative outside the institutional framework of religion.

The French story fits well within this pattern. In the pre-Revolutionary period France had a dominant Catholic Church, which both legitimated, and was legitimated by, a regime in which no religious minority was able to flourish. There can be no doubt, moreover, that the emergence of 'une république indivisible, laïque, démocratique et sociale' is a tale of bitter conflict, accurately described as 'la guerre des deux Frances' (the war of two Frances). The two Frances are represented historically by (a) the political right closely allied to an autocratic Catholic Church and (b) by a nascent republic itself sheltering the two minority religions of the period, the Protestants and the Jews. One consequence of this struggle can be found in the sociological nature of the counter system (the notion of *laïcité* itself); this in turn becomes 'church-like' in its dogmas and institutional requirements. The following citation describes its dominant characteristics:

> [it is] effectively a civil religion, provided with its own Pantheon, its own hagiography, its own roll of martyrs and its own liturgy; a liturgy which takes different forms in different places but which is ubiquitous, and which has invented its own myths and rites, constructed its own altars and temples, and multiplied its own symbols, statues, frescoes, street names and school books to produce a permanent educative spectacle.
>
> (Nora 1984: 651)

There were two particular sites of contestation in this struggle: the school system and the State itself.

The battle for control of the school system dominated the first period of the Third Republic; its legacy can still be felt. It is an interesting story (Ozouf 1963, Chevallier 1981; see also Chapter 9), not least for the fact that the Protestant minority, though tiny, played a crucial role in the system which eventually emerged. All three of the

Minister's (Jules Ferry) advisors – Steeg, Buisson and Pécaut – were Protestants, who acted as mediators between two hostile camps (the Catholics and the anticlericals); they exerted a powerful influence on the course of events. The debate culminated in a series of Acts in the early 1880s: these created a primary school system which was both compulsory and *laïque* and in which teachers were given a purely secular status (free from domination by the local priest). Much more contentious, however, was the form of morality to be taught in these schools. This too should be *laïque* in that it should have no connection with any religious system; from this point onwards, religious education as such was systematically excluded from the public education system in France, a very marked contrast with the British equivalent.

For students of sociology it is interesting to see the role of Durkheimian frames of reference in this contest. Durkheim's work on the 'conscience collective' became a key element in the creation of a universal system of public morality over and above a moral code based on a particular – and in the French case Catholic – theology. (Hence the hostility of the Catholic Church to Durkheimian thinking.) Such a system, moreover, must be appropriate to the needs of an emergent industrial society. For Durkheim *laïcization* and rationalization were necessarily connected; a connection which is under increasing scrutiny as industrial society gives way to a post-industrial one and ways of thinking alter yet again.[8] A second consequence of the absence of religious instruction in the French school system has resulted in a corresponding emphasis on philosophy and its place in the national curriculum. Not only have the French had such a curriculum long before us, its constituent elements reflect the basis of an educational system entirely different from its British equivalent. On this side of the Channel we continue to mix, some would say confuse, religious education with moral instruction (both public and private); we also reject the idea that philosophy is, or indeed should be, an integral part of the average child's learning.

The creation of a public school system in France based on the principle of *laïcité* took place before the separation of Church and State. The first shift did not lead automatically to the second, but the crucial role of the French state in the developing school system was bound to raise larger questions about its own freedom from religious influence. In the acrimonious debates which preceded the finalization of the Act of Separation – not least the repercussions of the Dreyfus Affair[9] – it was once again a Protestant, Aristide Briand, who brokered the deal. In the 1905 Act, religion became a private affair in French law, though freedom of conscience and freedom to worship are protected by the Constitution. The emphasis on privatization is critical, compared for example with what happened in Germany some fifteen years later. In France, the public functions of religion are systematically replaced by the State; more specifically by the school and the *mairie*, the new centres of communal life. The point to grasp is that the nature and form of the separation of Church and State in France emerges from a particular context. The constitutional arrangements are a product of the past, framed as much by the history of French Catholicism as by the promoters of *laïcité* itself.

What, then, does this term and its institutional embodiments signify a century or so later? Baubérot (1990, 1996) considers two different interpretations of the concept. The first of these remains 'exclusive', insisting on a relatively unchanging interpretation of *laïcité*; the anti-religious connotations of the word can still be seen in this line of thinking. The second is more flexible and 'inclusive'; it represents an ongoing effort to interrogate or redefine the principle in view of the changing nature of modern French society, not least the need to respect the growing diversity of religions and cultures now present on French soil. The tension between these two interpretations will form the thread that runs through the following section. One further point is also important. If it is clear that a developed version of *laïcité* depends for its existence on the awareness of a clericalized and dominant Catholic Church, what happens to such a notion when the Church which it resisted ceases in any meaningful sense to impose its will on public life? If religion, in other words, has been subject to a process of individualization, might not this also be true of *laïcité* as well?

Before turning to the case study which exemplifies this dilemma in the context of the 1990s, it is important to note that denominational schools have not ceased to exist in twentieth-century France; they have, rather, become part of the *école libre* sector of French education which caters for approximately one-fifth of French children. Most of these schools are Catholic but there are Protestant and Jewish examples as well. As yet, no Muslim school has been included in this category, which is vehemently defended by the French public.[10] Defended but within limits. In 1994 a second public demonstration rejected the notion of additional State finance for these institutions over and above the 10 per cent agreed by the *Loi*

Debré in 1959. It is also the case that private schools which started out as Catholic and remain so in a technical sense have themselves been 'laïcized'; in terms, that is, of their teachers, their pupils and their curriculum. It is equally clear that many parents choose such schools for reasons in which religion plays little part; they are, quite simply, perceived as good, and therefore attractive, schools.[11]

The *affaire du foulard*: A test case for *laïcité*

The *affaire du foulard* is inconceivable in a British context. That is not to say that the complex issues arising from the arrival of significant numbers of Muslims (or indeed Sikhs or Hindus) into a historically Christian society have been resolved without difficulty in the United Kingdom. Manifestly this is not so. It does, however, illustrate that the tensions in this process take different forms in different societies. The *foulard* controversy depends as much on French history as it does on the demands of the Muslim population. The *foulard* is the French word for the Muslim veil, traditionally worn by women and girls in Muslim communities. The French debate turns on whether or not the *foulard* should be seen as a religious symbol and whether or not such a symbol is acceptable in a school system which embodies *laïcité* as one of its basic principles. Since British schools are, by law, obliged to incorporate a number of religious elements (mostly in the form of daily worship), this particular dilemma was unlikely to occur on this side of the Channel.[12]

What, then, took place in France in the final decade of the twentieth century? The following offers a brief chronology of the principal events:[13]

October 1989   Three Muslim schoolgirls wearing the Islamic headscarf are sent home from the *collège* Gabriel Havez in Creil (north of Paris).

November 1989   The first *Conseil d'Etat* ruling which affirms that, in principle, the wearing of the Islamic headscarf as a symbol of religious expression in public school, though not encouraged, is not incompatible with the French school system and the principle of *laïcité*.

December 1989   Publication of the first ministerial circular (*circulaire Jospin*) stating that teachers must decide on a case-by-case basis whether or not to ban the wearing of the Islamic headscarf.

January 1990	Three girls are asked to leave the *collège* Pasteur in Noyon (north of Paris).
April 1990	The parents of one schoolgirl file a defamation claim against the head teacher of the *collège* Gabriel-Havez in Creil.
October 1993	Teachers at a *collège* in Nantua (eastern France) strike in protest against the wearing of the Islamic headscarf in school.
October 1993	Publication of the second ministerial circular on the need to respect the principle of *laïcité* in State schools.
September 1994	Publication of the third ministerial circular (*circulaire Bayrou*) which attempts to distinguish between 'discrete' religious symbols which should be tolerated and 'ostentatious' symbols, including the *foulard*, which are to be banned from public schools.
October 1994	Student demonstrations at the *lycée* St Exupéry in Mantes-la-Jolie (north-west of Paris) in support of the freedom to wear the *foulard* in school.
November 1994	Approximately twenty-four veiled schoolgirls are expelled from the *lycée* St Exupéry in Maintes-la-Jolie and from the *lycée* Faidherbe in the city of Lille.
March 1995	A *Conseil d'Etat* ruling confirms the expulsion of two veiled schoolgirls from the *collège* Xavier-Bichat in Nantua.
July 1995	A further *Conseil d'Etat* ruling indicating that the wearing of the *foulard* is not by nature 'ostentatious' – and so not in itself grounds for expulsion – unless it is accompanied by some other disruptive behaviour.

Even a cursory reading of this chronology reveals the degree of indecision and ambivalence which pervades the whole affair. Not only were there several attempts at buck-passing between the schools and central government, but the *circulaire Bayrou* requires a consistent definition of 'ostentatious'; a far from simple concept. Each case had to considered on its merits.

The issue generated an enormous public controversy in both the written and the broadcasting media. Baubérot (1998) discusses this in terms of the tensions between freedom of conscience (claimed by the Islamic families) and freedom of thought (claimed by the teaching establishment); if pushed to the extreme, the two are incompatible. The affair was further complicated by a significant number of middle-class intellectuals who interpreted the wearing of the *foulard*, not only as a challenge to the *laïcité* of the French school system, but as a restriction on the rights of women. There were, in consequence, two reasons to oppose its acceptance in State schools.

The *affaire du foulard* cannot, however, be properly understood without reference once again to the notion of *laïcité* itself and the two tendencies that have always existed within this. First, the universalist claim based on reason and excluding of all religions in the public space, and second, a more pragmatic emphasis which attempted to come to terms with the specificities of the contemporary situation in each generation (Baubérot 1990, 1997, 1998). Both existed from the outset. Despite the universalist claims of the Republican model, the French have always allowed for a free day in the middle of the week, in order that all children whose parents so wished could attend classes for religious instruction. This was a hard won compromise in the heated debates of the Third Republic. The same may turn out to be true of the *affaire du foulard*, with reference to which each understanding of *laïcité* points in a different direction. The first, fearful of the destructive forces of Islam in Europe, adopts a primarily defensive attitude. In so doing it is effectively – if not intentionally – discriminatory, for it implies that some religions are more acceptable than others. Christians and Jews get a better deal than Muslims. The second approach is more pragmatic and continues to look for new definitions of *laïcité* and new accommodations as France becomes an increasingly plural society. Questions however, are easier to come by than answers. The irresolution of the *affaire du foulard* is indicative of the difficulties involved in the second position. Realistic in its intentions, it has yet to produce an enduring solution to this problem.

A second, rather different, episode provides additional evidence for the changing nature of the French educational system. This was the proposal to re-introduce into the curriculum some sort of religious education, albeit of a historical or cultural nature. The background to this debate can be found in the introductory sections of a text containing the published versions of a series of classes on religious themes given within a Paris *lycée* in the early 1990s, itself a controversial episode (Azria *et al.* 1990). Both citations reveal the anxieties of a headteacher responsible for the education of students for the twenty-first century. The requirement for a better understanding of religion and religious issues (including the *affaire du foulard*) is evident:

> The idea of setting up a series of lectures on religion at the Lycée Buffon grew out of an observation. In the course of conversations with students wishing to specialise in the plastic arts, I began to grasp their almost total ignorance of certain fundamentals of European culture. These students possessed some vague notions about Greek mythology, but had almost no knowledge of the Bible. How could they possibly appreciate either literary texts or works of art from the past without minimum reference either to scripture or to the Christian religion?
>
> (Azria *et al.* 1990: 7)

> Or, from a more general point of view, how can young people today be expected to understand the events so widely reported by the media, without a better knowledge of the various cultures, very frequently religious cultures, that divide the populations of the world? How can they possibly comprehend the sometimes violent manifestations of fundamentalism in some Muslim countries, the passions and actions observed in various European countries – passions and actions directed against Islam or against Islamic communities – or, finally, the displays of anti-Semitism that have occurred in both western and eastern Europe in recent years?
>
> (ibid.: 7–8)

Either way there is work to be done. One answer can be found in the tentative re-introduction into French schools of some elements of religious instruction (Messner 1995, Messner and Woehrling 1996). Pupils at age 13 will be taught a religious element in literature, history and art, while students in their penultimate year of the *baccalauréat* will be taught an outline course on world religions. These courses, necessarily controversial given the history of the school system in France, began patchily in 1996 and 1997; it is too soon to judge the consequences of their introduction except to remark on the significance of the change taking place.

Celebrations and funerals:
A 1990s postscript

Three events took place in the mid-1990s in France which nicely encapsulate both the paradoxes of religious life in modern France and its unpredictability. One of these has already been mentioned in the section on 'Facts and Figures'; it concerns the phenomenal success of the World Youth Days in Paris in August 1997. Events such as these need to be kept in mind as a counterweight to the continuing decline in more conventional statistics. The second, the funeral of François Mitterrand in January 1996, astonished many observers. That the supposedly agnostic leader of the Parti Socialiste Français should choose (in a letter attached to his will) to mark his death, not only with a private Mass at the family home at Jarnac in south-west France, but with a public requiem in Notre Dame in Paris came as something of a surprise. This was effectively a State funeral, despite the *laïcité* of the system and the supposedly non-religious beliefs of Mitterrand himself.[14]

The last – the celebration of the Clovis centenary – in September 1996 brings a number of these points together. It seems that Mitterrand himself (always an *aficionado* of anniversaries), was strongly in favour of the invitation to Pope Jean-Paul II to participate in the celebrations of the fifteenth centenary of the baptism into the Catholic Church of Clovis, King of France. The anniversary itself was a strange and recondite affair with little relevance to modern French people. The decision to combine its celebration with a visit of the Pope to France provided, however, yet another trigger to the unresolved debate about the place of religion in the public life of the French State. Much of the controversy turned on the costs of the papal visit; how much of these were or should be borne by a secular state? It is clear, in this case, that the French Church paid by far the largest share. Unsurprisingly, and of interest for a chapter such as this, the visit also prompted a number of enquiries into the state of Catholicism in modern France (see, for example, *Le Point*, 14 September 1996). The statistics mirror those set out in the first section: Catholicism remains the majority religion in France but the disciplines are eroding fast, both in terms of practice and in terms of belief. Despite such erosions the visit was more a success for the Catholics than it was for the free-thinkers; the capacity of the latter to rally the troops is even more impaired than that of the Church. In the last analysis, moreover, the majority of

French people (70 per cent), are likely – like their former president – to return to the Church and to the familiar liturgies 'at the hour of their death' if not before. Intimations of mortality, it seems, concentrate the mind.

Notes

1 The term *laïcité* is almost impossible to translate into English; hence the decision to leave it in French throughout this chapter. It denotes the absence of religion from public space (from the State, from the school system, etc.) but is not in itself anti-religious. All religions meet as equals in the public arena; none receives favours, financial or otherwise.
2 Published in *Le Monde*, 12 May 1996; set in a sociological context by Willaime (1996).
3 The dramatic fall in the number of men coming forward for ordination undoubtedly has profound effects for both the present and the future of the Catholic Church in France. Its causes, however, are only partly religious. Demographic factors are also important: the section of the population (large rural families) from which significant numbers of vocations used to come, quite simply no longer exists in modern France. Economic and social (rather than religious) changes account for this shift. In itself it may not be an indicator of the decline in organizational religion, though the consequences of the changes taking place point firmly in that direction.
4 Eighty-three percent of the population indicate that individual conscience is their most important guide in the important decisions of life (ISA poll 1994).
5 The European Values Study is a major cross-national survey of human values, first carried out in Europe in 1981 and then extended to other countries world-wide. It was designed by the European Values Systems Study Group (EVSSG). Analyses of the 1981 material can be found in Harding *et al.* (1986) and in Stoetzel (1983). A restudy took place in 1990. Published sources include Timms (1992), Ashford and Timms (1992) and Barker *et al.* (1993). The latter includes a useful bibliography of the whole enterprise. Specifically French sources can be found in Riffault (1994) and a special issue of *Futuribles* (1995), titled 'L'évolution des valeurs des Européens'. A further restudy is planned for the turn of the century. The longitudinal aspects of the study enhance the data considerably.
6 A partial exception to this situation can be found in the eastern provinces of Alsace-Lorraine, which still adhere to the Napoleonic Concordat. These provinces were under German rule at the time of the Act of Separation and the Act does not apply in this part of France. It is an area of France where religious practice is relatively high; it has, in addition, a certain concentration of Protestants, Lutherans as well as Calvinists. This is one reason why this part of France has retained a specific regional identity (see Chapter 5).

7 There are two variations on this theme in Northern Europe: the Nordic countries which are almost exclusively Lutheran (with a relatively small though important Free Church presence) and the far more mixed religious cultures of the Netherlands or the United Kingdom. The Roman Catholic community in Britain, for example, is much larger than the Protestant equivalent in France. It comprises 10–11 per cent of the British population.

8 For a fuller discussion of this point within a British context, see Davie (1994), Chapter 10.

9 The Dreyfus Affair occurred at the turn of the century. The case involved a Jewish military officer wrongly accused of high treason and duly convicted. Alfred Dreyfus was made a scapegoat for others. Both the clerical and the political right felt that it was better to sacrifice one individual – and in this case a Jewish individual – rather than call into question the honour of the armed forces and those who supported them. It marks the high point of clerical anti-Semitism in French society.

10 Conspicuous here were the demonstrations at Versailles in 1984 against the *Loi Savary*.

11 The same, of course, is true of denominational schools in Britain, despite their difference in status. For very many children and parents, they are sought after as good schools rather than religious schools.

12 A partial exception can be found in a brief episode that took place in the Manchester area. The controversy turned, however, on the question of school uniform – a peculiarly British preoccupation. It was easily resolved, once the girls involved agreed to wear a scarf in the regulation colours. It was never the case that the scarf was regarded as an illegitimate garment for religious reasons.

13 For this account I am much indebted to the as yet unpublished work of Lina Molokotos Liederman, a doctoral student at the Ecole Pratique des Hautes Etudes. Her work takes the form of a close analysis of the print media during the time of the affair. Preliminary presentations have been given to the Association for the Study of Religion (New York 1996) and to the International Society for the Sociology of Religion (Toulouse 1997).

14 It is worth remarking that the British were, probably, more astonished about the presence of both a wife and a mistress at the private funeral in Jarnac than they were by the Mass in Notre Dame. A classic case of *autres pays, autres moeurs*.

Bibliography

Ashford, S. and Timms, N. (1992) *What Europe Thinks: A Study of Western European Values*, Aldershot: Dartmouth.

Azria, R. (1996) *Le Judaïsme*, Paris: La Découverte.

Azria, R. *et al.* (1990) *La Religion au lycée*, Paris: Cerf.

Barker, D., Halman, L. and Vloet, A. (1993) *The European Values Study 1981–1990. Summary Report*, London/The Netherlands: The European Values Group.

Baubérot, J. (1988) *Le Protestantisme doit-il mourir?*, Paris: Seuil.

—— (1990) *Vers un nouveau pacte laïque*, Paris: Seuil.

—— (1996) 'La laïcité: évolutions et enjeux', *Problèmes politiques et sociaux*, 768: 3–79.

—— (1997) *La Morale laïque contre l'ordre moral*, Paris: Seuil.

—— (1998) 'La laïcité française et ses mutations', *Social Compass* 45/1: 175–87.

Chevalier, P. (1981) *La Séparation de l'Eglise et de l'Ecole. Jules Ferry et Léon XIII*, Paris: Fayard.

Cholvy, G. (1991) *La Religion en France de la fin du XVIIIe à nos jours*, Paris: Hachette.

Davie, G. (1994) *Religion in Britain since 1945. Believing without Belonging*, Oxford: Blackwell.

Encrevé, A. (1985) *Les Protestants de 1800 à nos jours*, Paris: Stock.

Etienne, B. (1989) *La France et l'Islam*, Paris: Hachette.

—— (ed.) (1991) *L'Islam en France*, Paris: Editions du CNRS.

Harding, S. and Phillips, D., with Fogarty, M. (1986) *Contrasting Values in Western Europe*, London: Macmillan.

Hervieu-Léger, D. (1986) *Vers un nouveau christianisme. Introduction à la sociologie du christianisme occidental*, Paris: Cerf.

—— (1994) 'Religion, experience and the Pope: Memory and the experience of French youth', in J. Fulton and P. Gee (eds) *Religion in Contemporary Europe*, Lampeter: Edwin Mellen Press.

Kaltenbach, J.-H. and Kaltenbach, P.-P. (1991) *La France, une chance pour l'Islam*, Paris: Editions du Félin.

Kepel, G. (1991) *Les Banlieues de l'Islam*, Paris: Seuil.

Lambert, Y. (1994) 'Un paysage religieux en profonde évolution', in H.Riffault (ed.) *Les valeurs des Français*, Paris: Presse Universitaire de France.

—— (1995) 'Vers une ère post-chrétienne', *Futuribles* 200: 85–90.

Marrus, M. (1985) *Les Juifs français à l'époque de l'Affaire Dreyfus*, Paris: Complexe.

Messner, F. (ed.) (1995) *La Culture religieuse à l'école*, Paris: Cerf.

Messner, F. and Woehrling, J.-M. (eds.) (1996) *Les statuts de l'enseignement religieux*, Paris: Cerf/Dalloz.

Nora, P (ed.) (1984) *Lieux de mémoire*. I. *La République*, Paris: Gallimard.

Ozouf, M. (1963) *L'Ecole, l'Eglise et la République, 1870–1914*, Paris: A. Colin 'Kiosque'.

Riffault, R. (ed.) (1994) *Les Valeurs des Français*, Paris: Presse Universitaire de France.

Stoetzel, J. (1983) *Les Valeurs du temps présent*, Paris: Presse Universitaire de France.

Timms, N. (1992) *Family and Citizenship; Values in Contemporary Britain*, Aldershot: Dartmouth.

Willaime, J.-P. (1992) *La Précarité protestante. Sociologie du protestantisme contemporain*, Geneva: Labor et Fides.

—— (1996) 'Laïcité et religion en France', in G. Davie and D. Hervieu-Léger (eds) *Identités religieuses en Europe*, Paris: La Découverte.

—— (1998) 'La France religieuse entre l'Europe du Nord et l'Europe du Sud', *Social Compass* 45/1: 155–74.

Chapter 11

Healthcare

Bruno Dumons and Gilles Pollet

The gestation period (1890–1945)

According to the World Health Organisation (WHO), health is defined as 'a state of complete well-being, physical, psychological and social'. In other words, it is possible to assign objectives almost without limit to health systems and policies. But this conception, dominant today in industrialized countries, corresponds to a long historical evolution of an awareness of the social and sanitary aspects of the body. Since the eighteenth century, the individual has established him or herself in terms of both biological and sociological components. Thus, revolutionary France exalted the 'new man', born out of the philosophy of the Enlightenment, and who represented a real achievement in the process of civilization. This is a process which connects modern 'man' to a renewed awareness of 'affects' (or feelings),[1] an individual who – thanks to scientific progress – manifests a need and desire for a healthier body and an ever improved state of health (Vigarello 1985, 1993).

Due to these new needs and the responses resulting from them, there has been a real increase in life expectancy at birth from less than 29 years at the end of the *ancien régime*, to 47 years at the beginning of the twentieth century, reaching 73 years for men and more than 80 years for women in the 1990s. This shows the degree to which the setting up of a system of health policies, as well as a change in attitude, have borne fruit in the space of two centuries. Despite this, the France of the late-twentieth century is not the best placed among nations in terms of health indicators. Out of all the countries of the OECD, France is ranked only fifth (for women) and thirteenth (for men) for life expectancy at birth, sixth for infant mortality and as low as sixteenth for the perinatal mortality rate

(Join-Lambert 1994). The French system, one of the most expensive in the world, is not, therefore, the most effective. By exploring, first of all, the period of its conception and development and then that of its difficulties with regulation, and by looking again at the groups of people who made its slow institutionalization possible, this chapter will examine the plans for healthcare in France, characterized first and foremost by successive historical deposits set against a marked tendency to internal fragmentation.

The emergence of public hygiene and of effective medical science

Medical progress during the last century has not only increased longevity, it has also greatly improved the health of French people by eradicating certain serious illnesses such as smallpox, poliomyelitis and to a lesser extent tuberculosis, thus permitting a rediscovery of the positive values of the body (Guillaume 1992; Faure 1994; Lagrée and Lebrun 1994). The so-called 'Pasteurian' discoveries, from 1880 onwards, offered explanations based on microbes or viruses for a good number of diseases, making way for real progress in the field of vaccination, which gradually eradicated a number of serious illnesses. This experimental medicine did not, however, bring about any real therapeutic advance. It was necessary to wait for the middle of the twentieth century and the second medical revolution (the diffusion of antibiotics) in order to combat numerous infectious and parasitic diseases. Conversely, the further into the century we get, the more the retreat of pleurisy, tuberculosis or cholera underlines the advance of cancer and cardiovascular or cerebral illness, while still waiting for the arrival of molecular biology and genetic medicine – which have allowed the identification of serious afflictions such as cystic fibrosis and Alzheimer's disease. With increasingly effective therapies the results achieved by medication and pharmacology have made their contribution felt. These areas have, however, brought about new consumer habits and have developed into a veritable industry (Faure 1994).

One essential aspect which contributed to the better health of the French for at least two centuries is based on improvements in public and private hygiene. Both doctors and the hygienists of the nineteenth century greatly contributed to a reduction in infant mortality thanks to the careful attention paid to the feeding and clothing of the baby. They recommended, in addition, a properly aired building, a minimum of bodily cleanliness and more sporting activities. These practices, amended and revived by the 'Pasteurian revolution' found an echo among the urban élite and those elected to large municipal authorities. Towns were in the process of creating vast renovation sites at the heart of which plans were made for the installation of clean drinking water, the creation of parks and of wide avenues planted with trees. Finally, during the 1890s, the government worked towards the elaboration of a real public hygiene policy which led to the establishment of national and departmental organizations and a legislative body (Murard and Zylbermann 1996). The law of 15 February 1902, known as the 'public hygiene charter', constituted the first major piece of national legislation regarding the protection of public health. It insisted on the implementation of sanitary regulations in the municipalities and required the medical profession to declare certain diseases. Smallpox vaccinations became compulsory, standards of disinfection and hygiene in buildings were set down and the Council of Public Hygiene (Conseil Supérieur de l'Hygiène Publique) – a national consultative body – was created (Murard and Zylbermann 1996). By doing this, it was hoped to combat social plagues, such as venereal diseases and alcoholism, but real progress was made in reducing death from infectious diseases, notably tuberculosis, of which the cases were halved between 1920 and 1940 (Dessertine and Faure 1994).

Of course, all sections of the French population were not affected simultaneously by this success. Towns, formerly regarded as places of death and perdition, benefited to the detriment of the countryside during the course of the first part of the twentieth century – both from more sustained efforts at medicalization and more effective public health measures. It followed that the role of health policies from then on consisted in maintaining a balance between densely populated urban zones and the rural 'deserts' at the heart of the country, but also between different social groups and different generations. This concern with health and the body has, however, lapsed on occasions, with the appearance at the beginning of the twentieth century of eugenics, a doctrine proposing among other things the elimination of children suffering from incurable infirmities and which inspired, in particular, certain members of the medical profession during the inter-war years (Carol 1995).

Nevertheless, the quest for good health was increasingly legitimized during the first half of this century and gradually became an approved category of public intervention; for example, in the struggles of public authorities and entrepreneurs to prevent physical accidents and injury in the world of work (Ewald 1986, Dewerpe 1989). Similarly, within medical practices themselves, a sharper sensitivity towards suffering became evident, notably in attempts to mitigate pain with the development of anaesthesia and painkilling drugs. All these therapeutic changes contributed to the transformation of both patients' and doctors' attitudes; fewer and fewer illnesses were considered fatal. The result, however, was that the democratization of hygiene and medicine presupposed the establishment of a social security system which would keep up with the developments in healthcare.

The institution of health professionals and policies

French society has experienced progressive medicalization since the end of the nineteenth century with increasing professional special-ization, the development of specifically medical environments such as hospitals and the recourse to medicalized practices, for example in childbirth. Effectively, the functions of doctor and pharmacist have become increasingly professional with the rise of corporate trade unionism and the establishment of a more precise judicial framework which regulates conditions of entry into the profession (Jobert and Steffen 1994, Faure 1996, Hassenteufel 1997). From the end of the 1920s, demands for the professional regulation of doctors and a medical professional code of ethics became increas-ingly persistent due to pressure from trade union representatives. These led to the creation of the Medical Association (Ordre des Médecins) in 1940 in Vichy France (Hassenteufel 1997). Moreover, the law of 15 July 1893 on free medical assistance permitted the medical profession to intervene in the most needy cases, whilst still preserving the right to a liberal practice (Faure 1993). The status of doctor from then on required the acquisition of scientific and tech-nical knowledge recognized by a university, and was invested in return with a power which greatly surpassed the medical sphere; many practitioners found public recognition, in particular on the political scene (Ellis 1990, Vergez 1996). The power of medicine was also manifested in the role that the expert had now come to play in court cases and in the production of social legislation (Guillaume 1996, Hassenteufel 1997). However, the hospital remained the sphere where aspiring doctors were required to make their mark. Some accu-mulated private honours, becoming professors or consultants. As the place of social advancement and professional promotion, the world of the hospital had been greatly transformed; the more so since it had become a highly medicalized environment where patients met health professionals such as nurses, whose job has become increasingly secular and specialized (Knibiehler 1984, Faure 1993).

Consideration of this new behaviour in the face of illness led to the establishment of vast social security systems and to large increases in health expenditure, requiring contributions from the government, private enterprise, wage-earners and friendly societies. In this area France offers a unique way of organizing the health service, which is distinguished by progressive social benefits – a consequence of French history and the establishment of a public health policy (Immergut 1992). The widening access to healthcare was part and parcel of a process of democratization and the construction of citizenship in the nation as a whole. Effectively, illness was no longer considered as an expiatory plague attacking individuals; it was, rather, a collective danger from which society must protect itself. Tuberculosis, syphilis, and also alcoholism all manifest this social dimension which required a response from both private associations and public authorities.

Charity and philanthropy from the élite, in the form of religious works and charitable organizations, combined forces with the friendly societies. Since the second half of the nineteenth century the ethos has been a liberal one; by means of the 'notables', the public was educated to save and prepare for the possibility of illness. Then, with the law of 1898, mutual insurance schemes broke away from government authority, and became an area in which health risk took on an increasingly collective dimension. On the eve of 1914, there were about 15,000 friendly societies with over 5 million members. By 1938 there were 10 million members. Mutual insurance schemes constituted an important part of the awareness of health risk. This success was the result of the directors' ability to take on board the legislation which framed the ongoing development of French social security (Gibaud 1986).

In effect, the management of social risk became the responsibility of the collectivity, and in particular of the government. The liberal credo of the nineteenth century gave way to notions of solidarity and intervention, notions espoused by the Radicals who were then in power (Rosanvallon 1990, Gueslin 1992). The first years of the *belle époque* provided an opportunity to mark out the boundaries of the contemporary French social security system, organized around two main aspects: assistance and insurance (Renard 1995). These took into account certain risks such as old age for the working and peasant populations (Dumons and Pollet 1994). The plans were completed in 1928–30 by the institution of compulsory social insurance, covering a section of wage-earners against major social risks, among which was disease.

It was only in 1892 that medical training came under effective state control and the legal practice of medicine was gradually defined. Despite the delay, French doctors (organized the same year into legalized unions) found themselves soon enough pitted against collective partnerships (the financiers of healthcare), and had therefore to confront the question of negotiating the payment rates imposed on them. At first, however, the Association of French Medical Trade Unions (Union des Syndicats Médicaux Français – USMF), founded in 1884, favoured the institutionalization of compulsory social insurance, which, like the German model, set up direct payment by the insurers and negotiated rates for all practitioners (Léonard 1981; Dammame 1991; Faure 1994). But after the war, and especially during the 1920s, in the light of social insurance projects, the more liberal section of the profession organized itself into a group and provoked a reorganization of the unions.

In 1919, there were 3 million wounded people in France, of which 1 million were recognized as 'invalides de guerre'. In a gesture of national solidarity, the Pensions Bill of 31 March 1919 made provision for war pensioners to benefit from free medical and pharmaceutical care for the rest of their lives. This legislation safeguarded the free choice of doctor and pharmacist as well as direct payment, a system whereby the insurers (in this case the government), rather than the patient, paid the medical fees. However, the state and the USMF became locked in confrontation: the medical union persuaded the State to entrust it with the direct payment scheme; in other words, they obtained control of a large fund which should have been administered by a public body. This battle illustrated the recurring fear of State-run social medicine and created the basis for a professional corps of doctors who supported 'liberal medicine', and who would become an essential pressure group within the French social security system from the inter-war years onward (Merrien 1988).

The Confederation of French Medical Trade Unions (Confédération des Syndicats Médicaux Français – CSMF) then took up the baton from a declining USMF to defend 'French-style' – that is liberal – medicine, and in particular the direct agreement and the fixing of rates by doctors themselves. In 1927 the medical charter formalized the principles of liberal medicine in marked opposition to the idea of a State-run centralization of the healthcare system; an idea which was filtering in through the compulsory social insurance schemes, and notably through the first draft of the bill in 1921 – which instituted the creation of regional public funds, based more or less on the German model operating in Alsace-Lorraine, a region then reintegrated into French national territory. The charter asserts the patient's right of free choice of doctor, the doctor's freedom of prescription, direct agreement between doctor and patient with regard to fees, and the direct payment of these by the patient to the doctor. The pressure brought to bear by liberal doctors who made a stand against the earlier bill was not in vain. They were supported by the friendly societies, the employers, farmers, some Catholics, and certain left-wing trade unions such as the CGTU (Join-Lambert 1994, Jobert and Steffen 1994, Hassenteufel 1997).[2]

As for health risk, the law of 1928 decreed that the social insurance offices would repay the medical services with a lump sum, which varied according to the number of people eligible. The insurance offices were to set a payment rate that all doctors would then be obliged to respect. A patient's contribution, in the region of 15 to 20 per cent was introduced to avoid any over-use of the medical system. In fact, under pressure from the medical professionals the bill was debated again in Parliament, and this discussion brought about the legislation of 30 April 1930 which introduced social insurance and greatly amended the proposals by reducing the role of the government. Moreover, the basis of repayments made by social insurance funds applied only to the insurance offices and not to doctors. The latter, therefore, set their fees independently (fees which remained unfixed); the amount paid by the patient not only varied from one practitioner to another, it could be quite substantial. The health insurance scheme established comprised of five main benefits: the repayment of medical costs with a patient's contribution of 20 per cent in theory (but in practice depending on the doctor's fees), daily health insurance indemnities, inclusion of maternity benefit and protection from the risks of disability and death (Join-Lambert 1994; Jobert and Steffen 1994; Murard 1989; Beau 1995).

In a general way, the social insurance legislation established a compulsory social security system, covering health risks and old age, but it was in fact restricted to middle class wage-earners in industry and commerce since there was an affiliation threshold (15,000 francs per year at the beginning). In the mid-1930s, there were approximately 7 million members with a premium (for illness and old age only) of 8 per cent of the salary shared equally between employers and employees. In the end a different social regime was created for farmers, while the friendly societies emerged as the obvious winners among social insurance schemes as they had obtained a sort of quasi-monopoly over fund management (Murard 1989, Join-Lambert 1994).

Thanks to the steady growth and progressive democratization of entitlements to social welfare (developed by legislative and governmental action) healthcare gradually became incorporated into the welfare state. With the implementation of the first laws on free medical care (1893) and compulsory vaccination against smallpox (1903), recourse to the government and local collectivities – notably with regard to the 1902 public hygiene legislation – became a necessary part of the process of ensuring that citizens had effective protection against illness and a 'right' to health. The consequences of the First World War, in particular the number of wounded and with chronic diseases, contributed to the transformation of patients into a social group which had a priority within policies of national solidarity. Management of health problems took over from and in part replaced nineteenth-century preoccupations with hygiene. The former became even more of a priority due to the epidemic of Spanish influenza in 1918 which weakened minds and bodies. This led to the institutionalization of, and greater autonomy given to, health questions at the heart of government apparatus. Thus, in 1920, a Ministry of Hygiene, Assistance and Social Provision was created; it was presented as a great ministry of the people and which brought together the former services of the Ministry of the Interior, which had been responsible until then for public health matters. The boundaries between different remits remained fluid, however, until 1930 when the separation was finally clearly defined between, on the one hand, the Ministry for Public Health, and on the other the Ministry for Employment, to which was attached the sector of social provision (Gueslin 1992).

The context of two world wars, together with the economic crisis, thus legitimated to an even greater extent the state's capacity to intervene. Aspirations for a return to democratic freedoms after the Vichy regime led to a consolidation of the status of citizenship and contributed to the democratization of French society. Two acts symbolize this process at the Liberation: the right of women to vote in 1944 and the extension, the following year, of social security to the whole French population. Healthcare was then elevated to a 'right', the management of which was the State's responsibility and in particular that of those social partners who represented employers and employees. The time of the *Trente Glorieuses* (1945–1975) led on to the development of health policies, until the first cracks began to appear in the welfare state edifice – revealed by increasing spending on health.

The period of difficulties in regulation (1945–90)

The evolution of the care system and health spending

The post-Second World War period was marked by the establishment of a new social protection system: social security which followed the same pattern as the Social Security Act, passed in August 1935 in the United States. Influenced both by the transatlantic experience and by Lord Beveridge's Keynesian-inspired report on the Welfare State (1942) – the origin of the British model of social protection – those in the Provisional Government, close to the left-wing and to the National Council of the Resistance (Conseil National de la Résistance – CNR), attempted a complete renovation of the French system. A 'social security plan', born partly out of the CNR's reflections on the subject, was elaborated under the auspices of the government advisor Pierre Laroque, the future director of the Social Security Office (la Securité Sociale). This marked a desire to unify management bodies, to ensure management autonomy in the name of social democracy, to establish uniformity in the levels of benefits and subscription costs and finally to reach the entire population and to cover all risks. It was introduced in outline by the bill of 4 October 1945 (Galant 1955).

The legislation which followed between October 1945 and October 1946 still needed to accommodate a certain number of corporate pressures, which claimed the right to preserve their particular and diverse advantages. Very quickly, any universality was forgotten, as indeed was unity, since the general regime in fact only covered commercial and industrial employees. It has often been said that the

French attempted to put Beveridge's principles into practice with Bismarck's tools: i.e., a 'social insurance' type system with a decentralized and non-state-run management, in which only the waged were protected and only in proportion to their subscriptions and therefore their salaries. In this way, a mixed, or intermediary system emerged in the end, based on insurance but with certain clearly 'Beveridgian' elements. Managerial methods were also largely decentralized, and organized around primary, regional and national offices, but under State control. Equal representation was important, which led to the councils responsible for administering funds being managed by the union representatives for both employees and employers, of whom the former were in the majority at first. The system was financed by taxation but also, and to a greater extent, by social subscriptions (in the late 1990s, around 20 per cent comes from tax revenue, and 80 per cent from subscriptions). Finally, there was a certain necessary minimum which complemented the benefits determined by the level of subscription (*La protection sociale en perspective* 1995).

The setting up of this new system of social security created a problem for liberal medicine which attempted to defend its specificity and tried to organize resistance to the collective and generalized centralization of health spending. The Social Security Office's main innovation, contested by the doctors, was the adoption of a tariff principle, agreed jointly by funds and doctors, and which represented both the fees paid by the client and the basis of repayments to the insured party. In fact, extremely long negotiations on the practical application of this principle led in October 1971 to the first national contract for doctors and health insurance companies. Thus tariffs were introduced, universally applicable except to those doctors who explicitly did not wish to work within the health service. Since then, national contracts have regularly been signed (1976, 1980, 1985, 1990 and 1993). The contract of 1980 introduced Sector II, which concerns doctors working within the health service, but whose fees exceed the contracted rate. Those of 1990 and 1993, marked by a desire to bring health spending under control, saw the setting of expenditure targets (approximately 3.4 per cent in 1994).

As part of the same process, a hospitals policy was developed, dealing in particular with important new budgets for public hospitals. These became highly technical centres of excellence for medical care, but also for teaching and research, thanks mainly to a reform of medical and hospital studies in the so-called Debré Law of 1958 (Jamous 1969). This law created the university hospitals (*centres hospitalo-universitaires* – CHU), which permitted the formation of a full-time medical and university profession within hospitals. 'From now on the hospital elite would play a lone hand in its negotiations with the government' (Jobert and Steffen 1994: 78). The 'bosses' of the university hospitals thus occupied a hegemonic position in the French health service. They behaved, moreover, more like a lobby group – looking for strategic ways in which to increase their power even further and to safeguard their autonomy – than like an élite attempting to contribute to the regulation of the sector as a whole (ibid.).

In matters of public health, the Debré plan confirmed from 1945 the need to take health and social matters in hand on a national level. This programme was achieved in stages during the 1950s with the creation of a national health laboratory responsible for analyses, control of medication and health products (1950), the introduction of the Public Health Code (*Code de la Santé Publique*, 1953), which unified and harmonized previous arrangements, and the transformation of Social Hygiene management into the general management of Public Health (1956). These institutional tools permitted the formulation of an actual policy on preventive medicine, in particular with regard to maternity and child protection, which led to a considerable drop in the infant mortality rate between 1945 and 1970. Compulsory medical examinations for pregnant women and infants, compulsory vaccinations, and the introduction of a health card for all children were all part of this general preventive drive which led to a significant improvement in the general health of the population. However, from the 1970s, this public health policy lost some of its pre-eminence, due in part to its very success but also due to the comparative weakness of the public health sector *vis-à-vis* the rest of the medical profession. Above all, there was a growing tendency to capitulate when faced with the demands of the economy to bring health expenditure under control.

The main characteristic of the health service since the 1970s has been the rapid increase in spending in the face of weak central control. This exponential rise is due to two general factors common to all industrialized countries, but it also demonstrates specifically French problems. From a general point of view, there has been a growth in health expenditure since the 1960s, which is the result of several connected factors: medical progress and its expense, economic development, the need to provide ever-more efficient healthcare, and finally socio-cultural factors which urge the population to demand ever-higher levels of healthcare, and which encourage the emergence of new pathologies requiring treatment. However, most of these factors do not take into account the specificity of the French case.

Within France, health risk currently represents one third of social welfare benefits, a proportion which has remained stable for more than thirty years. It accounts for the second largest proportion of benefits after old age, which in the 1990s is equivalent to 700 thousand million francs. Of this over three-quarters goes on illness; disability and accidents in the workplace make up the rest. The share of the GNP spent on health is one of the highest among European countries, reaching almost 10 per cent in 1995 compared with 7 per cent for the UK (figures supplied by the OECD). Health spending per inhabitant is the second highest of all countries belonging to the OECD and is more than 50 per cent higher than the UK, without any real advantages relating to the efficiency of the system. The share of spending which goes on health has not stopped growing in terms of total consumption per household; it is now estimated that it will reach 20 per cent by the year 2000 (*La Protection sociale en France* 1995, Hassenteufel 1997). Public authorities and the various individuals concerned cannot simply do nothing when faced with figures like these.

Attempts to control the system

The health market in France seems to be difficult to regulate given the complexity of the system and the influence of its history. On the one hand this is because no attempt has been made to regulate the system, whether by administration – as in the United Kingdom, by organization – as in Germany, or by competition – as in the United States. In France, the regulators are up against a mixed system which attempts to manage both the supply and demand of healthcare, but with limited results. Furthermore, the collective and socialized financing of the system has not had the effect of establishing norms and regulations which (a) prevent the abuse of the system by consumers and (b) protect the system from wasting public money. On the other hand, due to the historical legacy mentioned above, the division of responsibilities between the major figures involved (the State, the Social Security Office and representatives of the healthcare system) remains delicate and unstable (Jobert and Steffen 1994, Join-Lambert 1994).

Initiatives relating to the demand for healthcare have always attempted to introduce regulation through pricing, by transferring part of the cost of care to households in an effort to limit their consumption. The progressive increase in the patient's share of the cost (see the Séguin 1987 and Veil 1993 plans) does have a limited effectiveness in the medium and the long term. The main consequence is that France is an industrialized country where the State shoulders less of the burden for the repayment of healthcare costs. This procedure has also led to a certain inequality in terms of access to healthcare, especially since the creation in 1980 of Sector II which allowed health service practitioners to set their own rates, leading to additional costs for the patient. However, despite lower repayments, health expenditure has continued to rise more rapidly than anywhere else. The State has, therefore, preferred to centre its policies on controlling both the supply and the framework of the medical system.

At first, regulation attempts targeted specific and therefore limited areas of healthcare supply. As we have seen, the 1958 reform established the basis for a first attempt at control and regulation of the hospital sector. Successive hospital legislation (in 1970, 1983 and 1991) aimed to transform hospitals into specialist health establishments and places of care which were more and more medicalized, rationalized, technical and effective. From this point, there emerged a policy of hospital management with, in 1970, the consolidation of recruitment and training for hospital directors, who (since 1958) have been nominated by the Health Minister for institutions with more than fifty beds. Then, two years later, came the reinforcement of the hospital directors' remit and powers, followed by the differentiation of types of illnesses according to seriousness, and thus the classification of beds into short, medium and long stay – once again in 1972.

This legislation also allowed the government to have more of a say in hospital management, by the means of regulated activity and supervision. The rulings of 1958 had already established the classification of hospitals. The law passed on 31 December 1970 introduced the public hospital service which attempted to rationalize the healthcare on offer, both in geographical and technical terms, and to ensure the co-operation of public and private sectors, by envisaging even the integration of the private sector (complete with profit motive) into the public hospital service, thanks to a number of government concessions. This law also introduced the health card, solely for so-called short-stay treatments (medicine, surgery, gynaecology and obstetrics) until the extension of the card to medium-stay treatments and psychiatry. The law of January 1983 introduced a general budget and in July 1991 the government re-launched health planning, while still proceeding with a certain thinning-out of hospital management as well as the reform of internal hospital structures. The health card, done away with by the Minister on the recommendations of regional and national commissions on health and social organization, had provided a framework for the country's health facilities, both public and private. Any supplementary installation, in order to get authorization, had to correspond to the agreed allocation, and thus to the needs which had been listed. Structural planning, forecasting of needs and a clear definition of the public hospital service were the three central aims of this legislation, which concentrated mainly on rational management of the hospital care on offer. It was, however, limited in its effectiveness (Jobert 1981, Catrice-Lorey and L'Huillier 1992, Join-Lambert 1994).

Faced with the difficulties of an overall reckoning of medical staff and of hospital spending, the new attempts at regulation first targeted doctors in towns, particularly from 1960 on, when the health service contract was adopted. The 'great watershed' in liberal medicine took place at this point; for this too had to reorganize itself in order to cope with a new context and new constraints (Hatzfeld 1963). Specialists and prosperous general practitioners broke away from the CSMF to found the more conservative Federation of French Doctors (Fédération des Médecins de France – FMF). Initially opposed to the health service, from the mid-1970s onward, the FMF became the senior partner of the funds in the health service contract, and the spokesperson for the whole sector. Nevertheless, at the heart of the CSMF, a section of GPs – whose interests were increasingly opposed to those of the specialists and the better-off GPs – formed an autonomous federation, MG-France. A fourth representative trade union, the Union of Liberal Doctors (*Syndicats des Médecins Libéraux* – SML), underlined, moreover, the persistence of liberal values in the medical sphere. In this way, one of the most essential characteristics of the French model was illustrated: the extreme fragmentation in the representation of interests within the medico-social sector, which has implications for decision-making and control-taking mechanisms, themselves very divided. From this stems the extreme complexity of the relationship between doctors and the state (Jobert and Steffen 1994, Hassenteufel 1997).

In an attempt to regulate medicine in towns, several factors were taken into account; medical demography, with a reduction in the number of students admitted in the second year; restricted intake, bearing in mind the needs of the population and the regulation of specialities; nomenclature, that is the rational classification of different medical treatments, attempts to restrict the number of prescriptions and to oversee the number of treatments. It must be recognized that the consequences of these virtually voluntary actions was limited. Control of spending with respect to medication is even more problematic, since it depends on individual people, as well as laboratories and industries in the sector – for whom the logic of commerce and productivity can be in conflict with the need to regulate spending.

With regard to ambulatory care, a programme of concerted control of health spending was organized very late – at the beginning of the 1990s; it was based on the German model under the direction of Claude Evin, Minister of Health in the Rocard administration. Tripartite agreements (between the State, Social Security offices and the medical profession) had to define the desired evolution of spending, and put in place decentralized tools of accountability and control. If some sectors (biologists, nurses, dentists) complied with good grace to the new rules, agreements with the medical unions were problematic due to the characteristic resistance of the credo of liberal medicine (Jobert and Steffen 1994). During the last two decades, this explicit desire to control health spending has to some extent distracted attention from other difficulties which have emerged within the sector. A number of problems figure prominently in the 1990s: the question of those excluded from the health service, the issue of dependency in old age as well as the need to take into account new pathologies such as AIDS. Politicians have not hesitated to address these problems with legislative proposals of greater or lesser scope (for example the Juppé plan and the white paper on managing dependency in old age).

The Juppé plan, presented by the Prime Minister Alain Juppé on 15 November 1995, constitutes the latest of these attempts at regulation and reformation of a social security system under constant renovation. It contained five essential points:

- the control of health spending linked with hospital reform and a desire to establish a universal health insurance scheme;
- the reform of special retirement schemes (quickly abandoned);
- the imposition and reorganization of family benefits;
- a new division of power between the different managing partners, with – in particular – the role of control and general orientation (with regard to aims and expenditure) devolved to parliament;
- the reform of the financing of social security.

From the point of view of health-risk it is necessary to note four main points. First, the plan aimed to harmonize existing health insurance schemes, of which there are nineteen, as well as the contributory schemes, in order to cover the whole population. The next proposal is for hospital reform. The redistribution of credit allocated on a regional level by the government must be more decentralized and suited to the regional finance agencies of public and private hospitalization. Indications of the quality of health care and security have been taken into consideration in order to achieve this redistribution. Moreover, for medicine in towns, a strengthening of spending control was envisaged. Finally, the social actors dominant in healthcare are expected to contribute within the financial framework. Thus, the pharmaceutical industry must provide an exceptional and provisional contribution of 2.5 thousand million francs. As for doctors, as well as contributing a subscription for the Repayment of Social Debt (*Remboursement de la Dette Sociale –* RDS), they must accept an increase in their family benefit subscriptions (for the 75,000 health service doctors in Sector I). The practitioners in Sector II (non-health service) must become affiliated to the general health insurance scheme. (*Droit Social* 1996a, 1996b).

Resistance from doctors has been fairly strong, although the government has once again been able to count on division within the ranks and internal antagonism within the medical sphere. Even if the opposition of hospital doctors has been less virulent, and the union MG-France has signed the new medical contact for general practitioners, the CSMF, the SMF and the FMF have fought Juppé's plan from the outset. The main stumbling block concerns the repayment of fees and the application of collective sanctions which would follow if the limits of the projected rate of health insurance expenditure were exceeded. These limits are now voted on each year by Parliament and were fixed at 2.1 per cent for 1996. The edicts of April 1996 mark a victory for practitioners since only individual sanctions survive and several measures, in particular financial ones (social costs, a tax of one franc per case sheet), were either introduced temporarily or suppressed while several points were amended to satisfy the medical lobby's claims (Hassenteufel 1997). The confrontation seems far from over.

In conclusion, it is important to stress that, following the dissolution of Parliament called for by the President of the Republic, Jacques Chirac, and the victory of the left in the parliamentary elections of May–June 1997 – as whenever political power has changed hands recently (1986, 1988) – the funding of the health sector has not been altered in any fundamental way. The general infrastructure of the system has not been questioned; rather a new phase of negotiation between the government and health service officials is beginning. Purely financial control seems to have been abandoned in favour of medical control, but it is not yet clear what is rhetoric, political strategy or deeply held conviction. Attempts at the general regulation of the French health service and the more fratricidal battles within the sector itself are likely to continue for some time yet.

Notes

1 'Affects' is the word used by Bourdieu, both in English and in French – it is not usually translated.
2 See Chapter 7 for more details on trade unions.

Bibliography

Beau, P. (ed.) (1995) 'L'oeuvre collective – Cinquante ans ans de sécurité sociale', *Espace Social Européen*: Observatoire Européen de la Protection Sociale.
Carol, A. (1995) *Histoire de l'eugénisme en France*, Paris: Seuil.
Catrice-Lorey, A. and L'Huillier, M.-C. (1992) 'Construction des politiques de régulation du secteur hospitalier', *Politiques et Management Public*, 10(2): 133–83.
Dammame, D. (1991) 'La jeunesse des syndicats de médecins ou l'enchantement du syndicalisme', *Genèses*, 3: 31–54.
Dessertine, D. and Faure, O. (1994) *La Maladie entre libéralisme et solidarité (1990–1940)*, Paris: FNMF-Racines mutualistes.
Dewerpe, A. (1989) *Le Monde du travail en France (1800–1950)*, Paris: Colin.
Droit Social (1996a) 'Le plan Juppé I': 3.
—— (1996b) 'Le plan Juppé II': 9–10.

Dumons, B. and Pollet, G. (1994) *L'Etat et les retraites*, Paris: Belin.

Ellis, J. D. (1990) *The Physician-legislators of France – Medicine and Politics in the Early French Republic (1870–1914)*, Cambridge: Cambridge University Press.

Ewald, F. (1986) *L'Etat-providence*, Paris: Grasset.

Faure, O. (1993) *Les Français et leur médecine au XIXème siècle*, Paris: Belin.

—— (1994) *Histoire sociale de la médecine (XVIII–XXème siècles)*, Paris: Anthropos.

—— (ed.) (1996) 'Médicalisation et professions de santé (XVI–XXème siècles)', *Revue d'Histoire Moderne et Contemporaine* (4): 571–743.

Galant, H. (1955) *Histoire politique de la sécurité sociale française (1945–1952)*, Paris: Colin.

'Généalogies de l'Etat-providence' (1995), *Lien Social et Politiques – RIAC* (33) printemps.

Gibaud, B. (1986) *De la mutualité à la Sécurité Sociale*, Paris: Editions ouvrières.

Gueslin, A. (1992) *L'Etat, l'économie et la société française (XIX–XXème siècle)*, Paris: Hachette.

Guillaume, P. (1992) *Histoire sociale de la France au XXème siècle*, Paris: Masson.

Guillaume, P. (1996) *Le Rôle social du médecin depuis deux siècles (1800–1945)*, Paris: CHSS.

Hassenteufel, P. (1997) *Les Médecins face à l'Etat – une comparaison européenne*, Paris: FNSP.

Hatzfeld, H. (1963) *Le Grand Tournant de la médecine libérale*, Paris: Editions Ouvrières.

—— (1971) *Du Paupérisme à la Sécurité Sociale*, Paris: Colin.

Immergut, E. M. (1992) *Health Politics, Interests and Institutions in Western Europe*, Cambridge: Cambridge University Press.

Jamous, H. (1969) *Sociologie de la décision : la réforme des études médicales et hospitalières*, Paris: Editions du CNRS.

Jobert, B. (1981) *Le Social en plan*, Paris: Editions Ouvrières.

Jobert, B. and Steffen, M. (eds) (1994) *Les Politiques de santé en France et en Allemagne*, Paris: Observatoire Européen de la Protection Sociale (Dossier spécial, 4, Supplément à *Espace social Européen*, 258, septembre).

Join-Lambert, M.-T. (ed.) (1994) *Politiques Sociales*, Paris: FNSP et Dalloz.

Knibiehler, Y. (ed.) (1984) *Cornettes et blouses blanches*, Paris: Hachette.

Lagrée, M. and Lebrun, F. (eds) (1994), *Pour l'histoire de la médecine*, Rennes: PUR.

Léonard, J. (1981) *La Médecine entre les pouvoirs et les savoirs*, Paris: Aubier.

Merrien, F.-X. (1988) 'La loi sur les pensions et le conflit avec le corps médical (1919–1921). Anticipation et genèse d'une relation socio-politique', *Colloque sur l'histoire de la sécurité sociale, Lyon 1987*, Paris: Association pour l'Etude de l'Histoire de la Sécurité Sociale.

Murard, N. (1989) *La Protection sociale*, Paris: La Découverte.

Murard, L. and Zylbermann, P. (1995) 'La Protection sociale en perspective', *Revue Française de Science Politique*, 45 (4), août.

—— (1996) *L'Hygiène dans la République: La Santé publique en France ou l'utopie contrariée (1870–1918)*, Paris: Fayard.

La Protection sociale en France (1995), Paris: La Documentation Française.

Renard, D. (1995) 'Assistance et assurance dans la constitution du système de protection sociale français', *Genèses* (18): 30–46.

Rosanvallon, P. (1990) *L'Etat en France de 1979 à nos jours*, Paris: Seuil.

Vergez, B. (1996) *Le Monde des médecins au XXème siècle*, Bruxelles: Complexe.

Vigarello, G. (1985) *Le Propre et le sale: L'hygiène du corps depuis le Moyen Age*, Paris: Seuil.

—— (1993) *Le Sain et le malsain: Santé et mieux-être depuis le Moyen Age*, Paris: Seuil.

Chapter 12

Leisure and consumption

Philip Dine

Introduction: France as a 'self-service' culture

In this chapter, I shall seek to show how leisure and consumption fit into the broader pattern of social restructuring which has occurred in modern France as the country moves, often reluctantly, from an industrially-based economy to a post-industrial one. As much an integral part of the public sphere as they are of the private lives of individual French citizens, these social phenomena may most productively be considered in terms of their joint contribution to the production of a distinctively French variety of 'everyday life'. In what follows, therefore, I shall highlight a number of culturally specific modes of leisure-based consumption (or of consumption-based leisure), which I take to be paradigms of French social relations in these inextricably linked fields. In consequence, little attempt will be made here to survey the whole of this vast sphere of highly diverse activities, but rather a number of case studies will be presented which are felt to be of particular significance to modern French society as it seeks to respond to global pressures and challenges. These sites of significant social change have been identified for their political, economic, cultural, or symbolic interest, or, indeed, a combination of all of these factors.

Two basic givens of French society may usefully be considered here before we go on to establish the statistical background to our three case studies. The first is the historical peculiarity that, in the case of this particular 'imagined community' – to adopt Benedict Anderson's celebrated term for the modern nation-state (Anderson 1983) – the state historically preceded the nation. Indeed, the final imposition of a unitary national culture by the Third Republic (1870–1940) was a process which one leading historian has likened to the simultaneous establishment of France's colonial empire (Weber 1977: 98). Moreover, the model of Frenchness which was imposed by the Parisian centre on the provincial periphery and the overseas empire alike in this period was a highly centralized and determinedly assimilationist one which left little room for genuine difference in spite of its individualist rhetoric. When subjected to stress as France emerged from the trauma of defeat and occupation (1940–4) into the brave new world of social and economic modernization, this model would be tested to its limits, and leisure and consumption would be key areas in which some of the most obvious cracks in the social fabric would appear.

The rapid and radical restructuring of the French economy in the period 1945–75 is the second of the key peculiarities of French society which we need to bear in mind as we consider leisure and consumption. For it was the affluence brought by unprecedented and sustained economic growth (averaging 5 per cent of GDP per annum) which ushered in a new age of mass consumption and mass leisure in France; as, indeed, it did elsewhere in western Europe, but nowhere more dramatically or with a greater impact on individual and collective identities (Parodi 1982, Vesperini 1987, Eck 1988). In particular, the new opportunities for self-realization which came with higher incomes and more leisure time would strain the homogeneous conception of Frenchness to breaking point at home, while the wars of decolonization in Indo-China (1946–54) and Algeria (1954–62), together with the Suez crisis of 1956 and the background rumblings of the Cold War, would reinforce France's determination to pursue a new, Europe-centred, vision of national development abroad. As Kristin Ross has argued in one of the very few studies of the *Trente Glorieuses* – the thirty years of France's post-war economic miracle – to link the narratives of modernization and decolonization, what we are dealing with here is nothing less than the complete overturning of the accepted norms of French society in the period 1945 to 1975:

in France the state-led modernization drive was extraordinarily concerted, and the desire for a new way of living after the war widespread. The unusual swiftness of French postwar modernization seemed to partake of the qualities of what Braudel has designated as the temporality of the event: it was headlong, dramatic, and breathless. The speed with which French society was transformed after the war from a rural, empire-oriented,

Catholic country into a fully industrialized, decolonized, and urban one meant that the things modernization needed ... burst onto a society that still cherished prewar outlooks with all of the force, excitement, disruption, and horror of the genuinely new.

(Ross 1995: 4)

The event in question, then, was nothing less than the overturning of 'everyday life', together with the mental attitudes on which it depended. Whether positively labelled as 'modernization' or negatively as 'Americanization', this radical transformation was accompanied by a process of social fragmentation which was primarily visible in the spheres of leisure and consumption. Whether hailed by contemporary French commentators as a 'civilisation of leisure' (Dumazedier 1962) or condemned by them as a 'consumer society' (Baudrillard 1970), the new social order would be marked, above all, by an ever increasing heterogeneity. The inexorable rise of this decentred and delegitimated mode of social interaction would, in time, result in its most striking post-industrial incarnation: the 'self-service' culture identified by Gilles Lipovetsky (1983: 14–17; see also Rigby 1991: 190–4).

Having lagged behind the United States, Britain and Germany in the pre-war period, when considered from both a technological standpoint and the socio-economic point of view, a France physically and psychologically scarred by the recent experience of defeat and occupation embraced modernity with a will. Indeed, the cult of modernization, so enthusiastically adopted as the economic and political creed of the French nation under both the coalition governments of the Fourth Republic and, *a fortiori*, the new semipresidential administration of General de Gaulle, was not to be seriously challenged until the social and political watershed of 1968, and not finally discarded until the economic watershed of 1974–5. Central to this process of developed industrial capitalism was the elevation of commercial products, and, of course, of the purchasing power required to obtain them, to a new position of centrality in French social life: what Walter Benjamin has famously identified as 'the enthronement of the commodity' common to all societies living in the condition of modernity (Rojek 1993: 105). As consumer durables such as refrigerators, washing machines, television sets and cars became available for the first time to the mass of French people, a new ideology of consumption – consumerism – arose both to justify and to encourage the widely shared affluence which resulted from state-managed post-war reconstruction and modernization.

Having come late and fast to France, the consumer society was to sweep all before it in the period 1945–75. Culture itself became, or was recognized to be, a commodity, which could be possessed by individuals or groups. On one level, this development represented a genuine democratization as culture – in the form of books, films, records, and the like – came to be purveyed like any other commodity, and thus, wherever possible, to a mass market. However, on another level, this new 'cultural capital', like any other form of capital, was liable to accumulation and hoarding by a few privileged individuals, families, or social classes. This observation is the foundation of Pierre Bourdieu's monumental study of taste in post-war French society, *La Distinction* (1979). Bourdieu's class-based analysis of cultural diversity argues that a fundamental dichotomy exists in modern France between a 'legitimate culture', which might also be called 'high culture' or 'bourgeois culture', and which is the exclusive preserve of the educationally and economically privileged, and an 'illegitimate' or, as his own preferred term has it, 'barbaric' culture of the lower orders. Brian Rigby helpfully captures the gist of what is a complex and highly detailed argument when he explains that:

> in Bourdieu's view, to be in possession and control of 'legitimate culture' is to occupy a position of power over those other people who are not in possession of it and who because of this are excluded from 'the social worlds in which this is required', and are thereby constantly made to feel a sense of their own inferiority.
>
> (Rigby 1991: 123)

In Anthony Giddens's terms, the 'allocative resources' of the economically privileged (most obviously their income and capital) are the foundation of their power-reinforcing 'authoritative resources' (manifested in areas such as status, taste and education) (Rojek 1993: 54).

Persuasive as Bourdieu's analysis may be as regards French society in the two decades after the Liberation, there must be serious doubts about its applicability in the new France(s) which emerged in the wake of the socio-political trauma of May 1968 and the economic shock of the 1974 oil crisis. For these very different watersheds in the post-war French experience were, together, to mark the beginning of the end of a society based on traditionally fixed class distinctions, and to point the way forward to new patterns of social convergence and divergence (Forbes and Hewlett 1994: xiv, 45). As both the post-war political consensus, based on industrially-based modernity and State-managed social harmonization, and the radical aspirations of the *soixante-huitards* gave way in the 1980s to a new pessimism in the face of the evident inability of French governments of whatever stripe to find solutions to an economic crisis which recalled for some the Depression of the 1930s, culture, whether 'high' or 'low', 'legitimate' or 'barbaric', 'bourgeois' or 'popular', could not long remain unaffected. More than this, the very existence of these widely accepted cultural distinctions has come to be challenged as the post-industrial France of the final decades of the twentieth century is increasingly perceived to be living not so much in the condition of modernity, characterized by a centrally organized and commodity-based mass culture, but rather in that of 'postmodernity', in which mass culture and the values on which it is based effectively implode.

The political crisis which has resulted from the failure of the traditional parties, and, with them, party politics as a whole, to find solutions to large-scale structural unemployment is only part of a broader crisis of legitimacy experienced throughout western Europe, but with particular intensity in France. Indeed, the post-modern age has been primarily perceived as a demolition of old ideologies and hierarchies, both social and aesthetic (Ory 1989: 209–17). In the words of Jean-François Lyotard, one of the first and still most influential of French theoreticians of postmodernity, 'we no longer have recourse to the grand narratives – we can resort neither to the dialectic of the Spirit nor even to the emancipation of humanity as a validation' (Rojek 1993: 127). So, in particular, neither of the two great frames of reference for French society in the pre-war and post-war periods, neither Catholicism nor Communism, are nowadays available as plausible sources of legitimacy, still less of certainty. The cultural implications of this sea-change were, as Pascal Ory argues, predictable enough: a tendency to individualism and nihilism, coupled with a highly vocal rejection of any and every political ideology and a shamelessly professed belief in the impossibility of anything other than individual salvation (Ory 1989: 217).

It is in the conjunction of this contemporary crisis of legitimacy with a consumerism reinvigorated by major technological (and commercial) developments in the sphere of information processing that are to be found the roots of the 'self-service' culture which increasingly characterizes French society. For in modern France, the system of social 'distinction' based on broadly accepted and essentially static definitions of 'legitimate' and 'illegitimate' cultural practices – the established order so diligently catalogued by Pierre Bourdieu – is presently being challenged, if not actually overtaken, by a non-hierarchical, intensely dynamic, and technologically mediated universe of 'delegitimized' (i.e., all equally legitimate and/or illegitimate) cultural possibilities. For Lyotard (1984), as for other major French analysts of postmodernity such as Jean Baudrillard (1970), this collapse of traditional value systems results in a generalized quality of 'depthlessness' being typical of contemporary cultural relations (Rojek 1993: 129–30). Prime examples of this are the globalized eclecticism of postmodern lifestyles and the all-pervasive nature of television culture. So, for instance, young French consumers are just as likely to listen to Jamaican reggae music, play Japanese video games, and eat McDonald's hamburgers as are their counterparts in the other developed industrial nations; while 94 per cent of French homes had a TV set by 1993 (20 per cent had two), with at least 83 per cent of the French public nowadays watching television on a daily basis (Maresca 1995: 142–8). Looking more specifically at contemporary French society, we might find characteristic examples of 'self-service culture' in the rise of the FNAC leisure chain, the development of France Telecom's Minitel system, and the advent of *le sport business*. Indeed, these distinctively French varieties of leisure-based consumption will provide our three case studies. Their significance may best be appreciated if we turn now to consider the development of leisure and consumption in France on the basis of some elementary statistical indicators.

Consumption, leisure and retail distribution

Given that leisure spending is only one relatively small part of total spending by French households, it is necessary to have an impression of patterns of consumption in general before moving on to consider leisure budgets in particular. As with French economic performance as a whole, it is useful to make a distinction between the 'thirty glorious years' of sustained growth on the Fordist model from 1945 to 1975, and the years of economic crisis since, which have seen France become accustomed to high levels of long-term structural unemployment. Indeed, some commentators have even begun to talk about the end of the consumer society as France approaches the millenium (Volatier 1995: 131–4). This may be an overstatement, but it is worth noting that patterns of consumption have certainly stabilized and even stagnated since the oil crisis of 1974–5, with a direct impact on retailing strategies which is considered below.

French economic expansion in the period 1945–75 was based on a sustained growth in demand for consumer durables such as household appliances and motor vehicles. A steady rise in salaries in this period – particularly those of industrial workers, made possible by constant increases in productivity as the French economy experienced the benefits of a state-managed 'virtuous circle' – combined with the demographic boost provided by the 1945–50 baby boom to generate consistently high demand for such goods. The result was a genuine closing of the gap between the lifestyles of rich and poor as all social classes benefited from the greater affluence of the *Trente Glorieuses*. Cars, washing machines and television sets thus became the familiar items in French homes that they did in other western European nations over the same period, but the transformation was all the more dramatic in the French context given the relatively low living standards which had characterized the pre-war period (Forbes and Hewlett 1994: 3, 42). Some of these emblematically modern objects became familiar fixtures in French homes later, and more rapidly, than others: thus only 2.1 per cent and 14.9 per cent of French households had a colour television and a telephone respectively in 1970, whereas 90.3 per cent and 94.9 per cent did by 1992 (Volatier 1995: 130). However, the general pattern of 'trickle-down' wealth distribution was maintained, and was in line with that in other European countries.

Thus, French patterns of consumption on essentials such as food, clothing, health and housing were by 1990 broadly in line with those of other developed industrial nations (Volatier 1995: 131, Forbes and Hewlett 1994: 42–6). However, the pattern of rapid expansion ended with the onset of the economic crisis in the mid-1970s. Although triggered by external factors, French difficulties were exacerbated by approaching saturation as regards the market for consumer durables, demographic stagnation, and an end to the chronic inflation which had hitherto favoured spending rather than saving, particularly on property, with all that this implied in the way of related expenditure (for the construction industry itself, but also on household equipment, gardening, DIY and related activities). All the evidence suggests that French households are nowadays both more cautious and more discerning in their patterns of consumption than was hitherto the case. Indeed, the only sectors where spending is continuing to expand rapidly are those where households have little or no control and thus market forces can function only imperfectly, such as health care and housing costs. One indication of both real and perceived differences in the way French households are spending today is the extent to which they are obliged to impose restrictions on their spending. So, in partic-ular, spending on leisure may have continued to increase as a proportion of total expenditure since 1970 (when it was 6.9 per cent), and today stands at 7.7 per cent of household budgets, but so has the willingness to cut back on leisure spending if needs be: with 42.2 per cent of households reporting such reductions in 1980, a figure which had increased to 46.6 per cent in 1992. It should be noted that these figures do not include spending on holidays, and that the whole leisure and holiday budget of the average French household is currently estimated at 17 per cent of total expenditure (Maresca 1995: 143, Volatier 1995: 130–3).

What exactly do we mean by leisure? At one level, 'leisure' may simply be defined as unconstrained time, and its history traced through a series of concessions made to French workers over the course of the century: such as the legal right to one day off each week in 1906; the 10-hour working day in 1912; the 8-hour working day in 1919; the introduction of paid holidays and the 40-hour working week under the Popular Front in 1936; up to and including the Socialists' extension of such *congés payés* to five weeks per year, and the reduction of the working week to 39 hours, both in 1981. To the list of symbolic dates just cited might well be added the year 1975, which is not only significant because of its position on the cusp between the *Trente Glorieuses* and the *vingt tumultueuses* (the post-boom period, 1975–95), but also as the moment at which free time began to overtake work time for the average French person:

> Free time rose on a weekly average, from 24 hours 16 minutes in 1975 to 28 hours 28 minutes in 1985; whereas work time dropped from 27 hours 7 minutes to 24 hours 44 minutes. We

seem to be witnessing what Marcuse termed an 'historic inversion'.

(Poujol 1993: 36)

Of course, 'the average French person' does not exist, and any consideration of leisure must take account of the additional constraints on the time of particular social groups, and thus include factors such as profession, class and/or income, gender, ethnicity and age. Such social stratification must also be borne in mind when examining changes in patterns of leisure spending, whether it be on holidays, sport, or the various products of the domestic leisure industry. However, it is here, in the establishment of the home as the primary cultural space of contemporary France – and particularly in the new (to France, at least) hegemony of television – that we also have to consider the phenomena of social homogenization and at least an apparent 'democratization', as Jill Forbes and Nick Hewlett have reminded us (1994: 45).

Leisure spending is clearly only one aspect of consumption, but it is proposed to focus on it in the present chapter, rather than to consider in-depth changes in patterns of expenditure on such basics as food, housing, transport, clothes and health, as well as the modern 'essentials' which the main consumer durables (cars, refrigerators, television sets, freezers, dishwashers, video-recorders, etc.) have undoubtedly become. However, the specificity of French ways of spending will be considered at some length, and it is here that we need to give some attention to patterns of retail distribution in France.

The French retail sector has undergone a profound modification since 1945, just as the relationship between consumers and shopkeepers has evolved constantly over this same period. A variety of factors have been responsible for this transformation, including particularly the following: the growth of towns and cities; increases in living standards; the generalized use of private motor vehicles; changes in employment patterns and rhythms, including particularly the increase in the number of working women and the generalization of the 'Anglo-Saxon' working week; the widespread introduction of advanced technologies (automation, computerization, refrigerated transportation); and the internationalization of purchasing patterns. The end result has been a phenomenon of concentration, both as regards producers and distributors, with a consequent increase in the size of both. The traditional pattern of small, specialized, and above all local shops has thus been replaced to a large extent by a new era of out-of-town shopping at hypermarkets of a kind which would be familiar to consumers in many other western European nations (Delbourgo and Taylor 1993: 103–7).

The first French supermarket was opened in Landerneau in 1949 by Edouard Leclerc, and the hypermarket chain which today bears his name is one of the 'big four' of French retailers, after Carrefour and Promodès, and just ahead of Intermarché and smaller chains like Auchan. With enormous stores (each having at least 2,500 square metres of floor space), these aptly named *grandes surfaces* sell everything from food to clothes to electrical appliances, and together accounted for 29.2 per cent of all retail trade in 1991 on the basis of some 900 hypermarkets (this figure had risen to over 1,000 by 1994). Such has been the impact on traditional shopping patterns of these enormous outlets, together with newer players such as the specialized chains Darty (electrical appliances), Conforama (furniture), Castorama (DIY), Decathlon (sports goods), and the FNAC leisure chain, that French governments have sought to protect traditional shopping patterns by means of legislation. The Royer law of 1973 has proved a generally unsuccessful attempt to prevent the expansion of hypermarkets; while the impact of legislation in force from 1 January 1997 to prevent industrial 'bake-offs', both inside *grandes surfaces* and elsewhere, from further eroding the commercial viability of the artisanal bakers who twice a day produce the archetypally French baguette remains to be seen (Delbourgo and Taylor 1993: 103–7, Frémy and Frémy 1995: 1803–10, Doyle 1997: 11).

Case study 1: the FNAC

As France's leading 'cultural supermarket' (Rigby 1991: 161), the FNAC provides a very appropriate first example of specifically French modes of leisure-based consumption. Its founders, André Essel and Max Théret, resembled Gilbert Trigano – the moving spirit behind that other icon of the French domestic leisure industry, Club Méditerranée – in their metamorphosis from obscure leftist political activists into leading lights of a qualitatively new, and distinctively French, model of cultural entrepreneurialism (Ory 1989: 159). Established in 1954, the Fédération Nationale des Achats began by selling photographic equipment, then diversified to include books, records and audio equipment, and now offers a range of associated products and services (such as ticket sales for concerts, shows and sports events). Initially organized on a co-operative discount (and for a while mutualist) basis, the FNAC is now a publicly quoted company in private hands. With stores in all of the major French population centres, the company had a turnover of 9.45 billion francs in 1993–4. Sales of records, CDs and cassettes nowadays make up the biggest item in the company's revenue (33 per cent), followed by books (21 per cent), computer hardware and software (15 per cent), and photographic equipment and services (11 per cent) (Frémy 1995: 428). It is arguably as France's largest bookseller that the FNAC and its characteristic distribution methods have been most visible and most far-reaching in their impact. It is not so much the physical enormity of the leisure chain's outlets (especially its numerous Paris stores) which is of interest here, but rather the company's role in the attempt to bring books fully into the leisure market as a commodity like any other in the 1970s and 1980s.

What was at stake, in fact, was the continued existence of France's extensive network of small- and medium-sized local booksellers; a distinctive pattern of retailing which was seriously threatened by the economic liberalism of the centre-right administration of President of the Republic, Valéry Giscard d'Estaing. David Looseley explains how this introduction of market forces into what had previously been one of the most closely regulated areas of French leisure spending came about:

> In July 1979 ... it was the Minister of the Economy, René Monory, who took the radical step of freeing book prices, regulated for the previous 120 years by the recommended-price system (*prix conseillé*). This, together with a decision to end the state's small subsidy to the CNL [Centre national des lettres] and the government's acquiescence to a proposed merger of the publishing firm Hachette with the industrial giant Matra, signified for many the rejection of a long-standing acceptance that books had to be treated differently from other commercial products.
>
> (Looseley 1995: 54)

This ministerial *arrêté* (decree) predictably altered the balance of power between the various parties involved in the French book trade: traditional specialist bookshops came under increasing pressure from those more modern retailers who were able to buy in bulk and pass at least a part of their savings on to consumers in the form of substantial discounts on the publisher's recommended price. To the fore were France's three biggest booksellers: the hypermarket chains Carrefour and Leclerc – the latter still very much a family-run business with a history of symbolic challenges to state controls on the retail sector – as well, of course, as the FNAC, whose business stood to gain considerably from the new relations of trade. However, the election in 1981 of François Mitterrand as the Fifth Republic's first socialist president was radically to change the position.

Mitterrand's charismatic and campaigning Minister of Culture, Jack Lang, made it a priority to attempt to secure the future of the specialist booksellers by limiting retailers, large and small, to a 5 per cent margin of flexibility on the publisher's recommended price; a system which eventually gained widespread support across the political spectrum and is still in place. However, as might be expected, the FNAC and the other major outlets were united in their hostility to the Lang law, which came into effect on 1 January 1982. While commercial motives were clearly paramount in this reaction, there was also something inherently questionable about the socialists' attack on an outlet which, in the case of the FNAC at least, had genuinely extended the appeal of books by marketing them in huge numbers and across a vast range: everything from the prestigious Pléiade editions of French literary classics to the latest *bande dessinée* (comic book) were sold in the same, unfussy, self-service, fashion by the leisure chain. As David Looseley explains, this was 'the paradox of a law which sought to democratize access by increasing prices and penalising those distributors like the FNAC who had unquestionably demystified books and introduced them to a wider public' (Looseley 1995: 99).

The real issue in this clash between the state and private enterprise was the right of all cultural products to compete for French leisure budgets on equal terms. For the time being, the Lang law has preserved the privileged cultural status of books, and thus the equally privileged commercial position of specialist booksellers. However, the FNAC's formula of promoting 'high' and 'low' cultural products on a resolutely equal basis seems sure to continue to prosper in an age of cultural 'depthlessness' and ever more eclectic lifestyles. For we are here at the heart of the continuing commodification, privatization, and fragmentation of French leisure – as of French culture as a whole – in the post-war period.

The social and ideological shock of 1968, the economic shock of 1974–5, and the political shock of 1981 may thus be regarded as 'defining moments' in the breakdown of the French cultural homogeneity of the pre-war and early post-war periods. That unitary model of national identity has increasingly been challenged by new political actors, new commercial players, and new cultural practices; as, very significantly, has the French State's once near-total monopoly of technologically mediated information. It is this last transformation which leads us now to consider France Telecom's 'Minitel' system as a nationally specific response to the transnational challenges of the global revolution in information technology.

Case study 2: Minitel

A uniquely French innovation, Minitel is also, on the face of it, a technological success story. From its experimental launch at Vélizy in 1981, the Minitel system had expanded to over 6 million terminals, used by both firms and individuals who together made 1.76 billion calls on over 17,000 services, by 1992 (Delbourgo and Taylor 1993: 1–4, Frémy 1995: 1541, Rincé 1990). The rapid growth of the Minitel was the result of what was at the time a revolutionary linking of technologies: telecommunications and computing (*l'informatique*). The result, *la télématique* or telematics, was as visionary in the early 1980s as were the France Telecom marketing specialists responsible for its launch. In a bold move, the State-run company offered its telephone subscribers a choice between the standard telephone directory for their area, or an electronic version for the whole of France, together with the Minitel terminal required to access the system, free of charge. Overnight, the Minitel unit – rather like a miniature personal computer terminal, with an integral keyboard and small black and white screen – became a familiar feature of French homes, and has steadily increased in popularity ever since. If we are to believe the postmodernist thesis regarding the putatively 'de-centring' impact on national cultures of the new information technology, then this structural linkage between the rise of the Minitel and the still highly centralized State must be reckoned a significant paradox, and perhaps even a characteristically French one.

The backbone of the Minitel system remains directory enquiries (the cheapest service), responsible for just under 45 per cent of all consultations by its 6.5 million users. However, the vast range of public and professional services now available has undoubtedly contributed to the steady increase in its popularity: some 23,000, from train timetables and reservations to dating agencies, and even the more dubious 'personal services' of the so-called 'Minitel Rose'. The simplicity of the system is undoubtedly part of its appeal: this includes easy installation and connection, a unit-based tariff-system which applies regardless of distance, and, most visibly, a set of easy-to-remember codes based on a limited group of numbers (3615, 3616, 3617) and the name of a product, firm, or service. Also of significance is its extension into such fields as banking (where it is linked to the increasingly standard use of *cartes à puces* ('smart' credit and debit cards), share-dealing and telesales. In addition, Minitel was used to place orders for 11.5 per cent of French mail-order purchases in 1994. Used regularly by over half of French households, irrespective of age, socio-professional category or geographical location, the extensive network of *vépécistes* (mail-order companies) might itself legitimately be regarded as a characteristic feature of French patterns of consumption, with the leading firm, La Redoute, set to become increasingly important in the European market, following its recent expansion into the UK and elsewhere (Frémy 1995: 1804).

However, the undoubted success of the Minitel is increasingly being recognized to be something of a double-edged sword. On the one hand, the phenomenal expansion of the system has permitted the rapid familiarization of a wide public with computer-based technology. Indeed, if the Minitel is included in the calculations, then France has the highest domestic use of computer terminals in the world. However, the fact that Minitel is limited to France and cannot be systematically used outside French territory – although France Telecom is currently working on a modem-based 'accelerator' to combat this problem – is a considerable handicap in the age of the Internet and the World Wide Web, as is the general reluctance of French Minitel users to upgrade to what has become established as the international standard for home and business computing, the personal computer or PC. According to a recent survey, only 15 per of French households are equipped with computers, and only 1 per cent of those who are not so equipped are considering buying a PC (Duval-Smith 1996). This situation may usefully be considered in the light of an important report made into the French failure to engage fully with computer technology, which was actually diagnosed as early as 1978.

The Nora-Minc report of that year was entitled 'Informatique Pour Tous' (Computing For All) and accurately anticipated the systematic computerization of societies around the world which has now occurred. Pointing to the slow take-up of the new technology by both private and business users in France, the report urged the extension of telematics as the key to a rapid expansion of computer use, but also pointed to the possible dangers of 'compartmentalization' (*cloisonnement*) which might result. This was a line which was echoed by the Agence de l'Informatique, itself set up by the government in 1979 in response to the Nora-Minc report, in a follow-up report written in 1986 by Norbert Paquel (Agence de l'Informatique 1986). Unfortunately, the Paquel report's prescient warning that France was 'a small country in a world market' (ibid.: 175) was to go unheeded as a result of the dazzling domestic success of the Minitel system. The results of this failure to plan for an increasingly globalized information age are daily more apparent in France, with the inability of the text-based Minitel system either to export its services or, crucially, to compete with PCs and the Internet in the key area of graphics being the domestic system's most significant weaknesses.

It need hardly be added that the French language itself also constitutes a significant, and highly symbolic, problem, with national identity perceived to be under threat from the use of English as the *lingua franca* of the Internet. In a test case in January 1997, the Association for the Defence of the French Language and the group Future of the French Language took 'Georgia Tech Lorraine', the Metz-based campus of the American Georgia Institute of Technology, to court over its exclusive use of English for its Web-site. Using legislation introduced in 1994 under Gaullist Minister of Culture Jacques Toubon to defend the use of French in advertisements, the two pressure groups attempted to ensure that the less than 500,000 French users linked to the Internet (of whom a mere 120,000 are private users) were at least able to understand the pages offered by producers based in France (Hughes 1997, Webster 1997). However, this state-sanctioned suspicion of what is perceived to be the latest manifestation of a creeping 'Americanization' of French society means that the French – relying on a modernized Minitel for access to the Internet not only as consumers but also, it is fervently hoped, as producers – are taking a considerable gamble on a system which, although once revolutionary, would now seem to have been decisively overtaken. François Fillon, as Minister for

Post, Telecommunications and Space, recently commented on the French technological paradox as follows:

> It is often hastily said that the French, and in particular 'decision-makers', are culturally impervious to information technology. It is true that computers and the Internet are not yet systematically part of the daily working life of executives, and PCs do not exactly have pride of place in politicians' offices, but that doesn't mean that the French are oblivious to the benefits of information technology.
>
> Indeed, we shouldn't forget that the French entered the era of mass telematics long before the Americans, with the success of the Minitel, which is present in millions of homes and businesses.
>
> (Fillon 1996)

A rather less charitable gloss is put on the present situation by François Benveniste, chairman of the French Association of Internet Professionals, who comments that 'the French love everything that moves fast and speeds through space – as long as the state is paying', but 'when it comes to everyday interest in technology, France is far from the Silicon Valley of Europe'. Or as one British journalist has put it rather more bluntly: 'France – land of the high-speed train, the Ariane rocket and the independent nuclear deterrent – drives a moped on the information highway' (Duval-Smith 1996).

Case study 3: le sport business

For Jean Baudrillard, in his critique of the consumer society, 'the finest object of consumption [is] the body' (1970: 199–201). Baudrillard goes on to examine in detail its role in advertising, but we might just as usefully look at another commercial representation of the body: that associated with modern, and especially professional, sports. Few commentators would doubt the significance of sport as a barometer of social change in France since its introduction by a combination of expatriate Britons and aristocratic Frenchmen in the 1880s. A talismanic figure in the development of the new games not only in his own country but also throughout the world was Baron Pierre de Coubertin, the founder of the modern Olympic Games. In the distance travelled by French sport from the élitist amateurism of pioneers like de Coubertin to the media circus that professional sports spectacles have become today, we are able to identify some of the key features of the development of leisure-based consumption as a whole in modern France. Moreover, in the rise and fall of one particular football club, and of its flamboyant owner, we have a privileged site for the examination of the relationship between the leisure industry and French society as a whole.

The apparent irony of Olympique de Marseille's name will not be lost on anyone brought up in the Coubertinian tradition of strictly amateur athletic competition. However, this is, in fact, only part of a tradition of reference to classical antiquity and its games which has been maintained since the earliest days of French sport. Thus it is, for instance, that France's leading weekly newspaper devoted to the non-Olympic (since 1924) sport of rugby union should be the Toulouse-based *Midi-Olympique*. In contrast, the real irony of this professional club's history is to be understood in terms of its status as the first French club to win the European Champions' Cup and the only club ever to be stripped of such a title. In order to understand this peculiar combination of glory and ignominy, we need to consider the role played in the club's meteoric rise, and even more spectacular fall, by the charismatic entrepreneur and politician, Bernard Tapie. However, we might also usefully note the expansion of both participatory and spectator sports as a central feature of the modern French leisure industry. In 1994, sales of sports goods were no less than eight times what they had been in 1960, while 68 per cent of French people claimed to practise a sport (although only 12 million of them in officially constituted clubs and federations) (cf. Yonnet 1985; Maresca 1995: 147).

Football is France's most popular team sport, both in terms of participation (with some 2 million *licenciés* or officially licensed players) and as a televised spectacle: over half of all French viewers are estimated to have watched the 1986 World Cup semi-final between France and Germany, while no less than 454 hours of TV schedules were given over to football in 1990 (Bourg 1994: 130–1). As such, the game is undoubtedly a major social phenomenon. In this, France is, perhaps, much the same as many other European countries, including most obviously Germany, Italy, Spain, Portugal and the United Kingdom. However, it is in the overlap between sport, the media, big business and politics, that the French case is worthy of particular note. More specifically, 1986 was not only a year of French footballing heroics in the World Cup, but also the one that Bernard Tapie, a self-made man who had risen to prominence as a result of a number of business deals which were as ethically dubious as they were commercially lucrative, took over control of the ailing Olympique de Marseille (OM).

Using an industrial empire which included some forty companies to finance his acquisition and transformation of the club, Tapie was to attract key French and overseas players to Marseille (such as Jean-Pierre Papin and Alen Boksic), where they would be taken in hand by the former manager of the highly successful national side, Michel Hidalgo. OM's success on the field was matched by its performance off it: French league champions for four seasons in a row between 1989 (when they also won the French knock-out cup competition) and 1992, the club was able to generate significant revenue from attendances, television rights, sponsorship and even local authority grants. A key element of Tapie's approach in this regard was his changing of the club's legal status. In fact, the club ceased to be a sports association in 1990, becoming instead a *société anonyme à objet sportif* (SAOS), that is to say a limited company, with a significantly enhanced potential for generating capital from private shareholders, in the expectation of future profits. However, both the (real) playing success and (apparent) commercial attractiveness of OM were only part of its ambitious president's strategy for personal advancement. As one French commentator has put it: 'Bernard Tapie transformed Olympique de Marseille into a real marketing tool, which helped him to gain access to legislative power (as a *député* [Member of Parliament]), executive power (as a minister) and the power of the media' (Bourg 1994: 130–1).

Sadly for the team's supporters – and the chronically depressed provincial city whose undoubted champions OM had become – Tapie's inevitable fall was to go hand-in-hand with that of the club which he had transformed into the leading French side and a major European force. In 1993, Olympique de Marseille became European champions when a headed goal by Basile Boli gave them a 1–0 win over A.C. Milan, to complete a season which should also have seen them crowned as national league champions for a fifth successive year, overtaking the great record of *les verts* of St-Etienne (1967–70). However, the club was to be suspended from the domestic championship and subsequently relegated to its second division by the game's ruling authority, the Fédération Française de Football (FFF), before being stripped of the European Cup by UEFA; all of this as a result of match-fixing allegations made by players from the small Valenciennes club. As if that were not enough, the FFF passed its file on the case to the police, who promptly launched a criminal investigation. Subsequent prosecutions for corruption would see Tapie stripped of the layers of political privilege and commercial protection with which he had surrounded himself, and would eventually result not only in his losing control of the financially troubled club, but also in his being sentenced to a prison term.

Yet this ignominious tale does not end there, and in the epilogue to these disciplinary enquiries and judicial proceedings we can glimpse some of the real forces at play in this most mediatized sphere of *le sport business*. The exclusion of OM should have meant that the runners-up in the national league went on to represent France in the following season's European Cup. However, the club in question, Paris-Saint-Germain refused, because its principal shareholder, the pay-per-view television channel Canal+, would not accept a move which was sure to boost the advertising revenue of its rival, the newly privatized TF1, who had already negotiated the rights to television coverage of the relevant matches. The next club in line, Auxerre, was in turn rejected by TF1 in favour of the theoretically stronger and certainly more marketable Monaco: a purely commercial move in which the FFF was obliged to acquiesce in order to protect its own interests. By the same token, the arrival times of the daily stages of the quintessential French sporting spectacle, the Tour de France, have steadily been pushed back from the traditional middle of the afternoon – a time which allows the competing cyclists the maximum time for rest and recuperation – and towards the 7–8 p.m. TV slot, which is much more attractive as an advertising vehicle to the event's major sponsors (Crédit Lyonnais, Fiat and Coca-Cola) (Bourg 1994: 130–1). A State-owned French bank, an Italian car manufacturer, and the soft drink which has become established as the epitome of American commercial interests – not to say cultural imperialism – abroad: a powerful triumvirate which neatly sums up modern France's globalized leisure market.

Conclusion

As so often before and since, Theodore Zeldin was remarkably acute when he observed in the early 1980s that France, having known three distinct phases in the construction of its self-image since the birth of the Republic in 1789 – nationalism, internationalism (both in its humanitarian and imperialist forms) and pluralism – seemed on the brink of a new age:

> individuals are becoming increasingly conscious of the multiplicity of their impulses and needs. A fourth, post-pluralist phase is in the process of replacing the 'France of minorities'. It is one in which individuals try to work out their own destinies for themselves, creating a unique identity from a combination of elements drawn from the many different groups and subgroups to which they feel they have an affinity. This has come not inappropriately at the same time as the computer: before its advent, the mind was accustomed to coping with relatively few simple categories: now individuals are emerging as infinitely varied permutations of qualities and choices.
>
> (Zeldin 1983: 510)

Not normally regarded as a prophet of postmodernity, Zeldin seems here to come close to such acknowledged commentators on the rapidly changing France (and developed world) of the latter part of the twentieth century as Baudrillard, Lyotard and Lipovetsky. It is in the overlapping fields of leisure and consumption that the 'infinitely varied permutations of qualities and choices' which go to make up contemporary French individuals are, perhaps, most readily apparent.

Of course, structural divisions remain within this area of French social relations, just as they do in those of education, employment, politics, religion, and so forth. However, as Forbes and Hewlett have argued, the class-based cultural divisions which characterized France in the 1950s have not been replaced by the complete uniformity – or, come to that, the 'Americanization' – which many feared would be the end result of the consumer society. Rather, new forms of convergence and divergence have emerged as 'the mass media and the domestic leisure industries have created both a degree of homogenization and different forms of stratification which have more to do with age than class' (Forbes and Hewlett 1994: 46). The myriad ways in which French citizens, young and old, spend their money and their free time are thus likely to continue to represent a privileged site for the study of sub-national as well as national specificities for the foreseeable future.

Bibliography

Agence de l'Informatique (1986) *L'Etat d'informatisation de la France*, Paris: Economica.

Anderson, B. (1983) *Imagined Communities: Reflections on the Origin and Spread of Nationalism*, London: Verso.

Baudrillard, J. (1970) *La Société de consommation*, Paris: Denoël.

Bourdieu, P. (1979) *La Distinction: Critique sociale du jugement*, Paris: Minuit.

Bourg, J.-F. (1994) 'Le sport, l'argent et les médias', in S. Cordellier (ed.) *L'Etat de la France 94–95*, Paris: CREDOC/La Découverte, pp. 130–1.

Delbourgo, F. and Taylor, P. (1993) *French For Business Studies*, London: Pitman.

Doyle, A. (1997) 'Baguette law may rescue bakers', *The Glasgow Herald*, 3 January 1997: 11.

Dumazedier, J. (1962) *Vers une civilisation du loisir*, Paris: Seuil.

Duval-Smith, A. (1996) 'Minitel Tales', *The Guardian*, 1 February.

Eck, J.-F. (1988) *Histoire de l'économie française depuis 1945*, Paris: Armand Colin.

Fillon, F. (1996) Interview for the *Singapore Business Times Online* (http://www.globalreports.com/)

Forbes, J. and Hewlett, N. *et al.* (1994) *Contemporary France: Essays and Texts on Politics, Economics and Society*, London: Longman.

Frémy, D. and Frémy, M. (eds) (1995) *Quid 1996*, Paris: Robert Laffont.

Hughes, S. (1997) 'Gauls upset by Anglo-Saxon Web', *Times Higher Education Supplement*, 17 January: 10.

Lipovetsky, G. (1983) *L'Ere du vide: Essais sur l'individualisme contemporain*, Paris: Gallimard.

Looseley, D. (1995) *The Politics of Fun: Cultural Policy and Debate in Contemporary France*, Oxford: Berg.

Lyotard, J.-F. (1984) *The Post-Modern Condition: A Report on Knowledge*, Manchester: Manchester University Press. (Originally published as *La condition postmoderne: Rapport sur le savoir* (1979), Paris: Editions de Minuit).

Maresca, B. (1995) 'Temps libres et loisirs: Grandes tendances', in S. Cordellier and E. Poisson (eds), *L'Etat de la France 95–96*, Paris: CREDOC/La Découverte, pp. 142–8.

Ory, P. (1989) *L'Aventure culturelle française*, Paris: Flammarion.

Parodi, M. (1982) *L'Economie et la société française depuis 1945*, Paris: Armand Colin.

Poujol, G. (1993) 'Leisure Politics and Policies in France', in P. Bramham and I. Henry (eds), *Leisure Policies in Europe*, Wallingford: CAB International, pp. 13–40.

Rigby, B. (1991) *Popular Culture in Modern France: A Study of Cultural Discourse*, London: Routledge.

Rincé, J.-Y. (1990) *Le Minitel*, Paris: PUF, Collection 'Que sais-je?'.

Rojek, C. (1993) *Ways of Escape: Modern Transformations in Leisure and Travel*, London: Routledge.

Ross, K. (1995) *Fast Cars, Clean Bodies: Decolonization and the Reordering of French Culture*, Cambridge, MA and London: MIT Press.

Vesperini, J-P. (1987) *L'Economie de la France depuis 1945*, Paris: Economica.

Volatier, J.-L. (1995) 'Consommation: Grandes tendances', in S. Cordellier and E. Poisson (eds), *L'Etat de la France 95–96*, Paris: CREDOC/La Découverte, pp. 129–34.

Weber, E. (1977) *Peasants into Frenchmen: The Modernisation of Rural France*, London, Chatto & Windus.

Webster, P. (1997) 'Netting the Web for France', *The Guardian*, 6 January 1997.

Yonnet, P. (1985) *Jeux, modes et masses: 1945–1985*, Paris: Gallimard.

Zeldin, T. (1983) *The French*, London: Collins.

Index